heart talk

heart talk

Say What You Feel In Thai

Christopher G. Moore

Heaven Lake Press

Distributed in Thailand by:
Asia Document Bureau Ltd.
P.O. Box 1029
Nana Post Office
Bangkok 10112 Thailand
Fax: (662) 260-4578
Web site: http://www.heavenlakepress.com
E-Mail: editorial@heavenlakepress.com

First Published in Thailand in 1992
by White Lotus Co., Ltd.

Third Edition 2006
by Heaven Lake Press
Printed in Thailand

Jacket design: Jae Song
Cover photograph: Ralph Tooten © 2006

ISBN 974-94118-9-7

preface
Third Edition

Most people would love to speak more than one language. Learning a new language after you become an adult is no easy task. It is like going back to school and starting all over. You are five years old again. *Heart Talk* is my small contribution to those wishing to learn an important aspect of the Thai language. As you study Thai you will come across words with the root word *jai* (heart) and at first you might not make too much of the fact these words which start as a trickle end up to flood your consciousness.

Fifteen years have passed since the first edition of *Heart Talk* was first written. During this time I have continued to live in Thailand. In 1998 I researched and wrote the second edition of *Heart Talk* and falsely believed that I had at last hunted down the missing *jai* phrases from the first edition. Writing a book such as *Heart Talk* is like picking up lovely shells from the beach. You fill the buckets and walk back to your house satisfied not one shell had been missed. The next morning the tide brings more shells onto the beach. My quest for *jai* phrases has been such a journey.

To use another metaphor, the word *jai* is like stem cells of the Thai language. It is difficult to imagine a conversation where a *jai* expression isn't used. *Jai* is the essential building block for a rich vocabulary of emotional, spiritual, mental and physical states and conditions. In the Thai language the heart is the center of thinking, feeling, shaping our moods, nurturing our spirit, bonding us to friends and family. The outline of what it is to move about in the home, office, and society can't be detached from the idea of *jai*. In our own language we have a vocabulary to express our deepest feelings of happiness, hope, fear, anxiety and sadness. *Heart Talk* is an on-going project to allow non-Thai speakers a way to expand their vocabulary to better express those feelings in Thai.

There are several new features in this edition. It is useful to know whether *jai* phrase is a verb, noun, adverb or adjective as this aide helps focus the correct grammar and makes usage easier and more reliable. There is a new Phonetic Guide prepared by Dr. Busakorn Suriyasarn, which has significantly improved the understanding of how to pronounce Thai words written in phonetic form. Also, I have added illustrations to open each of the chapters. Lastly, there is a new chapter on Thai *jai* proverbs. Learning a new language is becoming a child again. There is that sense of feeling helpless, powerless and overwhelmed. The chapter on *jai* proverbs is another way to take us back to our earliest experiences in learning: the world of proverbs, fables, and axioms. All cultures share an oral tradition were small saying carry large moral lessons. Many readers have children who may find the proverbs useful and fun to learn.

I have a feeling, one of dread, that while I have found many of the central *jai* phrases, there will always be omissions. But for the moment, I have swept the beach as clean as I can and offer up these beautiful shells of a beautiful language.

In researching and writing this edition I would like to acknowledge the contribution of Pairoh Sripattanatadakoon (Khun Jeab) and Kitirat Yothonsawadi (Khun Ying) my two research assistants who spent many hours helping me to discover and define many new *jai* phrases. They were patient and thorough, working closely with me to refine the definitions for many new phrases contained in this edition.

Paweena Plangprawat (Khun Nuch) worked diligently on the transliteration and the glossary, and made a substantial contribution in proof reading the text. Khwanruethai Jiamsomboon (Khun May) brought her considerable design and layout talents to the project. She created the new design for the third edition and deserves much credit for the polished, professional layout in the third edition.

Pakatip Dejaturat (Khun Tip) worked hard to bring a touch of humor and grace to the illustrations contained in the book. As a way of making *Heart Talk* more accessible, Khun Tip's drawings capture an important visual element of the *jai* phrases.

Also my wife, Busakorn, provided invaluable insight, support and advice, along the way rescuing me from many errors. She also prepared the index. Without her commitment, diligence and devotion this edition of *Heart Talk* would have been a lesser book.

For additional information, news, opinions and updates, as well as guidance to learn Thai language through *Heart Talk* please click onto www.thaihearttalk.info.

contents

Heart Talk: An Introduction

Phonetic Guide

Chapter 1 Heart Talk for the Good Times

Contentment 15
Desire 17
Entertainment & Relaxation 19
Excitement 20
Fulfillment 22
Happiness & Joy 23
Inspiration 27
Popularity 28
Relief 28
Security 30

Chapter 2 Heart Talk for the Hard Times

Anger 33
Annoyance 34
Anxiety & Worry 36
Depression 39
Discouragement 41
Disturbance 44
Doubtfulness 46
Fear 47
Frustration 49
Grief 50
Hopelessness 51

Loneliness 52
Regrets 53
Rejection 55
Sadness 56
Sensitivity 59
Shame 60
Weariness 61

Chapter 3 The Best of the Human Condition

CONDUCT & BEHAVIOR 65
Compassion 65
Confidence 66
Consideration 67
Honesty 69
Resolve 70
Trust 71
Willingness 71

CHARACTER TRAITS 72
Compassion 72
Confidence 73
Courage 73
Generosity 77
Goodness 78
Grace 80
Kindness 80
Nobility 82
Purity 83
Sincerity 84
Strength 85

Chapter 4 The Worst of the Human Condition

CONDUCT & BEHAVIOR 90
Arrogance 90

Complacency 91
Cruelty 92
Deception 93
Obsession 94
Self-centeredness 94
Surrender 96
Uncaring Behavior 96
Vengefulness 97

CHARACTER TRAITS 97
Cowardice 97
Cruelty 99
Impatience 100
Moodiness 101
Passivity 101
Selfishness 102
Showing Off 104
Treachery & Deceit 104
Unkindness & Selfishness 106
Unreliability 108
Weak-mindedness 109

Chapter 5 Compliments and Insults

COMPLIMENTS 113
INSULTS 118

Chapter 6 Heart Talk in Relationships

Appreciation 128
Betrayal 129
Character of the Heart 130
Convenience 134
Difficult Relationships 136
Fear 140
Grudge & Resentment 141

Heart Connection 144
Hypocrisy 147
Mistakes 149
Pain & Hurt Feelings 150
Pleasing Others 155
Respecting Others 157
Revealing the Heart 159
Revenge 160
Satisfaction 162
Secrecy 163
Sincerity 165
Suspicion 167
The Beloved 168
Trust 170
Truth 177
Vulnerability 177

Chapter 7 Heart Talk in Society

Class & Hierarchy 181
Community & Solidarity 187
Consensus 191
Consumer Society 192
Encouragement 194
Fairness 196
Friendship 197
Injustice 201
Justice 202
Persuasion 203
Pride 205
Responsibility & The Family 206

Chapter 8 Body Talk

Attributes 213
Breathing 214

Dying 219
Fainting 221
Kicking 222
Shake, Rattle & Roll 223

Chapter 9 Perception

Awareness & Realization 226
Concentration 227
Distraction 229
Forgetting 232
Imagination 233
Impression 233
Intuition 235
Knowledge 237
Satisfaction 238
Surprised, Amazed & Alarmed 241
Thinking 245
Truth 246
Understanding 247

Chapter 10 Self-Control

Calm & Composure 254
Patience 256
Peace 257
Restraint 258
Temptation 262

Chapter 11 Choice

DECISION-MAKING 268
Choices 268
Certainty 269
Decision-Making 270
Intention 272

Resolve 273
FREE WILL 274
Battle of Will 276
Uncertainty 278
Will Power 281

Chapter 12 Romance

Commitment 286
Cycle of Romance 289
Endearments 293
Infatuation 295
Intimacy 297
Love 299
Loyalty 302
Studying & Testing the Heart 303
Truth & Trust 304
Unfaithfulness 306

Chapter 13 Heart Proverbs

Benevolence 312
Concentration 313
Daydreams 313
Differences 314
Empathy 315
False Promise 316
Freedom 317
Guilt 318
Immature Acts 319
Indulgence 320
Marriage 322
Mistakes 323
Obedience 324
Self-Reliance 325
Sincerity 326

Skill 327
Spirituality 328
Treachery 329
Trust 330

Chapter 14 Hand Talk

Anxiety & Worry 334
Class & Hierarchy 334
Compassion 335
Confidence 336
Decision-Making 336
Dying 337
Encouragement 337
Endearment 338
Excitement 338
Free Will 339
Grudge & Resentment 339
Insults 340
Memory 341
Nobility 341
Nuisance 341
Satisfaction 342
Trust 342
Understanding 343
Unfaithfulness 344
Unreliability 344
Vengefulness 345

Glossary 347

Index 361

heart talk
an introduction

Heart is a powerful, pervasive and complex metaphor in the Thai language. In Thai, you can experience and understand heart or *jai* in a vast range of feelings, emotional and mental states. *Heart Talk* explores the basic emotional conditions such as happy, sad, kind, cruel, to the more descriptive expressions such as hard, soft, broad, narrow, open, concealed, confident, doubting, sinking, uplifting. Metaphors based on the heart are often puzzling to outsiders such as hot, cool, bland, salty, diamond, dog, monk, monster. While metaphors are the staple of novelists, poets, and playwrights, what is the relationship of heart as a metaphor to people interested in the Thai language and culture?

In *Metaphors We Live By* (1980) Lakoff and Johnson tell us that the "...human thought processes are largely metaphorical." Thus, whether you are a doctor, dock worker, lawyer, factory worker, merchant or jack-of-all-trades, then, you are pulling an oar in the same conceptual boat constructed from the same metaphors as everyone else in your language and culture. If you wish to row in the Thai conceptual boat, an understanding of the word *jai* is indispensable.

Many heart metaphors are universal such as *dii jai* (glad heart) and *sĕaa jai* (sorry heart), but others such as *kreeng jai* (awe heart), *jai jùuet* (bland heart) and *jai plaa siw* (silver fish heart) do not travel easily across cultural frontiers. This book provides a 'heart' guide to the human condition from love to hate, comedy to sorrow, hope to despair. The cumulative force of *Heart Talk* will help increase your awareness of how consciousness is shaped and defined in the Kingdom of Thailand.

The Thai language has the Thai word for heart in hundreds of different phrases. There is no single source in Thai or English where the heart phrases have been collected, organized and defined. One purpose of this book is to provide a lighthearted translation of Thai heart words and phrases into English. While the first edition of this book contained approximately 330 heart phrases, and 532 in the second edition, this edition adds over 200 more. Among the 743 heart words and phrases in this edition of *Heart Talk* are commonly used words and phrases, idioms and proverbs, as well as a selection of 40 sign language that contain the word *jai*.

Let's start with the basic notion of heart. In Thai, the word *jai* or the phrase *hŭaa jai* refers to both the physical organ that keeps you alive and the emotional condition and inclination and state of mind. *Jìt jai*—literally "mind-heart"—refers to emotional, mental or spiritual state. *Ní săi jai khOO* or *náam săi jai khOO*—literally "habit"or "true essence of the heart"—means the true nature of the heart, character trait, or spirit of the heart. *Jai khOO* suggests personality and natural disposition—good or bad, kind or cruel, mean or generous, etc.

Through these core *jai* words, you can glimpse the range of the Thai heart that covers an expansive, physical to existential, spectrum of the heart and the mind. Through understanding the Thai heart, you can also experience the sweetest words and the strongest condemnations, appreciate the best to the worst human conditions as seen from the eyes of the Thais, and see that there is a redemption even for the worst of evils.

♥

In Thongchai Winichakul's *Siam Mapped* (1994), a book to be treasured for its brilliant insight into the Thai mentality, the concept of language is addressed in this way:

> As a prime technology of imagining nationhood, a language works a nation out in different manners—for example, by a spoken vernacular, the written language, the printing press, a court's language, a state mechanism like education, or the unified language of a colonial rule. In short, a language enables a certain group of people of their community an unprecedented, spatiotemporal definition. Nationhood is an imagined sphere with no given identity or essence; it is a cultural construct.

In this context, it should be added, that the heart phrases in the Thai language are another way of imagining the nationhood of Thailand, the identity of the people, a looking glass peering deep into the cultural heritage.

The translation of the phrases in *Heart Talk* has been a highly personal one. How we describe our feelings and emotions in any language is highly individual. Not everyone will agree with each of the meanings or the examples used to support a particular meaning (nor would I expect universal agreement). And I have been selective. Not every possible meaning or shade of meaning has been included.

The intention has been to write a book that you, the reader, will find enjoyable, provocative, and useful in your day-to-day conversations. It is a book that will prepare you to walk around the markets, shops and streets of Thailand, and communicate in spoken or sign Thai from your heart. It is a book which, in a short space, provides a number of insights into the Thai way of experiencing what an English speaker would call matters of the heart, or to take Graham Greene's title, *The Heart of the Matter.*

If you are a native Thai speaker, the book may help you to create a bridge of understanding between the English and Thai languages. As with any bridge, everyone has his or her own idea on the right design and structure. Everyone visualizes the heart from a different angle or perspective. This book, if not exactly a perfect bridge, is a way of providing a language map to an English speaker who knows little about Thailand. It is not, of course, the whole story. But I hope it is a start in the right direction.

♥

To understand the Thai word *jai* is to understand the importance of *heart*, which provides access to the Thai way of looking at themselves, others and life. The word *jai* means both heart *and* mind. In the English language, these two perspectives, heart and mind, have become accepted as two separate categories. In English, one employs either words, which suggest to the listener that he or she is invoking the rational, logical mind to perceive the world or self, or words suggesting that the speaker has resorted to his or her emotional, non-rational side.

Since the Age of Reason, English speakers have become accustomed to viewing heart and mind as different. A common perception in English is to divide left-brain and right-brain *thinking* as an explanation for conduct and vocabulary. In Thailand, the consequences of the post-Enlightenment tradition did not split mind and heart into separate orbits of perception.

To comprehend the world with your heart in Thai often places you in many different contexts in which a native English speaker would not associate with heart but only with the intellect. The Thai language does not ignore the intellect, but the emphasis is on the emotive way of seeing and feeling. The mind and the intellect blend to become an essential and important feature of understanding the Thai language, culture and people. The Thais are rarely at a loss for an exact heart phrase to express a feeling or idea.

Have we in the West lost our range of communicating feelings? What would it be like to have a language where hundreds of phrases treat the state of our heart and mind as one? These are two questions you may ask when studying the phrases and examples in *Heart Talk*. You may discover some aspect of yourself that has been surrendered, forgotten or neglected in English. That realization may bring a smile or a tear. *Heart Talk* may open up the vast possibility of feelings that lie beneath the surface of our rational, logical, empirical world.

♥

The Thai language uses *jai* or heart to generate meaning in many contexts. For a native Thai language speaker, who is raised to understand that *jai* is a word with hundreds of shadings, an ever-present force within daily language, it is an evocative word that echoes with a sense of emotion. A leading Thai scholar, Weerayudha Wichiarajote, has commented that in Thailand:

> [T]he basic drive is to establish extensive networks of personal relationships [which establish] the basic motivational drives . . . for

friendship, love, warmth and social acceptance. In general, feelings are counted more than reason.

With this emphasis on feelings in Thai culture, the language of the heart assumes a place of central importance. In a social or business context, the native language of a person is the way she or he reacts to you, or your ideas. In English, the heart connotes a sense of romance or medical science. We fall in love with our hearts or have heart transplants. The word heart in English, though of importance, occupies a secondary position to the logical or analytical path. Or at least it appears so when compared with the diverse uses of *jai* in the Thai language.

The Thai language requires us to reevaluate the way we perceive reality, in the home, a restaurant, bar, business meeting, or traveling on traffic-choked streets. If we seek insight into another language, culture and people, we need some clue as to the ways they react when challenged by an idea, thought, book, newspaper, TV, or in the street, conference room or parlor. Understanding the uses of the *jai* takes one into the private backyard of the Thai language—a place where ideas are shaped, feelings formed, moods transformed, and relationships sealed or split apart.

♥

Many Thai language books have been written that prepare you to buy a cup of coffee or ask for directions to the train station. This book has a different purpose. It is a short tour of the heart words, which, in the Thai language, explain some of the reasons Thailand is known as the Land of Smiles. This book provides an introduction to the source of those famous smiles; and explains, in part, the cultural difference when someone from the West meets and interacts with a Thai speaker. The way we talk (or don't talk) about matters of the heart exposes something about what we feel is important, true, or possible about ourselves.

Some *Heart Talk* expressions are descriptive of the nature of a person: A person with an impatient nature is *jai rÓOn* (hot heart) and a person with a sensitive, touchy nature is *jai nÓOy* (small heart). Other times the *Heart Talk* phrase is connected with an emotional state and not necessarily the nature of the person experiencing the emotion. Thus a feeling of panic translates as *jai túm túm tÒOm tÒOm* (panic heart). Another feature is the reversal of order in certain expressions. Thus *jai dii* (good heart) refers to the nature of a good-hearted person while *dii jai* (glad heart) refers to the emotional state of gladness. In a number of cases, the switch can turn a negative feeling into a good personality trait. For example, *ÒOn jai* (worn out heart) means weary-minded, while *jai ÒOn* (soft heart) refers to someone who goes out of their way to help others.

If you ask a Thai speaker to explain if they had ever experienced one of the states embodied in a *Heart Talk* phrase, the answer may reveal a great deal about that person's past because for the native Thai speaker there is a stored-up library of feelings and experiences he or she connects with each heart phrase. These heart phrases can become emotional road maps exploring the terrain of another's feelings and the way language defines the nature of another's personality. But be prepared to have the same courage to reveal your own heart, your own feelings, in return. What *Heart Talk* does is to provide a key to what is locked inside us all: A yearning to understand how another person feels.

In Thailand, the concept position and presentation are not stage props; they are the drama. Every drama needs a script. In many instances, the script is drawn from *Heart Talk*. Position can mean a number of things, including your social rank, your job, your education, or your family background. The expressions of *Heart Talk* allow for dramatic interaction between members occupying the same or different positions. The way people occupying their roles see themselves can be found in the grammar of *Heart Talk*.

It is difficult for many foreigners to master oral and written Thai. *Heart Talk* is a way to master a narrow range of the language—a vocabulary of the heart. This is your how-to guide. It gives you the means to talk about your heart and from your heart in the Thai language. You can ask questions about the heart in Thai, and how, in the process of using *Heart Talk*, you may find yourself better equipped to express and understand a rich variety of phrases. In learning this new technique of language study, you can become expressive and, with enough practice, might begin to do what the Thai speakers do by instinct: Look, evaluate, decide, react, and judge as if their heart and mind were one.

phonetic guide

There is no universally agreed-upon system to write Thai in romanized letters. The phonetic guide originally adopted in first edition of *Heart Talk* was suggested by Dr. Theraphan L. Thongkum, Department of Linguistics, Faculty of Arts, Chulalongkorn University. For the second edition, Gaynor de Wit has made a number of useful additions to this guide.

For this third edition, Dr. Busakorn Suriyasarn has revised and reorganized the phonetic system of the vowels and consonants into a more accessible format, adding more examples and clarifications. The revision partially benefits from the Royal Thai General System of Transcription and the Thai language phonology page on Wikipedia, the free encyclopedia website.[1]

Vowels

Learning to pronounce the vowels in the Thai language can be intimidating at first, as there are over 30 combinations of vowels. Fortunately, many of them are the short and long pairs of the same sounds. Short vowels in Thai are vowels that are pronounced in short duration, while the long vowels are those pronounced in longer duration. Two words with the same vowel sound but with different duration usually have different meanings in Thai. There are 9 pairs of basic Thai vowel sounds and over 20 other vowels and vowel combinations (of two or three basic vowels). The single or the first dash (-) in the table below indicates the position of the initial consonant after which each vowel is pronounced, for example อะ, อ, อุ, เอะ, โอะ. The second dash represents the final consonant, for example อัด, อีก, อูด, เอก, โอด.

1 http://en.wikipedia.org/wiki/Thai_language#Phonology.

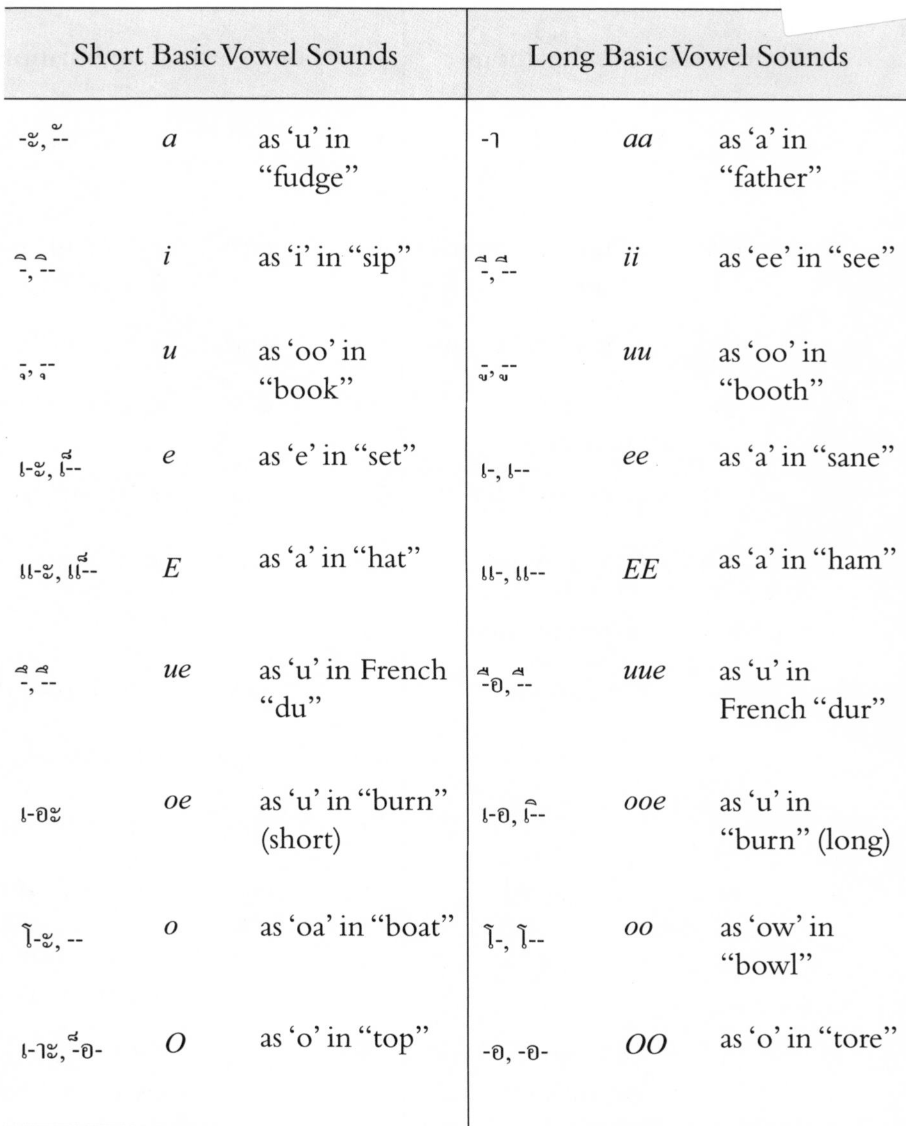

Short Basic Vowel Sounds			Long Basic Vowel Sounds		
-ะ, -ั-	*a*	as 'u' in "fudge"	-า	*aa*	as 'a' in "father"
-ิ, -ิ-	*i*	as 'i' in "sip"	-ี, -ี-	*ii*	as 'ee' in "see"
-ุ, -ุ-	*u*	as 'oo' in "book"	-ู, -ู-	*uu*	as 'oo' in "booth"
เ-ะ, เ-็-	*e*	as 'e' in "set"	เ-, เ--	*ee*	as 'a' in "sane"
แ-ะ, แ-็-	*E*	as 'a' in "hat"	แ-, แ--	*EE*	as 'a' in "ham"
-ึ, -ึ-	*ue*	as 'u' in French "du"	-ือ, -ื-	*uue*	as 'u' in French "dur"
เ-อะ	*oe*	as 'u' in "burn" (short)	เ-อ, เ-ิ-	*ooe*	as 'u' in "burn" (long)
โ-ะ, --	*o*	as 'oa' in "boat"	โ-, โ--	*oo*	as 'ow' in "bowl"
เ-าะ, -็อ-	*O*	as 'o' in "top"	-อ, -อ-	*OO*	as 'o' in "tore"

Short Vowel Combinations			Long Vowel Combinations		
ไ-, ใ-, ไ-ย, -ัย	*ai*	as 'I' in "I"	ไ-, -าย	*aay*	as 'eye' in "eye"
-ำ	*am*	as 'um' in "mum" (short)	-ำ	*aam*	as 'um' in "mum" (long)
เ-า	*aw*	as 'ow" in "chow"	-าว	*aaw*	as 'ow' in "cow"
-ัวะ	*ua*	as 'ewe' in "brewer"	-ัว, -ว-	*uaa*	as 'oor' in "poor"
เ-ียะ	*ea*	as 'ier' in "pier"	เ-ีย, เ-ีย-	*eaa*	as 'ee' in "beer"
เ-ือะ	*uea*	*ue* + *a* sound	เ-ือ, เ-ือ-	*ueaa*	*ue* + *aa* sound
-ิว	*iw*	as 'ew' in "new"	-	-	–
เ-็ว	*ew*	*e* + *o* sound	เ-ว	*eew*	*ee* + *oo* sound
-	-	–	แ-ว	*EEw*	*EE* + *oo* sound
-	-	–	เ-ียว	*iiaw*	*ii* + *ee* + *oo* sound
-ุย	*ui*	*u* + *i* sound	-ูย	*uuy*	*uu* + *ai* sound
-	-	–	โ-ย	*ooy*	*oo* + *ai* sound (as 'oe' in "Chloe")
-็อย	*Oi*	*O* + *i* sound (as 'oy' in "boy" (short))	-อย	*OOy*	*OO* + *ai* sound (as 'oy' in "boy" (long))
-	-	–	เ-ย	*ooey*	*ooe* + *ai* sound
-	-	–	เ-ือย	*ueaay*	*ue* + *aa* + *ai* sound
-	-	–	-วย	*uaay*	*uaa* + *ai* sound

Consonants

There are 44 letters in the Thai alphabet, producing 21 initial consonant sounds (i.e., in the initial position of a syllable) and 6 final consonant sounds (i.e., at the end of a syllable).

Letters	Initial Position	Final Position	English Equivalent Sounds in Initial Position
ก	k	k	as ‘k’ in “skate,” unaspirated, plosive (also used to transliterate the English letter ‘g’)
ข ฅ ค ฆ	kh	k	as ‘c’ in “car,” aspirated, plosive
ง	ng	ng	as ‘ng’ in “linger,” nasal
จ	j	t	as ‘j’ in “jet,” unaspirated, affricate
ฉ ช	ch	t	as ‘ch’ in “chat,” aspirated, affricate
ฎ ด	d	t	as ‘d’ in “dale,” unaspirated, plosive
ฏ ต	t	t	as ‘t’ in “stale,” unaspirated ‘dt’ sound, plosive
ฐ ฒ ถ ท ธ	th	t	as ‘t’ in “tale,” aspirated, plosive
น ณ	n	n	as ‘n’ in “nail,” nasal
บ	b	p	as ‘b’ in “bark,” unaspirated, plosive
ป	p	p	as ‘p’ in “spark,” unaspirated ‘bp’ sound, plosive
ผ พ ภ	ph	p	as ‘p’ in “park,” aspirated, , plosive
ฝ ฟ	f	p	as ‘f’ in “fee”/“fake”/“fail,” fricative

Letters	Initial Position	Final Position	English Equivalent Sounds in Initial Position
ม	m	m	as 'm' in "male," nasal
ญ	y	n	as 'y' in "you," approximant
ย	y	-	as 'y' in "you," approximant
ร	r	n	as 'r' in "rake"/"rail," thrill
ล ฬ	l	n	as 'l' in "lake," lateral approximant
ว	w	-	as 'w' in "wee"/"wake"/"whale," approximant
ซ ศ ษ	s	t	as 's' in "see"/"sake"/"sail," fricative
ห ฮ	h	-	as 'h' in "he"/"hen"/"hale," fricative
อ	-	-	This letter is silent if appearing before a vowel, or a glottal plosive sound *OO* if following a short vowel without a final consonant.

* Note: Letters ฉ ซ ผ ฝ ห ฮ never appear at the end of a syllable.

Tones

Thai is a tonal language. Understanding its five tones is an essential part of usage as using the wrong tone may cause confusion because different tones of words with the same sound usually convey different meanings in Thai. In *Heart Talk*, the tones are indicated by unique symbols in the Thai transliteration of each heart phrase as shown in the chart below.

Tone	Tonal Mark in Thai	Symbol	Thai	English
middle tone	*săaman* (no tonal mark)	*naa*	นา	rice paddy
low tone	*èek* (–่)	***nàa***	(น้อย)หน่า	custard apple
falling tone	*thoo* (–้)	***nâa***	หน้า	face
high tone	*trii* (–๊)	***náa***	น้า	maternal aunt/ uncle
rising tone	*jàttàwaa* (–๋)	***nǎa***	หนา	thick

Comfortable Heart

sà baay jai (adj., v.) สบายใจ

yen jai (v.) เย็นใจ

1
heart talk for the good times

When you experience feelings of contentment, happiness, inspiration, relaxation or other pleasant emotions that create a sense of well-being, the phrases in this chapter provide a range of ways to express yourself in a fashion that is connected to your heart. In Thai culture and custom, it is from and through the heart that the language locates these feelings of well-being.

The good times and good feelings cover a wide emotional terrain, from getting what you wished for to being cheerful, satisfied or at ease. You are not suffering or in turmoil or conflict. You are relaxed, happy and controlled (or give that appearance to another) if you hear a Thai speaker refer to you by employing one of these *Heart Talk* phrases.

Contentment

Comfortable Heart

sà baay jai (adj., v.) สบายใจ
yen jai (v.) เย็นใจ

Use these heart phrases for the experience of feeling the absence of problems or burdens in life. You have entered a state of feeling perfectly in tune with yourself emotionally or a state of comfort and pleasantness. You feel comfortable inside yourself and with those around you; there is an inner peace and sense of calm. You may have this feeling as a result of the presence of another in a relationship, to which there are no rough edges and in which the personal connection is natural, fluid and mellow. Alternatively, you may have eaten a perfect mango and sit back with a big grin, stomach full, heart comfortable.

Contented Heart

ìm jai (v.) อิ่มใจ
ìm òoep jai (v.) อิ่มเอิบใจ
chûm jai (v.) ชุ่มใจ
chûm òk chûm jai (v.) ชุ่มอกชุ่มใจ

The heart is like a gasoline tank. Often it is running on half full or, worse, it is running on empty. Good feelings are the fuel that best drives the heart forward. Thus, *ìm jai* is a general catch-all phrase to express a feeling of happiness at its peak. The expression comes close to the English notion of being contented. Completeness and depth of the feeling are important. The Thai word *ìm* is normally used to say that one is full after a meal. Thus *ìm* alone refers to the full stomach and *ìm jai* the full heart, and with both organs filled the result should be a state of contentment. *Ìm òoep jai* has the same general meaning but is flowery language. *Chûm jai* and *chûm òk chûm jai* also have the same meaning and are a little old-fashioned. The emphasis is on meeting your needs or desires. If you are thirsty and drink a glass of cold water you will feel *chûm jai*.

Heart at Ease

săm raan jai (v.) สำราญใจ
preem jai (v.) เปรมใจ

These are two more variations for expressing the feeling of a comfortable, happy heart. They cover the same situations that make you feel *sà baay jai*. These literary phrases are mostly used in Thai writing and are not frequently used in spoken Thai. For the literal person, though, the occasional reference to "heart at ease" (in the appropriate context) will no doubt improve one's linguistic score card with a Thai speaker. You are sitting on the beach with a cool drink and reading a good book. No one disturbs you. You feel *preem jai* or *săm raan jai*.

Pleased Heart

khrúem jai (v.) ครึ้มใจ
khrúem òk khrúem jai (v.) ครึ้มอกครึ้มใจ

When someone either gives another a special gift or bestows a favor, the recipient experiences a sense of pleasure or "pleased heart." When you get an email from your girlfriend sending kisses and hugs and a smiley face, you feel *khrúem jai*. This state of being pleased derives not only from the gift or favor but also from the sentiment that the person who is giving has shown that he or she cares. *Khrúem jai* is the feeling of being valued by another person and the good feeling that comes from being appreciated. Also, whenever anyone faces a difficult obstacle and manages to succeed in spite of it, there is a feeling of being pleased with oneself and this *jai* phrase becomes an appropriate description of that feeling. Another example occurs when a student finishes a difficult examination and leaves feeling pleased with herself for having answered all of the questions correctly. The demonstrative expression of this sentiment of *khrúem òk khrúem jai* includes smiling, dancing or singing.

Satisfied Heart

krà yìm jai (v.) กระหยิ่มใจ

When you experience the feeling of satisfaction, you feel *krà yìm jai*. The phrase is used to express a sense of happiness from getting what you desired. There is also a sense of glee. You bought a new iPod, got a hot date, formed a new partnership for your import/export business or managed to keep your job in a period of economic decline. A second usage is similar to *lam phOOng jai* and carries the negative connotation of arrogance. The third usage is similar to *im òoep jai*.

Desire

Desirous Heart

yuaan jai (v.) ยวนใจ

yûaa yuaan jai (v.) ยั่วยวนใจ

Your impulses are triggered by the sight of something or someone that causes a feeling of desire. What is tempting to possess causes desire in your heart. In the presence of such a desirable object or person you feel *yûaa yuaan jai*. This object of desire—or what seduces—may be any number of temptations: from an artfully prepared Thai dish, to a vintage bottle of French wine, to a beautiful sexy woman. The person or object which is *yûaa yuaan jai* acts as a seduction, and when confronted with the person or object you may try to remember to *yáp yáng châng jai,* or to control or restrain such impulses and desires.

Pander to the Heart

prà loom jai (v.) ประโลมใจ

The usual meaning, especially in written form, is associated with comforting or consoling others. However, there is a second meaning that usually occurs in a conversational exchange where the phrase has become associated with provocative images, words and music designed to arouse sexual desire (or excitement). The thing panders to the heart of the viewer, reader or listener. The source of such appeals may be movies, magazines, TV or cyberspace. Rock videos often employ erotic images indicating that the producers or promoters are pandering to the sexual desires of the audience, thus the rock video is *prà loom jai*, the movie is *prà loom jai*, or *Playboy* magazine is *prà loom jai*. An erotic calendar is *prà loom jai*. A person can also pander to the heart of another by relating an evocative love story. The story is *prà loom jai*.

Wake up the Tiger's Heart

plùk jai sǔeaa pàa (v.) ปลุกใจเสือป่า

This heart phrase is slang and is typically used to describe sexually provocative clothing, actions, photos, words, advertisements, movies, etc. The long-legged starlet appearing in a beer or automobile commercial on TV is intended to wake up the hearts of the tigers watching the starlet sell the product. The desire is evoked through images, words or actions. The photograph of Mr. Universe pumping iron might wake up the tiger's heart in a woman. The second meaning is stimulation or arousal of a group of people. An example of this would be instilling patriotism or nationalism in a group of people, to bind them together, whether as a fighting force or a political one.

Entertainment & Relaxation

Cheerful Heart
bòoek baan jai (v.) เบิกบานใจ
jai baan (v.) ใจบาน
baan jai (v.) บานใจ
phlooen jai (v.) เพลินใจ

When you feel cheerful and happy in your life, then you feel *bòoek baan jai*. The other *jai* phrases under the same heading can also be used to express this state of cheerfulness. It is appropriate to use these phrases when you experience a sense of your heart opening up like a lotus flower, with petals unfolding in peace, happiness and contentment. The essence is the overriding feeling of being in a cheery mood, experiencing a sense of merry entertainment.

Entertained Heart
rûuen rooeng ban thooeng jai (adj.) รื่นเริงบันเทิงใจ

A person who has an "entertained heart" is able to kick back, relax and enjoy an activity that takes him or her away from the multiple obligations of the day and/or the dreary routine of day-to-day living. What entertains is highly personal to each person. It might be solitary activities such as a game of chess, a good novel or a walk in Lumpini Park, or social activities such as a party with friends, dining in a restaurant on Kata Beach in Phuket, or a fun night out. In each case, the activity allows a person to enter into a state of enjoyment and well-being. In a Thai context, this feeling is most often felt as a member of a group. And anyone who can assist others to entertain their heart is a highly prized companion.

Entertained Heart
sà nùk sà nǎan bòoek baan jai (v.) สนุกสนานเบิกบานใจ

This phrase describes a feeling of fun, happiness and entertainment—a combination of "cheerful heart" and "entertained heart" above. Your girlfriend feels *sà nùk sà nǎan bòoek baan jai* that all of her close friends have come to her birthday party, and everyone is having a blast. The host of the party is such a good and entertaining host that the guests feel happy. They joke with one another and are obviously enjoying themselves. The guests feel *sà nùk sà năan bòoek baan jai*.

Relax One's Heart
yÒOn jai (v.) หย่อนใจ
phák phÒOn yÒOn jai (v.) พักผ่อนหย่อนใจ

The *yÒOn jai* experience arises when you emotionally withdraw from the woes and cares of the world. You disengage from your personal or business life in order to achieve this emotional state of relaxation. Perhaps you had a fight or argument with your spouse, children or a friend, or had a conflict or problem in the office, or your car isn't working, but, despite all of this, you can go into your personal study, lean back in your chair, sip a glass of wine, listen to your favorite record and read a book. You can relax your heart when others may feel discontent. As you withdraw from your troubles and close that world off from your heart, then you will feel *yÒOn jai*. When you see a friend or colleague working too hard and becoming stressed out, you can use this *jai* verb and ask that person to *yÒOn jai*—to chill out.

The phrase *phák phÒOn yÒOn jai* is used when you wish to get away from it all for a longer period. You may wish to take a long weekend or a vacation to escape to Hua Hin in order to walk along the beach, enjoy the sand and sun in an environment free of obligations connected with work.

Excitement

Excited Heart
tùuen taa tùuen jai (v.) ตื่นตาตื่นใจ

A person who has never encountered or seen something before experiences excitement. Villagers in a remote village in Thailand would feel *tùuen taa tùuen jai* to see a strange-looking, tall foreigner with white skin, long nose and blond hair (known locally as farang) for the first time. Or that new action film starring Tom Cruise has such breathtaking scenes and state-of-the-art special effects that the audience feels *tùuen taa tùuen jai*. The essence is novelty, and the awesome feeling that comes from experiencing something unusual for the first time.

Jerkily Dancing Heart
jai tên (v., adj.) ใจเต้น
jai tên mâi pen jang wà (adj.)
ใจเต้นไม่เป็นจังหวะ
jai tên túm túm tÒm tÒm (adj.)
ใจเต้นตุ๊มๆต่อมๆ

Something has caused the heart to flutter (*jai tên*) or dance madly (*jai tên mâi pen jang wà* or *jai tên túm túm tÒm tÒm*). This is the feeling of excitement experienced in relation to a person, thing or event. It might be the rush and thrill of an amusement-park ride. Or it may be that Lek is so overwhelmed by seeing the current Thai TV heartthrob that her heart starts pounding out of control. Vinai, who is a highly regarded and kind person, asks Noi out for dinner. She has had a secret crush on Vinai, so the invitation causes Noi to *jai tên mâi pen jang wà*. Her heart is jerkily dancing about in her chest.

Titillated Heart
ráw jai (v.) เร้าใจ

When Nid goes to her favorite club and she hears a song from her favorite singer, this causes her heart to beat faster and she is in the mood to dance. When the hordes of Thai children waited for the bookstores to open so they could buy the latest copy of *Harry Potter* their little hearts were filled with excitement and they felt *ráw jai*. A woman with a lot of sex appeal can cause men (and some women) to feel *ráw jai*. Something in your experience draws you in, captivates you, holds your attention: it might be a film, music or a perfect body on the catwalk.

Fulfillment

As One's Heart Wishes
sŏm jai (v.) สมใจ
sŏm dang jai (v.) สมดังใจ
sŏm khwaam tâng jai (v.) สมความตั้งใจ

When you wish to express your feeling of fulfilled desires or expectations, these *jai* phrases can be employed. The receiving of the thing you wished for is the essence of these heart phrases. For example, you receive a gift of flowers or a ticket to a concert of your favorite singer from another person, which you anticipated receiving; you feel *sŏm jai*—fulfilled. You have always wanted to go to Paris, get that dream job or get your book published. Now your wish is answered, you feel *sŏm jai*. You get what you have wished for *sŏm dang jai* or *sŏm khwaam tâng jai*.

As One's Heart Desires
sŏm jai núek (v.) สมใจนึก

Most people harbor a secret wish or dream. Making the wish or dream come true is longed for by the person holding it. The focus of attention may be an event, a thing, a state of affairs, or a person you want to come into your life. You are convinced the realization of this dream will make your life better and more fulfilled. Similar to the above phrases, the essence of the expression is in the wishing and desiring and having your wish fulfilled. In this state, it is appropriate to use *sŏm jai núek*. The object of your desire may be a beautiful companion, a loyal son or daughter, a Rolex watch, a BMW, a scholarship, or dinner at a five-star restaurant. Whatever it happens to be, this is what you wish to come true.

Wishing for Others Heart
sŏm jai rák (v.) สมใจรัก

You may wish others to succeed in their efforts so they can achieve what they desire in their life. In this case, you feel *sŏm jai rák* for them, and provide encouragement for their desires in life by a display or expression of support for them. It is common to feel *sŏm jai rák* for your spouse, lover or close personal friends. This state of heart is a powerful combination of emotional support and empathy offered to others as they pursue their quest for happiness.

Happiness & Joy

Glad Heart
dii jai (v.) ดีใจ

This is the emotional feeling of gladness. Gladness may arise in many circumstances, including when friends throw you a surprise birthday party or when you are served your favorite deserts. In these circumstances, you feel *dii jai*. In another context, if Lek is an evil person and she comes to a nasty end, those who suffered as a result of Lek may feel *dii jai* over her fate. If Lek is a lovable, kind, decent person and something good comes her way, such as a job promotion, those connected with Lek will feel *dii jai* for her success.

Over-the-moon Glad Heart
dii òk dii jai (v.) ดีอกดีใจ
dii núeaa dii jai (v.) ดีเนื้อดีใจ

Hysterically glad describes this emotional state. This isn't just having-a-good-day kind of happiness or gladness. The person has won the big lottery and is trembling, crying, jumping up and down. Lek has received notice that she's placed number one in her class at Chulalongkorn University and she is more than just ordinarily happy; she is over-the-top happy at being the best student in her class. The actress who receives the Oscar is often captured by the cameras as being in the midst of experiencing *dii òk dii jai*. The modern phrase *dii òk dii jai* has largely replaced *dii núeaa dii jai* which is old-fashioned.

Happy Heart

sùk jai (adj.) สุขใจ

The basic meaning of *sùk jai*, as in *sà baay jai*, "comfortable heart," applies to the definition of "happy heart." If your heart is comfortable, it is necessarily happy as well. The essence is a state of peace and contentment with your life, work, spouse, children and friends. You are living in the center of a balanced, contented life. Another lesson in *Heart Talk* is that acquiring a comfortable, happy, at-ease heart requires an extended vocabulary.

Very Happy Heart

rooeng jai (v.) เริงใจ

This *jai* word describes a feeling of extreme happiness and is usually accompanied by a visible, outward sign of this happiness, such as a wide smile. When Lek wins the big lottery she would feel *rooeng jai*. When Daeng finally asks Lek to marry him and she has a long-lasting smile, you can be sure that she feels *rooeng jai*. Also, when a child has long wanted a toy and finally receives it from his or her mother, the child will feel *rooeng jai*. This is one of those *jai* words that is often felt by the person experiencing the happiness but is rarely expressed. It is an old-fashioned *jai* phrase and isn't heard often in conversation in modern times.

Joyful Heart

phlôoet phlooen jai (v.) เพลิดเพลินใจ
râa rooeng jai (adj.) ร่าเริงใจ

The state of being associated with a joyful heart occurs in the circumstances when you feel a sense of comfort, entertainment or concentrated interest. Accompanying this feeling is your absorption in the moment; external distractions and annoying factors are filtered out and you are able to enjoy the moment totally and purely. The feeling of joy and pleasure cause you to forget time and all of your worries. This state of joy may come from being with your favorite person, listening to your favorite music, reading a good book, or playing a video game.

Merry Heart

jà rooen jai (v.) เจริญใจ

This phrase is used in oral communication. It can describe an act that makes another person happy. For example, if you give your friend a surprise birthday gift, he or she may feel happy. Your friend's feeling would be expressed as *jà rooen jai*. On Mother's Day, when the daughter tells her mother that she loves her and she's a special mother, you can be sure the mother feels *jà rooen jai*. The feeling may, in other words, come from words genuinely and honestly spoken. It doesn't have to come from a material gift. A beautiful sunset on the beach can also make you feel *jà rooen jai*.

Overflowing Heart

tûuen tan jai (adj.) ตื้นตันใจ

Happiness and joy overflow the heart on certain occasions. When you learn of the extraordinary efforts made on your behalf by another, you feel *tûuen tan jai*. The phrase applies when the person who performed the act of kindness did so at some personal sacrifice or cost to himself. Usually this feeling arises out of gestures within the context of a personal relationship, such as between a parent and child, between lovers or spouses, or between friends. For instance, the daughter has lost her job and has very little money but spends most of what she has left to buy her mother a birthday present. The mother, knowing the sacrifice her daughter has made, will feel *tûuen tan jai* by such act of love and affection. The husband has an important business meeting in Singapore but cancels the trip to stay at home to celebrate his wedding anniversary with his wife. His wife will have an overflowing heart (*tûuen tan jai*) as a result of her husband's decision.

Pleased Heart
chÔOp jai (v.) ชอบใจ
thùuk jai (v.) ถูกใจ

For most purposes, *thùuk jai* and *chÔOp jai* cover the same notion. If Lek is asked to go and see the classic film *Titanic*, a film that she wishes to see again and again because it is romantic and sad, then she may feel *chÔOp jai* when she receives the invitation. When someone does something that pleases you or indulges your wishes, then you will feel *chÔOp jai* or *thùuk jai* toward that person.

Swelling Heart
hǔaa jai phOOng too (v.)
หัวใจพองโต

This emotional state of happiness occurs when someone receives a special gesture or gift at an unexpected time or place. It applies to the person giving as well as to the person on the receiving end. A mother and father will feel *hǔaa jai phOOng too* after making a gift to their son or daughter—their hearts swell—as a result of seeing the surprise and happiness on their child's face. Another example would be if Lek does not expect her boyfriend to collect her from school or work, and plans to take a taxi to meet him for dinner. But, to Lek's surprise, the boyfriend arrives in his car and they drive to the restaurant together. Lek feels *hǔaa jai phOOng too*. A sense of pride combines with happiness to form a very happy heart.

Uplift the Heart
Inspire the Heart
chuu jai (v.) ชูใจ

To uplift another's heart is to say or do something that brings the person encouragement and happiness. Lek announces to her husband that she is taking him for a holiday to London, and produces two airline tickets. Lek *chuu jai* her husband. The employee who receives a raise and a compliment from his or her boss will also have an "uplifted heart." The lover or spouse who surprises his or her other half with flowers will likely inspire this state of happiness as well. This phrase is formal and somewhat old-fashioned. It is not commonly heard in today's conversations.

Inspiration

Inspired Heart
don jai (v.) ดลใจ
ban daan jai (v.) บันดาลใจ
daan jai (v.) ดาลใจ

All three phrases are associated with the concept of personal motivation or inspiration. To inspire or motivate others to complete a task or accomplish a goal is the role of leaders, teachers, officers in the military and employers who are the role models. It is their obligation to inspire those under their command, supervision or control to excel at their duty. In traditional society, supernatural beings—good or bad deities (angels or devils)—are also thought to inspire people to do or not to do certain acts. By providing a good example, fair and just standards, and following through on what is promised, the soldier, the student, the employee, the voter will listen and follow.

Another example of *don jai* occurs as you are driving to work and you remember that you forgot to turn off your computer and lock the front door; you have this realization that some higher deity is inspiring (*don jai*) you to do something. Once this feeling is in your heart, you will likely turn your car around and return to your home, turn off your computer and lock the door behind you. *Ban daan jai* is used in the exact same way as *don jai*, while *daan jai* is not as frequently used.

Inspiration Heart
rEEng ban daan jai (n.)
แรงบันดาลใจ

Inspiration may also comprise emotional support, guidance, insight and knowledge conveyed to others. Perhaps you see a movie about a chess grandmaster and are inspired to learn the game of chess. Or you read a book about cross-country skiing and are motivated to take up the sport. A moving story about mistreated orphans can provide an inspiration (*rEEng ban daan jai*) for you to contribute money or otherwise work to support the cause of orphans.

Popularity

Win Someone's Heart
chá ná jai (v.) ชนะใจ

You may feel that you have won the heart of a friend, lover or employer, or these individuals may feel that they have won your heart. A very diligent, hard-working employee will likely win the heart of his or her employer. A faithful, considerate and compassionate friend will win your heart. Often the winning-over takes effort and time. For instance, the girlfriend's mother disapproves of her daughter's boyfriend, and the boyfriend, knowing of the mother's disapproval, does his very best to win her heart. He may invite the mother to go out for a Chinese dinner, knowing that she likes Peking duck. You can also win your own heart in a struggle over doing the right thing. Here you decide to do right rather than taking advantage of another, or doing what you know is wrong. The feeling of *chá ná jai* arises after this struggle is won inside your own heart. An athlete who competes with grace, sportsmanship and integrity may fail to win the gold but may win the hearts of those watching his or her performance.

Relief

Reassured Heart
jai chúuen (adj.) ใจชื้น

This *jai* phrase is used to describe an emotional state of relief after you have regained hope and the trouble has passed from your life. When you face an obstacle and overcome it successfully, you will feel *jai chúuen*. For example, you are caught in heavy traffic on the way to an important meeting but manage to arrive in time, upon walking into the boardroom, you feel *jai chúuen*. If Lek's brother is injured in a car crash, she rushes to the hospital with her parents. The doctor tells the family that the brother will survive his injuries and can be discharged in a couple of days. Lek and her family will feel *jai chúuen*.

Also, you can use this phrase to describe a feeling of relief that comes from the discovery that there is no problem after the initial feeling of one lurking on the horizon. You might believe that you're short of money to pay the rent, and then you check your bank account and find a balance larger than you remembered. Or you mislay your car keys, then find them under the newspaper on the dining-room table.

Relieved Heart

lôong jai (v.) โล่งใจ
lôong òk lôong jai (v.) โล่งอกโล่งใจ
pròong jai (v.) โปร่งใจ

This emotional state of being arises when your initial overwhelming feelings of panic, gloom or despair are followed by relief. A passport, credit card or travelers' checks are misplaced. The distressed feeling of the time, trouble and expense required to replace such valuables suddenly vanishes once the articles reappear—you feel *lôong jai* or *lôong òk lôong jai*. You may have an appointment with a friend who is two hours late and you have no way to contact her. You are worried sick that something bad might have happened to her. The stormy emotions that build up during the long wait are released once your friend arrives safely. The heavy, negative feelings in your heart suddenly disappear. When the clouds of worries are lifted, you feel *pròong jai*. The temple sparrow is released from a wooden cage. The sense of relief and freedom is the hallmark of this heart expression.

Give a Big Sigh of Relief
thǑOn jai (v.) ถอนใจ
thǑOn jai yài (v.) ถอนใจใหญ่
thÔOt thǑOn jai (v.) ทอดถอนใจ
thǑOn hǎay jai (v.) ถอนหายใจ

You let out a big sigh, *thǑOn jai* or *thǑOn hǎay jai*, at the end of a grueling Friday at the office. You feel relieved because the work that has occupied you all day is behind you and you leave the office and enjoy yourself for the weekend. Used in this sense, the phrase carries with it a good feeling. It is also used when you feel a sense of defeat. Perhaps you want your son to become a doctor and instead he has made up his mind to be a beachcomber. He won't listen to you. He simply goes off and lives on a beach, making a living picking up discarded bottles. Your feeling of powerlessness to stop him from this life-choice brings often causes you to give a big sigh. Only that the big sigh will not necessarily give you a sense of relief. During a troubling time, *thǑOn jai* can be used in circumstances similar to *thǑOn jai yài*. The sense of relief in the case of *thǑOn jai yài* is much greater, stronger and lasts longer. However, *thǑOn jai yài* is an old-fashioned *jai* phrase and has fallen into disuse. *ThÔOt thǑOn jai* is found in novels or poetry.

Security

Secure Heart
ùn jai (adj.) อุ่นใจ
ùn òk ùn jai (adj.) อุ่นอกอุ่นใจ

Emotional security arises when a person feels comfortable and the threat of external hardship appears remote. A person who receives a large monthly amount from a trust fund would feel *ùn jai*. Having salted away several million dollars in the bank would be a cause to feel *ùn jai*. The soldier who goes into battle wearing an amulet or carrying a photograph of his wife or sweetheart would feel *ùn jai* from having the amulet or photo in his possession. Having a professional qualification such as a doctor, nurse, dentist, lawyer or computer programmer would also bring this state of security. Presumably Bill Gates has an abundance of *ùn jai*.

When someone is feeling at their most secure in life, then they will feel *ùn jai*. The degree of warmth in the heart is a metaphor repeated in a number of heart phrases. The sense of warmth, as used here, translates into a sense of security. If someone feels secure in their relationship with their friends, lover or parents, then they feel *ùn jai*. The operative emotional state is one marked by feelings of security, serenity and peace.

You can think of certain *jai* phrases as heart temperature gauges. On the one hand, to feel *rÓOn jai*—the heart is hot—is to feel anxiety and worry. On the other, if to feel *yen jai*—the heart is cool—is to feel content and happy. A *jai rÓOn* ("hot heart") person is impatient and angry, while a *jai yen* ("cool heart") person is composed, in control and collected in circumstances where the *jai rÓOn* person might explode in a rage. To have a heart that is warm or *ùn jai* is to feel secure, so the temperature is just right.

Protected Body, Comfortable Heart

ùn kaay sà baay jai (adv.)

อุ่นกายสบายใจ

Ùn kaay sà baay jai translates as happiness in physical and mental well-being. There is a sense of being safe and protected. For instance, a small baby in the mother's arms will feel *ùn kaay sà baay jai*, literally "warm body, comfortable heart." The perfect husband will elicit this expression from his wife. The phrase is used almost exclusively within the context of the family. It would not, for example, be used among friends or colleagues at the office.

Child Disturbs the Body, Husband Disturbs the Heart

mii lûuk kuaan tuaa mii phŭaa kuaan jai (proverb)

มีลูกกวนตัว มีผัวกวนใจ

2
heart talk for the hard times

When you have a bad case of the blues or feeling out of sync with life, there may be no better language than Thai to express the extent of your emotional funk. The phrases contained in this chapter cover a wide range of feelings experienced in various states of emotional difficulty and turmoil. For example, there is a rich vocabulary of expressions for the many different states of loneliness, sadness, depression, discouragement, frustration, anxiety, weariness, and fear.

This region of emotion also covers feelings of unease, as well as the feelings of being disturbed, off-balance, lost, lonely, annoyed, impatient, hurt or lacking in confidence. Chances are you will find the right *Heart Talk* phrase to express the exact nuance of an ill feeling. A number of the phrases serve to describe more than a transitory emotional state—they are used to describe the nature or personality of a person. A person who is tired, depressed, moody, bored or has a trigger temper may well hear a Thai speaker use one of the phrases in this chapter to describe his or her personality.

Anger

Boiling with Anger Heart

dùeaat jai (v.) เดือดใจ

The person is boiling over with anger. Often the person who feels *dùeaat jai* has clenched jaws, sweat pouring down the face, and lips narrowed as the anger shoots through his or her body. The cause of such anger could be any number of things including an insult, assault or rudeness. A driver cutting in front of you, nearly causing an accident, might cause you to boil over with anger. A person has insulted you by saying that you have been born to the life of a dog (*Î châad mǎa*). This is guaranteed to cause a reaction of anger in a native Thai. When you are robbed at gunpoint, it is likely (after the robber flees the scene) that you would feel a great deal of anger or *dùeat jai*.

Annoyance

Annoyed Heart
ram kaan jai (v.) รำคาญใจ

Thai people wish at all costs to avoid conflict. Behind a smile might lurk a person who feels *ram kaan jai*. If you go to the health club and the music is cranked up to the point your eardrums are ready to burst, most of the Thais would say nothing (but would feel *ram kaan jai*) while the farangs would be screaming and jumping up and down, much to the great amusement of the Thais. When the suitor continues to call the woman who has made it clear that she doesn't wish to hear from him, she feels *ram kaan jai* as soon as she hears his voice on the telephone. When the nagging child at the department store runs around picking up every toy and dragging them back to his mother, his mother and the staff of the department store will feel *ram kaan jai*.

Irritated Heart
khueaang jai (v.) เคืองใจ

In every interaction with others, there are conventions and rules to be followed, and when those conventions and rules are violated, someone may feel annoyed in their heart. For example, a person wais another and if that other person does not return their wai they may feel irritated. There is a heavily pregnant woman on the bus who stands in front of the young male who sees her but pretends that he is sleeping so that he doesn't give up his seat. The pregnant woman will feel *khueaang jai*. The feeling of irritation will pass when another passenger volunteers her seat for the woman.

Pestering Another's Heart

nâa kuaan jai (adj.) น่ากวนใจ

Nâa kuaan jai is an adjectival phrase that describes a state of annoyance caused by an annoying person. Lek is trying to study in the library or to work at her desk in the office and someone keeps interrupting her with an invitation for a conversation. Lek feels frustrated by this person's constant interruptions and tells him to stop. Her request is ignored and the intruder continues to interrupt her concentration. The intruder is *nâa kuaan jai*—a pester. When a small child begs for toys in the department store and nags the mother, the child is *nâa kuaan jai*.

Vexed Heart

khùn jai (v.) ขุ่นใจ

This *jai* phrase describes a state of being displeased or in conflict with another person. The underlying causes are usually the actions or words of the other person. A client has cancelled an important appointment because he claims to be too busy to see you, and as a result the deal you've been negotiating falls through. You had no advance warning this was going to happen. As a result, the heart quickly goes from a peaceful state to one of irritation. You may have had an argument with a friend over something she said or did that was irritating or annoying you. A colleague may have criticized your work. The emotions experienced in such circumstances are often short-lived. People recover from irritation and annoyance quickly. In this emotional state, you feel a desire to withdraw from other people, deal with your irritation and then return to the world of others with a smile.

Anxiety & Worry

Ill At Ease Heart

mâi sà baay jai (v.) ไม่สบายใจ

This is probably the most common *jai* phrase Thai speakers use to express their anxiety and worry. *Mâi sà baay jai* is the opposite of *sà baay jai* or "comfortable heart"(*mâi* is a term for negation). When you feel *mâi sà baay jai*, you have lost the sense of comfort, contentment and inner peace that you enjoy when you have a "comfortable heart." In this emotional state, you feel ill at ease, worried or distressed about something or someone. Perhaps you said something that upset your close friend, or your father just told you that he is experiencing frequent dizziness and you are worried about him. *Mâi sà baay jai* also applies in many other situations. It is a catchall phrase for whenever you are emotionally out of tune with yourself.

Butterflies in One's Stomach

hăay jai mâi thûaa thÓOng (v.) หายใจไม่ทั่วท้อง

A person in this emotional state has some deep-seated worry, fear or troubles on his or her mind. The emotional state can be described as when your worries are so intense that you cannot draw a breath. A person is riding a bicycle along Sukhumvit Road (not to be recommended) and a motorist drives too close, accidentally knocking down the cyclist. The cyclist's father arrives on the scene and he is an influential person and threatens to have the motorist sent to prison for a long period. The motorist, in the face of this threat and the powerful father, will feel *hăay jai mâi thûaa thÓOng*.

Boiled Flesh, Steaming Heart

dùeaat rÓOn jai (v.) เดือดร้อนใจ
dùeaat núeaa rÓOn jai (v.) เดือดเนื้อร้อนใจ

From the dramatic translation you have a hint of the active drama that causes you to face a situation where there is no good alternative. You don't have peace of mind. The mother who, at the start of the school term, doesn't have the money for the school uniform and books for her child, is beside herself and doesn't know what to do.

This heart phrase is reserved for the big-time personal worries. Someone is worried they don't have enough money to meet their daily living expenses and may have to go without food or shelter. In times of economic gloom, terrorism, natural disaster, one has such a worried heart as to whether employment and life will continue. Without a job, the car, the house and the family disappear. The prospect of such losses would naturally cause extreme anxiety to the point where your heart steams or *dùeaat rÓOn jai*. *Dùeaat núeaa rÓOn jai* is similar with the added feature that not only does your heart steam but your flesh also boils.

Hot Heart, Hot Chest

rÓOn jai (v.) ร้อนใจ
rÓOn òk rÓOn jai (v.) ร้อนอกร้อนใจ
à naa thOOn rÓOn jai (v.) อนาทรร้อนใจ

If someone walks around with a set of fundamental worries they can't shake free from then their emotional state is appropriately described as *rÓOn jai* or *rÓOn òk rÓOn jai*. The background emotional condition is associated with profound concern, fear, anxiety or insecurity. Someone is afraid that something will happen outside of their control and that they, or someone they love, may suffer harm as a result. They may fear that they will fail to complete a project assigned by their boss. Other examples include: being afraid that their best friend will not recover from a major operation, or their child will fail in school, or their spouse or lover will abandon them. *À naa thOOn rÓOn jai* is used in the same context.

Turmoil in One's Heart

krà won krà waay jai (v.) กระวนกระวายใจ
rÓOn rûm klûm jai (v.) ร้อนรุ่มกลุ้มใจ

You have fears or worries that something terrible has happened or is about to happen. Often these worries are connected to the intense pressures from work, family and friends. For example, your boyfriend has turned off his cell phone for the last three days. Your child is absent from school and no one knows where he is. You have heard rumors that your company is going out of business and will lay off the staff in two weeks. Such possibilities can overwhelm you to the point where you are in turmoil. In circumstances where another person experiences depression caused by the crush of daily pressures or resulting from a decision or course of events outside of his or her control, either of these two heart phrases may be used to describe the emotional impact.

Worried Heart
jai mâi dii (adj.) ใจไม่ดี

This is a common informal *jai* phrase used to describe someone who is worried. Perhaps children are left alone at home and the parents are unusually late in coming back for dinner, and the children start to worry about their parents. Wondering if maybe they have been in an accident. Lek's boyfriend calls every Friday but he fails to phone one Friday or for the following five days. Lek doesn't know what has happened to him, and her worry causes her to have *jai mâi dii*. Less commonly, this *jai* phrase is used to describe a person who is moody.

Worried Heart
klûm jai (v.) กลุ้มใจ

In this emotional state, your feeling of worry may arise from a rapidly approaching deadline when you know there is insufficient time to successfully complete the task. Given the traffic jams in Bangkok, businessmen who sit in their cars knowing they will be late for a multimillion closing, which will fall through if they are not present, will feel *klûm jai*. A mother may feel *klûm jai* that her daughter is doing something wrong in her life—perhaps associating with friends who smoke, drink and hang out in nightclubs with gun-carrying gangsters—and feel powerless to stop her daughter from making a mistake. If a daughter wants to marry someone her mother disapproves of, she will feel *klûm jai*. The tone conveyed is serious concern and represents the emotional state of anxiety or worry in the absence of any good alternative courses of action.

Worried Heart
kang won jai (v.) กังวลใจ

A worried mother, waiting for her child to return from school when he or she is late, feels *kang won jai*. The emotional stakes causing the worry are less serious than *klûm jai*. There is, in other words, less to fear and the fear or concern is for a shorter duration. Still the ache of fear is inherent in this emotional state. The emphasis is on the nagging worry that something bad may have befallen you or someone for whom you feel responsibility.

Heavy Heart
nàk jai (v., adj.) หนักใจ
nàk òk nàk jai (adj.) หนักอกหนักใจ

When a person experiences deep worries or concerns for which finding a situation is a great challenge then his or her emotional reaction may be one of heavy heart or *nàk jai*. Feeling *nàk jai* or *nàk òk nàk jai* is similar to feeling *klûm jai* but with an added sense of great burden. For example, a child has been chronically disobeying the wishes of his parents, so that his father and mother feel *nàk jai* about his future. A company made much less profit than in the previous quarter. The CEO feels *nàk jai* as he has to answer to the unhappy shareholders in the next shareholders' meeting.

Depression

Depressed Heart
jai hòt hùu (adj.) ใจหดหู่

This *jai* phrase conveys the sense of being dispirited by the failure of purpose or plan. The failure zaps your spirit. You go into a state of depression. You feel despondent at the absence of some essential ability, trait or characteristic that is regarded as necessary to cope with a situation or other person. In this depressed state, you may be judged by your friends and family as being *jai hòt hùu*—your heart has withered, shrunken.

Despondent Heart
jai hìiaw (adj.) ใจเหี่ยว
jai hÊEng (adj.) ใจแห้ง
(jìt) jai hÒO hìiaw (adj.) (จิต)ใจห่อเหี่ยว
(jìt) jai hìiaw hÊEng (adj.) (จิต)ใจเหี่ยวแห้ง

Whether the metaphor for this emotional state is withered as in *jai hìiaw* or dry as in *jai hÊEng*, the effect is the same: you are feeling sad, unhappy and depressed. You feel sad or dismayed about something, or about what someone did or said, or with your own actions. Or you may have witnessed a terrible event like a major injury or death of a child. Emotionally, you are like yesterday's donuts, or three-day-old flowers. Wilted and demoralized, you feel no will to claw yourself out of the emotional hole you've fallen into. The feeling is the same as when using *(jìt) jai hÒO hìiaw* or *(jìt) jai hìiaw hÊEng*. A young woman who is rejected by her boyfriend may fall into this state; it doesn't need to be a permanent condition but it is one that at the time makes the person feels as though the dark clouds will never clear and life is without hope.

Cheer-up One's Heart
yÓOm jai (v.) ย้อมใจ
chúp náam jai (v.) ชุบน้ำใจ

This heart phrase comes into play when you are feeling a little depressed or feeling despair, and what you need is someone to brighten your spirits. Who would be better than friends to rally you out of a funk? You have just been dumped and are moping at home. Your friends are worried about you so they come to get you for a night out. They have a plan to *yÓOm jai* you—bring your heart back to life—with bar hopping and many rounds of drinks.

Similarly, *chúp náam jai* is literally dipping or soaking the heart in water to bring it back to life. Actual usage focuses on the emotional encouragement to make the heart return to a state of comfort. You may listen to music, read a book or drink a glass of wine to *yÓOm jai* yourself.

Discouragement

Cut Courage in the Heart
tàt kam lang jai (v.) ตัดกำลังใจ

When you feel empowered or encouraged, then you are up for any challenge. When someone "cuts" the power of your heart, the effect is to discourage, disempower you. Sometimes the loss of encouragement is inflicted as the result of a remark or the action of another. When your girlfriend proclaims that you are getting fat and bald, she has likely cut the courage in your heart: *tàt kam lang jai*. Such a remark might well cause you to lose confidence (or *mòt kam lang jai*) and destroy your positive image as a slender, handsome guy. The employer who tells her secretary, Khun Vinai, that his typing skills are terrible may cause him to feel discouraged. The boss's criticism is described as *tàt kam lang jai*.

Discouraged Heart
thÓO jai (v.) ท้อใจ

You may feel *thÓO jai* by the undesirable outcome of an event, the undesirable behavior of a person you care about or critical opinions others have expressed about your performance, character or appearance. You may have lost out on a promotion to a younger colleague. The political party you supported in the last election lost. Following a sudden currency devaluation you find that you've lost thirty per cent of your buying power. In these circumstances, you may well feel the loss of courage and enthusiasm about the future. In another example, a child may wish that her father stops smoking and tries to convince him to cut down or stop but the father continues his old bad habit. The father ignores the child's warning even though he knows about the health hazard. When the child sees the father is unable to stop, she will feel *thÓO jai*. The feeling is one of being discouraged.

Lose Power of the Heart

sěaa kam lang jai (v.) เสียกำลังใจ
mòt kam lang jai (v.) หมดกำลังใจ

This is the feeling associated with broken will power. The wind has gone out of your sails and you feel powerless. The person has a sense of being overwhelmed or fearful about the future. When a non-Thai speaker first learns to read Thai, he finds great difficulty and spends many long hours in sorting out the forty-four consonants, confusing *khor khwaay* with *dor dèk* (or the water buffalo with the child). In this process of starting over in a new language from the beginning, or reverting to a childlike level of language ability, one may feel discouraged or *sěaa kam lang jai*. A student wishes to apply to a famous university. He studies hard but he is only an average student. His friend—apparently not a very good one—tells him that he's wasting his time applying to the university as the standards are higher than he can reach. The student, upon hearing this verdict, will likely feel *sěaa kam lang jai* and experience a diminished sense of self. If he wants to give up all hope and his will power is gone, then his feeling can be described as *mòt kam lang jai*.

Lost Heart

jai sěaa (adj.) ใจเสีย

A person who is *jai sěaa* feels discouraged or disheartened by an event or fears something bad will happen. The feeling that underlies *jai sěaa* is one of being *jai mâi dii,* "worried heart." For example, you just fell of a motorbike and don't feel any hurt or pain. But upon picking yourself up, you discover a large amount of blood on your leg. The sight of blood makes you feel *jai sěaa*—feeling afraid that you might have sustained a serious injury. When the grandmother receives news from her doctor that she is in an advanced stage of cancer, both the grandmother and her family members will feel *jai sĕaa.*

Sinking Heart
jai pÊEw (adj.) ใจแป้ว
jai fÒO (n., adv.) ใจฝ่อ

You lost all of the data on your hard drive. You have a crush on a woman in your office and on the way to the sky train you see her walking hand in hand with another man. These mini-dramas, though not really as bad as a divorce, loss of life, job or spouse can still make you feel a mini-collapse inside your chest—your heart sinks. The feeling is *jai pÊEw*. It can be either direct, as a result of what you experience, or the empathy of feeling another's loss or pain as your own.

Wasted Heart
plueaang jai (v.) เปลืองใจ

Daeng looks after many children in her household. The children don't listen to her, ignoring her every request. After a day of chasing around after all these wild, undisciplined children, she collapses in a chair and feels *plueaang jai*: she feels exhausted and resentful that all her efforts with them are for naught—her heart has been wasted. The premise is of someone who has a goal or task to complete but is not receiving the reciprocity they need. The dispirited, tired, weary state of the poor person who fights battles with such unhelpful, thoughtless people and problems leads to the feeling contained in this *jai* phrase. It is also used in a relationship where the man, after many years of living with a devoted, caring, loving woman, dumps her for a younger woman. The woman who is dumped feels *plueaang jai*, rejected.

At One's Wits' End Heart
jon jai (v.) จนใจ

This heart phrase can be defined as hitting an emotional dead end despite your best efforts. *Jon jai* describes a personal failure to obtain something of value or to perform according to expectations. Your friend asked to borrow some money but you are broke yourself, so you say you feel *jon jai* that you cannot lend any money. Frequently, the *jai* phrase is used as an excuse to tell someone that you can't do what they have asked.

Disturbance

Difficult Heart
lam bàak jai (adj.) ลำบากใจ

This *jai* phrase is used when you feel uncomfortable, especially in the sense that you are unable to respond to another's request, or you are put in a difficult situation. You are incredibly inconvenienced, in conflict of interest or in conflict of your own conscience. For example, your friend's spouse is seriously ill and needs an expensive medical care. You friend asks you for a loan but you need the money to pay for your child's new school term. Or your friend lost all his money in gambling and asked you for a loan. Money is not a problem but you don't want to support his gambling habit. However, you know that if you don't lend him the money, his young wife and children will suffer. In both cases, you feel *lam bàak jai*, and are in a conundrum. But eventually you will have to make a choice and deal with the situation one way or another.

Disturbed Heart
wûn waay jai (v.) วุ่นวายใจ
pùaan jai (v.) ป่วนใจ

In this state of emotional turbulence, you find yourself locked inside an emotional wind tunnel with the fan turned up full blast. You feel mentally disturbed. Any number of incidents, slights, actions, moods can engage the rotary blades and stir up a terrible storm to disturb the normal equilibrium of the heart. What does it feel like to be inside such a place? One explanation is *wûn waay jai*—a state of internal chaos. Your heart is out of control and you've lost your peace of mind. It can happen if you have too many demands from others and too little time to satisfy them. Everyone is pulling on you, asking you for something, and you feel in turmoil.

Troubled Heart

yûng yâak jai (adj.) ยุ่งยากใจ

If you face a difficult choice falls into a state of emotional chaos. This *jai* expression is similar to *lam bàak jai*, "difficult heart," above. This troubled feeling can arise as a result of small or big trouble in your life, such as your child is having difficulties adjust to his or her new school, your dog has bitten your neighbor, or you have a difficult time choosing between Employee A and Employee B for a promotion because both are equally deserving. If you have more than one lovers, then it is likely that you frequently fall into this state of *yûng yâak jai*.

Child Disturbs the Body, Husband Disturbs the Heart

mii lûuk kuaan tuaa mii phŭaa kuaan jai (proverb)

มีลูกกวนตัว มีผัวกวนใจ

This *jai* proverb expresses the concern of many women (both single and married) who have to combine the demands of child-rearing with looking after their husband's or boyfriend's needs and desires. Such a woman feels that the domestic pressures leave her very little personal time and freedom. This heart expression has become more common as more women enter the workplace and have the same time constraints placed on them as their male counterparts, while the traditional view of what is expected of woman has not changed as rapidly. This is a *jai* phrase that a Thai woman would use with her husband, lover or child when she's in a complaining mood. She's expressing a feeling that has a germ of truth but is not intended seriously; it is more an expression of being tired, and it allows her to vent her sense of feeling disturbed. It can also be used as a warning from married women when their single girlfriends want to get married. This may explain why so many Thai women choose to remain single.

Doubtfulness

Doubtful Heart
khÔOng jai (v.) ข้องใจ

With this heart phrase we enter the realm of unresolved doubts. This is a more serious feeling of uncertainty than *mâi nÊE jai*, "unsure heart." The wife may suspect that her husband has a minor wife. The feeling of not knowing whether her suspicions are true or not gives her a feeling of *khÔOng jai*. When haunted by feelings of doubt, or when one believes another person is suffering from such doubts, this heart phrase is a useful expression. It is a call for reassurance and a request for the other to restore trust. Another example is when a student receives a low score on her examination. She feels *khÔOng jai* because she believes she did very well on the exam. She goes to the teacher to clear her doubt. The teacher shows her the correct answers and she now understands that she misread many questions and gave the wrong answers.

Doubting Heart
khaa jai (adj.) คาใจ

This heart phrase is used when you face an unresolved problem. It was made popular in a Thai love song and expresses the doubts felt by a lover. The doubt may, for example, focus on the degree of commitment to the relationship by the other person. The person who experiences the doubts may have some evidence that his or her lover is seeing another person. This suspicion would cause him or her to feel *khaa jai*. But *khaa jai* is not limited to the doubting-lover situation. Another example is when Lek goes to the market and buys many items and believes the amount will be about one thousand baht; the vendor says Lek owes two thousand baht. On the bus back home, Lek thinks about the cost of each item. She becomes obsessed about the cost. Her friend asks Lek to forget about it. But she can't stop calculating the price of each item because if she stops working out the numbers she feels *khaa jai*. Her doubt will be put to rest by the final round of calculation.

Fear

Lost Heart

jai hǎay (adj.) ใจหาย

Jai hǎay applies to the emotional state of feeling frightened. The person is stunned by an unexpected event or thing. For example, you almost dropped your expensive laptop by accident. Or you had a close call on the road; another car just ran the red light and almost broad-sided your car. The *jai* phrase applies to less dramatic circumstances as well. For instance, you are driving your car and you remember that you forgot to lock the front door of your house. Or you get out of a taxi, walk away, and a few minutes later discover that you left your cell phone inside the taxi. In both of these cases, *jai hǎay* is a good expression to capture the feeling that you feel at the moment of the realization.

Lost and Overturned Heart

jai hǎay jai khwâm (adj.) ใจหายใจคว่ำ
jai mâi yùu kàp núeaa kàp tuaa (adj.) ใจไม่อยู่กับเนื้อกับตัว

Jai hǎay jai khwâm is *jai hǎay* with an additional exclamation mark. It is a more dramatic expression of *jai hǎay*. For example, in the middle of the night at home you hear a sudden noise, a breaking glass; you realize that your house is being broken in. You suddenly feel the chilling fright. Your heart is pounding inside; what you feel is *jai hǎay jai khwâm*—your heart is lost and overturned. Another similar expression is *jai mâi yùu kàp núeaa kàp tuaa*—your heart is frightened out of your body. The latter phrase is also used in the context of a person being absent-minded.

Fearful Heart

rá thúek jai (v.) ระทึกใจ

Faced with a sudden flash of fear you feel *rá thúek jai*. Your heart pumps harder, you feel it inside your chest. The translation falls in the territory somewhere between fear and thrill. If you are walking down a jungle path and meet a tiger, a "fearful heart" will no doubt be pounding in your chest. The same applies to someone who is trying to cross Sukhumvit or Silom Roads. Watching a horror film in which the monster jumps out and makes a grab for the hero may cause a collective feeling of "fearful heart" in the audience. Another example is at a sports event when one set of supporters express their collective support. Fans who are cheering feel *rá thúek jai*. You may experience the same thumping-heart feeling when you are in the midst of reading a thriller and you aren't certain whether the hero will emerge alive from the trap set by the villains.

Shuddering with Fear Heart

sĭiaw jai (v.) เสียวใจ

This heart phrase is not commonly used. It can be employed to describe a state of being scared or afraid. The fear in this case is often irrational. You can't pin down exactly why you are fearful. Fear of the unknown causes you to feel *sĭiaw jai*. Also the situation may be scary and the outcome uncertain, and this leads to a feeling of fear falling within the ambit of this phrase. For instance, a boss makes a threat to an employee that unless his job performance improves the employee will be fired. The employee so threatened would feel *sĭiaw jai*. Extreme sports, such as jumping out of planes or off cliffs with a parachute, would cause a person to experience this feeling. If you are making a horror film then sending the lead actors into a cemetery at night to confront a hungry ghost would cause the audience to feel *sĭiaw jai*.

Trembling Heart

ngan ngók tòk jai (v.) งันงกตกใจ

An experience may be so intense and overwhelming that you tremble with fear. In the case of child abuse, when someone inflicts mental or physical torture, the child would feel *ngan ngók tòk jai* as the person inflicting the punishment appeared. In the case of a battered or abused wife, the abusive, violent husband who approaches the wife with his fist raised will cause her to feel *ngan ngók tòk jai*. Police officers or prison officials who use physical force to extract information from a suspect or prisoner, would find their charge trembling with fear as the beatings resumed.

Frustration

Frustrated Heart
àt ân tan jai (v.) อัดอั้นตันใจ

When you keep your feelings bottled up inside because you feel helpless about your situation, or you are unable to express your frustration or control what is being said or done to you, your heart is frustrated (*àt ân tan jai*). You are invited to stay as a guest in the house of an old friend you haven't seen since school. He has a wife and two children. The bathroom is never vacant. The phones are always being used by the children. The TV is blasting at high volume after midnight. Your friend and his wife both smoke two packs of cigarettes a day. You don't have a lot of money for a hotel so you put up with the annoying situation until you reach a breaking point. At some stage you'd rather sleep in the park than stay in what is an intolerable environment. Thais seek to avoid confrontation if at all possible and might get out of this situation by saying they had to return home urgently to assist an ailing relative. In this way the frustration can be relieved without causing a loss of face or hard feelings.

Stricken Heart
kháp jai (v.) คับใจ
kháp òk kháp jai (v.) คับอกคับใจ
kháp khÊEp ÈEp jai (adj.) คับแคบแอบใจ

These expressions are used to convey a serious emotional discomfort. A person who says he or she feels *kháp jai* may be signaling suicide. The tone of this expression indicates a serious bad feeling, and the person with such feelings is filled with anxiety, stress and often a sense of hopelessness. Such a person may have trouble coping with the sense of being overwhelmed by such negative emotions and should be listened to carefully and offered assistance to alleviate this dreadful feeling. The circumstances or context of an event, along with a question of the person's temperament are to be taken into account; what emotionally affects one personal substantially may have less impact on another.

Uncomfortable Heart
ùet àt jai (v.) อึดอัดใจ

This heart phrase literally means stifled, obstructed or clogged heart and is used to cover feelings of discomfort. A person who feels uncomfortable through some social situation or circumstance, or from a conflict, experiences *ùet àt jai*. A guest insists on giving all the details of a gory auto accident that he witnessed. Out of politeness you are unable to express your desire for the person to change the subject. You may feel uncomfortable in strange surroundings, or when you quarrel with a friend. The range of events, objects, meetings and encounters that cause feelings of discomfort are legion. Inevitably, what makes one uncomfortable in the heart is highly personal to each person, and part of the exploration of other people is to determine zones of comfort.

Grief

Grieving Heart
hŭaa jai rá thom (v.) หัวใจระทม

This is a heart expression to describe your broken-heart condition. In this state, you possess a deep, profound sense of *rá thom,* meaning sadness and emotional pain of the gravest kind. Perhaps it is the death of a parent or friend that causes this penetrating sense of sadness to envelop your heart and soul. It may also be used in a romantic context.

Hold Breath Until Death Heart

klân jai taay (v.) กลั้นใจตาย

Extreme, unbearable grief can cause someone to wish to die. It is as if you wished to hold your breath and exit this veil of tears and enter the next life. When a couple breaks up, one person may be so distraught at the loss of the relationship that he or she wishes to hold his or her breath until death. In Thailand, like in most countries, this is a fairly difficult threat to carry out. The second sense of the *jai* phrase applies when someone is spoiled and wishes to have their way. A small child might use this expression with her mother because the mother refuses the child's request to buy the latest computer software game.

Shattered Heart

jai sà lăay (v.) ใจสลาย

Wimol sees her boyfriend walking along Sukhumvit Road holding hands with another woman who is obviously pregnant. She believed that she was the only woman in his life and is shattered to the tender treatment of the pregnant woman. The phrase applies in other emotionally painful situations as well. In times of war, if a child witnesses the execution of his parents by an invading force, he would feel *jai sà lăay* for life. An upcountry woman who believes that she is going to work in a restaurant abroad but is forced into prostitution would also have a shattered heart. The phrase is used to express extreme states of sadness. Having your wife or child killed in a terrorist attack would cause the kind of sadness represented by this *jai* phrase.

Hopelessness

Hopeless Heart

mâi mii kà jìt kà jai (v.) ไม่มีกะจิตกะใจ

mòt kà jìt kà jai (v.) หมดกะจิตกะใจ

Something has happened or has been said that causes you to lose your desire to deal with a situation. Emotionally, the condition is one of feeling powerless. Events are beyond your ability to influence or control or the problem is so paramount that you feel a lack of will to fight on and, being overwhelmed by the sense of defeat. You are paralyzed into inaction. In this state (which often can be merely temporary) you lose any desire to go out with friends or to be around family. You wish only to be left alone. For example, Lek has been given a notice of termination by her employer of seven years. She is devastated, knowing that there are few jobs now being offered because of economic problems. Having lost her job, she feels *mòt kà jìt kà jai*. Lek feels that she cannot shape the events of her own life. These phrases can be used in less extreme situations, such as when your partner has criticized your performance on a joint project, blaming you for the loss of the client.

Loneliness

Forlorn Heart
wáa wèe jai (adj.) ว้าเหว่ใจ

"Forlorn heart" expresses your feeling of aloneness. Being alone in the heart comes from living in isolation from others, especially family and friends. The Thais are a very social people and maintain close connection with their family and friends. Great value is placed on this social support structure. Someone banished from this nurturing set of relationships would likely experience *wáa wèe jai*. When you live in another culture and country, sometimes you look around and see no familiar face, and everything and everyone seems alien to you. At that moment, you feel.

Lonely Heart
plìiaw jai (adj.) เปลี่ยวใจ

The phrase is used to describe emotional states of isolation with a hint of sexual connotation. In many cases it can be used in the same circumstances as *wáa wèe jai*. You are fed up with eating dinner alone, or sleeping alone night after night.

You experience an empty, hollow feeling in the core of your life. And something wakes up inside you and you discover that you are all alone. With this realization comes a feeling of unhappiness or desolation arising out of the sense of loneliness. Perhaps your spouse or lover has gone, causing you to feel lonely. Maybe your spouse or lover is beside you physically but the love has vanished from the relationship. The use of the phrase may be a cry for rescue from this solitary state of being.

Lonesome Heart
wang weeng jai (adj.) วังเวงใจ

This is a difficult heart phrase to translate into English. The English word, "lonesome" only partially captures the meaning. Visualize a late-night street in a dark neighborhood. You are alone walking down the street. In order to go to your destination you must pass a cemetery. It is dark and stormy. The overpowering quietness of this moment in this situation creates a certain emotional state, which the Thais call *wang weeng jai*. One's heart is on full red alert, waiting for some invisible force of danger or evil to make itself evident. It is also used in the context of feeling lonely. A child left alone at home will feel *wang weeng jai* in the sense of loneliness. After the husband dies, the widow who is left home alone also feels loneliness or *wang weeng jai*.

Regrets

Sorry Heart
sĕaa jai (v.) เสียใจ
rúu sùek sĕaa jai (v.) รู้สึกเสียใจ

This is a common *jai* phrase used for feeling sorry. You may feel sorry (*sĕaa jai* or *rúu sùek sĕaa jai*) in several different situations: (i) for something bad that has happened to you; (ii) for something that you said or did to another that you regret; and (iii) for a misfortunate that has befallen another. In the first sense, you may feel sorry because your boyfriend or girlfriend has left you, or that your close relative has passed away. In the second sense, the expression is used in the context of asking for forgiveness. You may have said harsh words to someone or did something to hurt their feelings, and want to express your regrets by saying you feel *sĕaa jai*. In the third sense, it is used to express sympathy. For example, you wish to convey your condolence to a friend whose father has died; you can say, "*Sĕaa jai dûaay ná khráp/ khá*," which means "Please accept my sympathy."

Lose Chest, Lose Heart
sĕaa òk sĕaa jai (v.) เสียอกเสียใจ

You are feeling very sad when you have this heart. This *jai* expression is normally used to express profound sorrow for a major misfortune that has befallen oneself. Examples are many, including (unwanted) termination of a relationship, death in the family, failure in life or career, etc. While this feeling is felt by the person who experiences that sorrow, it is, however, not usually expressed by the person who is feeling the sorrow, but by a third party. For instance, Gung tells her friends about John who has just been divorced by his wife. Gung describes John as being *sĕaa òk sĕaa jai* over the breakup. In another example, Apple studied very hard for the university entrance examination and failed to get into her first choice of university. Apple feels *sĕaa òk sĕaa jai*.

Returned Heart
klàp jai (v.) กลับใจ

To repent for what one has done to wrong another is to *klàp jai*. Repentance is a return of the heart. There is an element of redemption. A criminal may wish to become a good person, and his change of intention or plans may be evidence of an act of *klàp jai*. The emotional content is one's acceptance of responsibility for a wrong or harm caused to another, and implicit is the message that the person causing the harm will not do it again. In another context, *klàp jai* means to change one's mind (normally a

180-degree kind of change). For example, the husband who has kept many mia nois and mistresses may *klàp jai*, end all his affairs and return with complete faithfulness to his wife.

Rueful Heart
sěaa jai phaay lăng (v.)
เสียใจภายหลัง

You were given a warning not to buy (or sell) those shares on the stock market, or you would regret it later (*sěaa jai phaay lăng*). But you thought you would make a killing. Instead you lost your entire investment. Now what you feel is *sěaa jai phaay lăng*—that sick feeling in the gut that you were stupid not to listen when you had the chance to do so. *Sěaa jai phaay lăng* is the feeling of knowing you did wrong, regretting your past actions, and applying self-criticisms. You don't need anyone to point out that you were a fool. You know it and feel it yourself.

Rejection

Lost Sympathy Heart
sěaa náam jai (v.) เสียน้ำใจ

Your best friend made a special trip to a distant market in order to buy New Zealand lamb, then drove in heavy traffic to buy a bottle of imported red wine. When you arrive for dinner, rather than appreciating the efforts you have a negative reaction to the food. You announce: (i) you have hated lamb since you were a boy; (ii) the wine is of an inferior vintage; and (iii) you've already had a snack with some colleagues and you are no longer hungry. Given such insensitive and thoughtless behavior, your friend would feel let down and maybe a little miffed, or *sěaa náam jai*. She has made an effort on your behalf and those efforts go unappreciated. You rejected her heart, her *náam jai*, her expression of caring.

In another context, the phrase may be used by someone who insists on giving you a gift that you feel uncomfortable accepting. The person may say to you, don't make him or her feel *sěaa náam jai*, please accept the gift. In this situation, if the gift does not make you feel too uncomfortable, you may have to accept it, or the person will feel really let down.

Sadness

Almost Breaking Heart
hǔaa jai thÊEp jà khàat (v.)
หัวใจแทบจะขาด

You experience an attack of *hǔaa jai thÊEp jà khàat* when you feel that your heart is about to tear apart. It might be because you feel heartbreaking grief over the death of a loved one. This wretched feeling may be caused by a variety of circumstances and can be used in a hyperbolic sense, for example you want a new BMW so much it breaks your heart but you can't afford to buy one. Or your spouse or lover is out of town and you are overcome by longing. Or you have expectations that your son or daughter will become a doctor and instead he or she is caught in a club with drugs and an unregistered firearm. Someone won the lottery but lost their ticket. In such circumstances, they may use this expression of *hǔaa jai thÊEp jà khàat*. They experience despair that makes them feel heartbroken. As the following heart phrases suggest, the Thai language has a rich arsenal of heart expressions for the English language notion of sadness that comes from a broken heart.

Broken Heart
ráaw raan jai (v.) ร้าวรานใจ
ráaw jai (v.) ร้าวใจ

You feel that another has chipped off a piece of your heart. If the heart is a crystal vase, it has a crack down the center. You can still use the vase. Just as you won't die in this state of being, you definitely feel what happened has caused you to feel loss and sadness. You are experiencing a classic case of heartache. You may have been away from the country for a couple of months and your lover has established a new relationship with someone else. You feel *ráaw raan jai*.

Hurting Heart

sà thueaan jai (v.) สะเทือนใจ

Sà thueaan jai means that you feel sadness or hurt as a result of events. Your heart aches. There are many causes for heartaches. The feeling can be a reaction to the misery or suffering of others. For example, if you are in a restaurant where a terrorist attack kills several patrons, after the blast you will feel *sà thueaan jai*. The feeling may also be caused by hurtful words said by someone you care about.

Miserable Heart

thúk jai (adj.) ทุกข์ใจ

This heart phrase is the classic expression of misery. *Thúk jai* is commonly used to express the daily, garden-variety states of unhappiness in life. You wake up in the morning to find that your car has been broken into the previous night and the radio has been stolen. You are likely to feel *thúk jai*. Or if you are laid off or fired from your job, you would also use this expression (among others) to express your emotional state of being. You can't pay your rent, your son is on drugs, or your spouse is upset with you over the lack of money for the household—these are a few examples of the misery that can be visited upon you.

Miserable Body, Comfortable Heart

thúk kaay sà baay jai (adj.) ทุกข์กายสบายใจ

This expression suggests a state of mental well-being that transcends material well-being. In the not too distant past, when life was less defined by what people owned and was more about other factors determining the quality of life, *thúk kaay sà baay jai* described an attitude towards life where happiness and contentment arose from a sense of family and community. A poor family worked hard, lived hand to mouth, was often engaged in manual physical labor, but at the end of the day the family members were happy and content with their life. The phrase is also connected with the Buddhist state of happiness and contentment.

Saddened Heart
sà lòt jai (v.) สลดใจ
à nàat jai (v.) อนาถใจ

When you witness another's true misfortune in life, then you may feel *sà lòt jai.* This is sadness in the sense of empathy or sympathy for another's black luck or harm. You become sad in the heart about the misadventure suffered by others. You may have come upon a terrible automobile accident and witnessed the suffering of those injured. School children are killed in a mudslide. People in the thousands are killed in an earthquake. Victims in these circumstances make you feel *sà lòt jai.*

A second situation for using *sà lòt jai* is to describe a major disappointment. The feeling may arise when someone who is close to you commits an act or says something which is disappointing. A child may be caught out in telling a lie and this disappoints his mother. The event in question is significant. It would not refer to a trivial disappointment. But what is trivial to one may be of profound significance to another. On the other hand, some misfortunes are universally significant. If a newspaper reports a plane crash with all passengers dead, then most readers would experience a "saddened heart." Another variation of this heart phrase *à nàat jai* is used in the latter context.

Shrivelled Heart
hŭaa jai lîip (n.) หัวใจลีบ

"Shrivelled heart" is a slang phrase (now rarely used) to express the sense that someone has a broken heart. The word *lîip* has a meaning similar to the English word shrivelled. Alternatively, this heart phrase can be used to mean one suffers from heart disease. The metaphysical state of the heart must be distinguished from its physical condition and this is usually evident from the context in which the phrase is used.

Sensitivity

Touchy Heart

nÓOy jai (v.) น้อยใจ

nÓOy òk nÓOy jai (v.) น้อยอกน้อยใจ

There are two categories for the variations of *nÓOy jai*. In the first example, you suffer from being ignored or slighted. When you forget your wife's birthday, she will feel *nÓOy jai*. You are left off the list for the annual office party, and when you discover that you are the only one not invited, then you will feel *nÓOy jai* or *nÓOy òk nÓOy jai*. In this first category, you are reacting, or those around you are reacting, to the small slights that come along in ordinary life. You feel bad about being slighted. This is a normal emotion.

In the second category, there are people whose personality makes them far more likely to feel touchy or belittled or ignored. There are those individuals who are sensitive to any hint of disapproval, limitation, restriction or criticism, for a lifetime. In this case, *nÓOy jai* is an adjective rather than a verb. Small things cause them anguish and they may be wounded by a disapproving glance as well as by a thoughtless word. Criticism is something that is not tolerated by a person with a "touchy heart." These are the truly touchy-hearted amongst us.

Belittled Heart

nÓOy núeaa tàm jai (v.) น้อยเนื้อต่ำใจ

tàm jai (v.) ต่ำใจ

NÓOy núeaa tàm jai has the same meaning as *nÓOy jai* and *nÓOy òk nÓOy jai*. This phrase, however, has an additional dimension of a heightened sensitivity towards one's own status in the family or social hierarchy. A childless couple adopts a child and a year later they have a child of their own and begin to neglect the adopted child. At six years old, the adopted child feels a deep-seated inadequacy or insecurity about his status in the family and this feeling can be expressed as *nÓOy núeaa tàm jai* or *tàm jai*.

Such a child may cry often, may be withdrawn or may seek constant reassurance that he or she is loved. A poor janitor or security guard from upcountry working in an upscale condominium in Bangkok can sometimes feel *nÓOy núeaa tàm jai* about his life when he sees how rich people live the life style he can never reach. The feeling may readily arise especially if he is not treated well by these rich people. He feels belittled and depressed.

Shame

Abashed Heart
khŭaay jai (v.) ขวยใจ
krà dàak jai (v.) กระดากใจ

This is one way of expressing your shame or embarrassment for having done the wrong thing. For instance, you have had a quarrel with your neighbor who normally takes care of your dog when you are out of town. Now you feel too *khŭaay jai* or *krà dàak jai* to ask him to babysit your dog. In your reaction to others, you have miscalculated their true intention, morality and commitment. Perhaps you have accused your maid of taking money but later you discover the missing sum in your desk drawer. The maid was blameless; you, as the accuser, have mistakenly attributed wrong conduct to her.

Ashamed Heart
lá aay jai (v.) ละอายใจ
rúu sùek lá aay jai (v.) รู้สึกละอายใจ
aay jai (v.) อายใจ

When you feel that you've done something dishonorable or unworthy, you feel ashamed of your actions. You may have treated your child, your spouse or your friend unfairly or without due consideration for their feelings. Or you have committed an act in which there is a lie, half-truth, deception or dishonor involved. The act of being caught in a lie is a surefire way of being delivered to this heart state. In the middle of the night, having announced that you have stopped smoking, you sneak out for a cigarette. Your spouse or child comes into the kitchen and catches you smoking. Two nights earlier, when you were discovered sneaking a cigarette, you promised an oath to never touch another one. Having been caught breaking this promise, you may feel *aay jai* or *lá aay jai*. Another example, you come across the scene of a road accident. There is no one else on the road and you see several injured people at the crash site. You are in a hurry for an important meeting, so you tell yourself you can't stop to help. Not long afterwards, you feel shame in your heart for failing to stop and help the injured.

Weariness

Tired Heart

nùeaay jai (v.) เหนื่อยใจ

The feeling is one of being tired and discouraged. The underlying cause is likely to have been a breakdown of communication with another person. Maybe, you have tried on many occasions to express your point of view on a subject and to explain how important your view is, but each time the other person fails to understand you or to act appropriately. Perhaps the feeling might arise when your spouse or lover fails to understand your intention. She or he may have made every effort to understand your point of view, but simply cannot comprehend the true meaning. For example, one person may place a high premium on being punctual but your friend, spouse or lover is chronically late. You explain the importance of being on time. The explanation is listened to but never acted upon.

Heartbreaking Tiredness

nùeaay jai thÊEp khàat (v.) เหนื่อยใจแทบขาด

The phrase describes a person who has an extraordinary sense of dedication that pushes him or her to the point of physical and mental exhaustion. A single mother who works two or three jobs to support her children and will often be exhausted to the point where the tiredness overwhelms her. This expression is often used by the person who experiences such exhaustion in a call for sympathy. For example, the single mother may tell her children to study hard because she feels *nùeaay jai thÊEp khàat* working to support them.

Weary Heart
rá aa jai (v.) ระอาใจ
ìt năa rá aa jai (v.) อิดหนาระอาใจ

This heart phrase is employed when you are fed up or wearied by an activity or another person's behavior. A student may sit in his or her room reading an English language book for hours. But he or she does not understand the grammar rules; after hours of attempting to master them, the student becomes totally weary from the effort and throws the book at the wall. A small child may run around a shopping mall picking up items, and the mother runs after the child, putting the items back. After a certain period, the mother will feel *rá aa jai*. In another example, a mother has lectured the son to study hard but the kid loves to party. When the mother later finds his marks, which are all D's, she feels *ìt năa rá aa jai*. It's as if all her efforts have failed and she is weary with her son and helpless about what to do next.

Worn-out Heart
ÒOn jai (v.) อ่อนใจ
ÒOn òk ÒOn jai (v.) อ่อนอกอ่อนใจ
ÒOn jìt ÒOn jai (v.) อ่อนจิตอ่อนใจ

This is the universal feeling of tiredness that bubbles to the surface for most people during the course of ordinary day-to-day living. It is brought on by the trivial inconvenience such as the car that won't start, the phone that is engaged for seven straight hours, the constant engaged signal when trying to log on to the Internet, the electrical blackout in a person's neighborhood for the weekend. This is the sense of being weary in mind.

Your son refuses to give up his spot in the rock'n'roll band and resume his computer studies. You have tried every known means to persuade him that good education is important for his future, yet you continue to fail in your effort. As the parent you will likely experience this feeling of fatigue. The sense of weariness comes from repeated failed attempts to change another's behavior or course of action.

Exhausted Heart
lá hèaa jai (v.) ละเหี่ยใจ
phleaa jai (v.) เพลียใจ

The feeling experienced is similar to *ÒOn jai*. These phrases are appropriate to describe of a state of emotional exhaustion. This emotional state often arises after keeping strong emotions stored inside and at a rapid boil for a long period of time. At the end you feel that your mental stamina has been spent and you experience a burnt-out feeling; you feel *phleaa jai* or *lá hèaa jai*. You are way beyond the feeling of anger and descend into a sluggish state of lethargy. Constant complaints from your parent or spouse may cause you to enter into this advanced state of exhaustion. The son may hear his parents bickering and feel *lá hèaa jai*. A wife with a complaining husband may feel *lá hèaa jai*. There is a well-known expression for a constantly bickering couple, *phǔaa meaa lá hèaa jai*.

Water Heart

náam jai (n.)

น้ำใจ

3
the best of the human condition

In the Thai language you learn how to express yourself with regard to the best of the human condition. Certainly most people feel that giving and receiving genuine compliments is uplifting and pleasurable. A life marked by happiness and joy is one worth living. And when our family, neighbors, circle of friends and colleagues are able to work in harmony we are also happy. In a perfect world all we would require to make our way in life would be a vocabulary of words to express our feelings of compassion, generosity, goodness, kindness, sincerity and nobility, making references to the appropriate *jai* phrase. The chapter is divided into two sections: (i) conduct and behavior, and (ii) character traits.

CONDUCT & BEHAVIOR

There are patterns of conduct displayed through acts or deeds that bring happiness to others. The thoughtful act of a friend who remembers your birthday and brings you a gift. The considerate neighbor who drives you to the airport to pick up your mother. The friends who give you words of comfort in the face of challenge.

Compassion

Empathetic Heart
aw jai khăw maa sài jai raw (v.)
เอาใจเขามาใส่ใจเรา

This is a Thai idiom that translates as taking another person's heart into your own heart. It is useful advice, teaching people to be considerate and thoughtful to others. This notion is taught to children at an early age, in school and in Thai households, in an attempt to instill the importance of showing compassion and sympathy to others.

Sympathetic Heart
hĕn jai (v.) เห็นใจ
hĕn òk hĕn jai (v.) เห็นอกเห็นใจ

When you know someone who has suffered some personal misfortune or setback, you show your sympathy to them, giving them comfort in a time of hurt, anguish or suffering. By your act of sympathy you are "seeing" their pain with your heart, and this feeling of empathy and compassion is *hĕn jai*. Noi's wife has left him, and he is miserable. He is your friend and you *hĕn jai* him and invite him out to dinner in order to cheer him up. You feel sympathy for his plight and hope the dinner will take his mind off his troubles. Someone who *hĕn jai* another person sees the suffering in their heart. *Hĕn òk hĕn jai* is another expression that is used to show a more intense level of sympathy.

Words of Comfort Heart
chá loom jai (v.) ชโลมใจ

This poetic *jai* phrase is appropriate in times of uncertainty when a person needs comforting words to feel more secure. The context is when someone is emotionally upset, worried or concerned, and a friend, parent or spouse provides comforting words of support. A student is worried about whether she has passed her examination and her mother takes her aside and tells her that she has faith that her daughter has done well and that she shouldn't worry, the results will be just fine. The mother's words are *chá loom jai*.

Confidence

Confident Heart
mân jai (adj.) มั่นใจ

This phrase conveys the certainty or confidence that you feel. It may be about another, your career, your abilities, your health or your language skills. In the context of a personal relationship, this heart phrase ranks as a high compliment. When another person feels *mân jai* about you, that means feelings of distrust, suspicion or doubt have disappeared. A feeling of great intimacy is required before this state of the heart is achieved.

This heart phrase is frequently heard on Thai TV and in radio ads. The assumption is that product sales will increase through ads promising consumers that they will have a confident heart if they wear, display, eat or drink an advertised product. This commonly used phrase is used to describe the self-confidence people feel in themselves and their abilities. The kick-boxer who gets into the ring and stares at his opponent before the match feels that he can beat the other fighter. He feels *mân jai* in his abilities and skills as a boxer.

Another contemporary feature of *mân jai* is its application to women. This is a relatively new development as women find that confidence is a desirable and admirable quality. In traditional society, Thai women are expected to defer to others, especially their elders. This view is giving way to the aspirations of Thai women who wish to be *mân jai nai tuaa eeng* or *mân jai nai ton eeng*, as this *jai* phrase fits the modern image of a woman who is intelligent, attractive and self-confident.

Consideration

Water Heart

náam jai (n.) น้ำใจ

mii náam jai (v.) มีน้ำใจ

When you make an effort to remember someone, or take into account his or her feelings, for example, by bestowing a small gift or after returning from a trip abroad or when invited to dinner. Traditional recipients of such gifts are friends, family, an employee, staff, or servant. If you make this gesture you are said to possess *náam jai*. The phrase translates literally as water of the heart.

Everyone likes to feel they are important, that they matter, and that others take them into consideration. In Thailand, one way of expressing your *náam jai* is through a simple gesture of appreciation. Often *náam jai* translates as acts of common courtesy. Giving up your seat on the bus for an elderly person or a pregnant woman, allowing the person with one or two items to go ahead of you at the check-out in the supermarket, or permitting another car to enter the traffic in front of you. *Náam jai* doesn't take much effort. Inside such a heart is the understanding that these small gestures are part of the glue that holds society together, and make us all a little more human and decent. It reminds us that there is something to admire in people who take into account the fact that other people have feelings. The way a person with a *náam jai* treats another touches all of us. If you demonstrate *náam jai* through your actions, Thais will describe you as *mii náam jai.*

Nurturing Heart

thà nǑOm náam jai (v.) ถนอมน้ำใจ

thà nǑOm jai (v.) ถนอมใจ

léaang náam jai (v.) เลี้ยงน้ำใจ

One aspect of being considerate to others is sparing their feelings. The essence is to show *náam jai* to others and not hurt or deflate their spirit—to nurture the water of their heart. In the case of "nurturing heart" that may require a person to tell a little white lie. In other words, telling someone what they want to hear rather than the reality or truth of a situation. For instance, it is Lek's birthday and her sister bakes her a birthday cake. Unfortunately, the sister is a terrible cook and the cake is filled with all the wrong ingredients and no one, not even the soi dogs, would eat it. However, Lek puts on a good face in the presence of her sister and makes an effort to consume a small piece of the cake, smiling and telling her sister that it is wonderful. What Lek does is *thà nǑOm náam jai* her sister.

Honesty

Pure Heart
bOO rí sùt jai (adj.) บริสุทธิ์ใจ

BOO rì sùt jai means to have a pure intention or innocence, free from guilt. An example of *bOO rí sùt jai* is in the context of a court hearing where a neighbor's wall has been destroyed and the neighbor sues for damages. The defendant may say to the judge that his heart is innocent and that he wasn't the person responsible for the destruction of the fence. Another example is the taxi driver who finds your cell phone in the back of his taxi and returns it to you. You offer him a reward and he declines it, saying this wasn't his intention. The return of the cell phone was done with an innocent heart, meaning to do the right thing rather than expecting something in return.

Honest Heart
sùt jà rìt jai (v.) สุจริตใจ

"Honest heart" is similar to *bOO rì sùt jai*. The heart phrase indicates that although there has been a misunderstanding or something has gone wrong, the person had no bad intentions. Since blame often follows the assignment of bad motive or harmful intentions, to plead that one is *sùt jà rìt jai* is to plead that one is innocent. For example, a patron leaves the restaurant; the waitress flies out after him or her claiming that the bill has not been paid. But the patron thought a friend had paid it. He or she claims to be *sùt jà rìt jai* and explain there has been a misunderstanding. No fraud or wrongdoing was intended. Whether the "honest heart" explanation is accepted is another matter. But with an accusation of dishonesty, the honest person may claim to be *sùt jà rìt jai*. Another meaning describes a person who, without ulterior motives, helps others. The volunteers who assisted in the tsunami relief efforts were helping from the goodness of their hearts and did not expect anything in return.

Honest Heart
thŭue jai sûue (v.) ถือใจซื่อ

When a person speaks directly and truthfully, he or she is said to *thŭue jai sûue*. When Lek asks her boyfriend whether he likes her new dress, and he replies that he doesn't like the color and thinks the style doesn't suit her, he is speaking *thŭue jai sûue*. Though his girlfriend might wish he were a little less truthful. The basic idea is that the person doesn't color his feeling by trying to please others. Such a person would rather take the consequences and speak straight from the heart. Most politicians worldwide would fail the *thŭue jai sûue* test. In fact it is a rare person whose honesty overcomes all temptations to please others in order to convey what he or she truly feels.

Resolve

Good Heart Fights the Tiger
jai dii sûu sŭeea (adj.) ใจดีสู้เสือ

This heart phrase means that the person with a good heart can overcome an adversary who may be stronger. The notion of *jai dii* in this context isn't referring to a "good heart" so much as the ability to keep calm in adverse circumstances. It also suggests that you can find the courage to meet the challenge of a threat. The adversary may be a wild animal, or it may be a madman or an armed robber. For example, when a police officer faces a madman who is holding a knife to a child's throat, while he is still waiting for back-up, he tries to keep calm and in control of the situation by feeling *jai dii sûu sŭeea*.

Unyielding Heart
sûu jai khàat (v.) สู้ใจขาด
sûu jon khàat jai (v.) สู้จนขาดใจ

Someone who may be in a losing fight doesn't give up even though they know that at the end they may lose. There is some quality that makes the person keep fighting despite knowing the fight is lost. People with such quality don't accept defeat. You can tell them to give up or surrender but they would rather die first. Some people simply will not yield under any circumstances. This is a good quality in a soldier or athlete. In others it is not always good, for example, in criminals who refuse to give up and would rather shoot it out with the police.

Trust

Trust with the Heart
wái jai (v.) ไว้ใจ
wái waang jai (v.) ไว้วางใจ

You trust another with your heart. Whether the person you are relying on is your spouse, child, employee, driver or friend, this is a person who you trust with your secrets, your confidence, or personal information that is most important to you. To reach this stage of "trust with the heart" means that you have made a judgment about this person's loyalty and faithfulness. And you believe she or he will not let you down. When you give the "green light of trust" you are saying, in Thai, that you *wái jai* that person. The central aspect of this heart phrase is "My heart trusts you." Trust has a universal meaning in every language. The elements include truthfulness, not deceiving or betraying another, and believing and relying upon the honorable intentions of others.

The phrase *wái waang jai* is another way to express trust. An example is where a young mother works in Bangkok and it isn't possible for her to look after her child. So she takes the child to live upcountry with her parents who promise to look after and educate their grandchild. The daughter feels *wái waang jai* about her parents and their ability and desire to provide a safe home environment for the child.

Willingness

Willing Heart
tem jai (v.) เต็มใจ
tem òk tem jai (v.) เต็มอกเต็มใจ

Tem jai is a willingness and predisposition to do something to help others without any thought of receiving a reward or recognition for the act. You can feel *tem jai* to fulfill your duty, make an extra effort to help others or show an act of great kindness and generosity to others. For example, you tem jai to support your mother in her old age; to pick up your friend's child and drop her off at her soccer game; or to lend some money to your friend in a difficult time.

Sometimes someone with a "willing heart" is willing to do things for others at their own cost. Your wife's best friend is opening a new restaurant and you and your wife are invited. Even though you have another commitment on that day, you *tem jai* to cancel the previous commitment in order to accompany your wife to the opening. Such acts of kindness and friendship come from the good nature of a person whose heart is set by default to automatically go out to provide support and comfort to others in need.

CHARACTER TRAITS

Some people are fundamentally good, kind and decent. The person who never displays anger or loses his temper is an example. There are many *jai* phrases to describe someone who has such a character or personality. Thais value a calm, peaceful and agreeable personality. The Land of Smiles is more than a slogan; it is an aspiration to be joyful and happy and show this state of being to others with the simple gesture of a smile.

Compassion

Compassionate Heart
jai mêet taa (adj.) ใจเมตตา
jai kà rú naa (adj.) ใจกรุณา
mii jai ûeaa fúeaa phùeaa phÈE (adj.) ใจเอื้อเฟื้อเผื่อแผ่

The Buddhist concepts of compassion and generosity are implicit in these *jai* phrases and the values inherent in them are highly prized by Thai culture. Parents instruct their children to have a compassionate heart (*jai mêet taa*) and a kind heart (*jai kà rú naa*). You exhibit these qualities by being willing to help others and by feeling compassionate toward others less fortunate than yourself. *Mii jai ûeaa fúeaa phùeaa phÈE* is another formulation to describe the quality of compassion and wiling to help others.

Confidence

Firm Heart
jai nàk nÊEn (adj.) ใจหนักแน่น
jai khOO nàk nÊEn (adj.)
ใจคอหนักแน่น

Most Thai women would want their men to be *jai nàk nÊEn*—to have a "firm heart." Someone with a "firm heart" has the kind of personality that has an edge, a highly developed sense of personal confidence. Such a person is not easily taken in or deceived, does not waver or change his mind easily. There is the outward appearance of being in control and being on top of the situation. There are many beautiful women around a certain man but he doesn't fall for their charms and continues to be devoted and loyal to his wife. Women would refer to such a man as having *jai nàk nÊEn* or *jai khOO nàk nÊEn*.

Courage

Brave Heart
jai klâa (adj.) ใจกล้า

If you are the kind of person who does not show fear or is not afraid, and others sense this about you, then you may hear someone comment that you are *jai klâa*. A little girl who is not afraid of the bullies at school is *jai klâa*. This heart phrase defines a person's appetite for risk, which in turn shapes and defines bravery and courage. A person who is not afraid of the uncertainty of a situation, or the unknown consequences of an action, has a "brave heart."

Riding on the back of a motorcycle taxi through heavy Bangkok traffic is having a large dash of *jai klâa*. Helping someone who is

being mugged on the street is *jai klâa*. The threat may be less visible. Going unescorted to an ATM machine late at night might be another example of *jai klâa*. A woman, wearing several two-baht gold chains, walking alone on an unlit, isolated soi at two in the morning, is *jai klâa*. An investor who buys shares on the SET as the market drops like an anchor is *jai klâa*. To ignore risk or danger and to proceed requires the possession of *jai klâa*. The line often blurs between brave and reckless behavior.

Daredevil Heart
jai thŭeng (adj.) ใจถึง

A person who is *jai thŭeng* is fearless. The first meaning is similar to *jai klâa* but with the added ingredient of boldness and recklessness. The swimmer who dives from the top of a 70-meter cliff into the sea and the beautiful actress who shaves her head for a role in new movie are *jai thŭeng* in this first meaning. The second meaning of *jai thŭeng* is in the context of acts of generosity. Like *jai pâm*, "sporting heart," it is a compliment to say a generous person is *jai thŭeng*. The boss who knows the company had a bad month and dips into his own pocket to take his staff on a weekend retreat is *jai thŭeng*.

It is interesting to place *jai thŭeng* in the wider context of Thai culture, where the art of indirect expression is often accepted (but not by all) as the norm. The concept of *kreeng jai* limits the full expression of opinions or views that might be taken as confrontational or disrespectful to authority. A person who is *jai thŭeng* overcomes the inhibitions of *kreeng jai* and speaks straight. A student might say to her professor that his explanation is incorrect. Another example occurs when a politician claims that he has the perfect plan to solve Bangkok's traffic problem, and once his plan is in place traffic jams will vanish in six months. Such a person is *jai thŭeng*. It doesn't matter whether the traffic problem is solved; what matters is the direct, confident promise that is made in circumstances where others would not be willing to tread.

Intrepid Heart
jai dèt (adj.) ใจเด็ด
jai khOO dèt dìiaw (adj.) ใจคอเด็ดเดี่ยว
mii náam jai dèt dìiaw (adj.) มีน้ำใจเด็ดเดี่ยว

This may be a compliment, depending on the context. In the face of adversity and danger you do not flee but remain determined and resolute. When you make a difficult decision and stand your ground, when you are fearless in the face of a threat or adversity, then you are *jai dèt*. These *jai* phrases are a comment on your personal attribute as one who has a courageous determination and who can withstand panic in the face of fear.

A *jai dèt* person is blessed with an incredible amount of courage and determination but not always common sense. For example, you walk out on Sukhumvit Road and expect traffic to stop for you to pass—you may be said to be *jai dèt*. The spin, in such circumstances, turns the compliment into something that is not necessarily a compliment: it translates to mean that you are bold and stupid—a dangerous, if not fatal, combination. A man splits up with his girlfriend and later he wishes to return, but she remembers all of the bad things he said and did and she refuses to take him back. Her friends would call her *jai dèt*. The others two phrases are used in the same way.

Lion Heart
jai sĭng (adj.) ใจสิงห์

Another *jai* phrase related to courage is *jai sĭng*, "lion heart." *Jai sĭng* is the quality of bravery that allows you to do what others are afraid to do and wish to avoid doing. A lawyer who represents difficult cases involving allegations of police brutality or official wrongdoing would be said to have *jai sǐng*.

Robust Heart
jai chà kan (adj.) ใจฉกรรจ์

This is not commonly used in oral communications. It is more usual to find *jai chà kan*—which is variation of *jai klâa*—in literature or written Thai. The great general who fought with his troops and won a decisive battle might be referred to as *jai chà kan*. The term is especially used in the context of a physical confrontation or fight and denotes the person who does not back down.

Rogue Heart
jai nák leeng (adj.) ใจนักเลง

The central quality is lack of fear and the courage to accept the consequences of one's own action. It is not necessarily bad even though the term incorporates the phrase *nák leeng*, which on its own refers to a gangster or street thug. The person (man or woman) with *jai nák leeng* fits the profile of a rogue. Such a person lives by a code of conduct that comes from the streets and is outside normal convention. For example, a politician who is *jai nák leeng* may circumvent the law but provides for his or her constituents. In other words, a "rogue heart" may also have a populist tendency.

In the Thai cultural context, a true *nák leeng* usually possesses more courage, is more generous and loyal under the unwritten code but at the same time has a dark side that manifests itself in acts of cruelty, brutality and viciousness. In the afternoon he may be Robin Hood, and at night a killer for hire. On occasion the rogue may be on the side of the weak person and appear to be a hero (his Robin Hood, good side). Other times, he may seek to intimidate others with threats of force or violence, causing them to be fearful (Mafia kingpin).

Generosity

A person described as having *náam jai* is generous, compassionate and willing to lend a hand of assistance when others are in a time of need. While *náam jai*, which translates as "water heart," doesn't have an equivalent expression in English, the qualities of generosity lie at the heart of this *jai* phrase. There are other *jai* phrases that are also used to describe a generous person or acts of generosity.

Big Heart
jai yài (adj.) ใจใหญ่

If you are *jai yài*, you are the kind of person who pays for your friend's children's school fees because their mother does not have money. You might have adopted several orphans and paid to put them through school. You are often the person who picks up the check when your group of friends or colleagues go out for a dinner at the expensive restaurant. In performing these acts of grace, you demonstrate that you are *jai yài*—you have a big heart which knows no bound of generosity. You treat everyone as if they were part of your extended family. Because of this boundless generosity, this *jai* quality may sometimes be viewed as a flaw of someone who is doing more than is normally expected or spending beyond their means.

Broad Heart
jai kwâang (adj.) ใจกว้าง
jai khOO kwâang khwǎang (adj.) ใจคอกว้างขวาง
náam jai an kwâang khwǎang (n.) น้ำใจอันกว้างขวาง
jai pen mÊE náam (adj.) ใจเป็นแม่น้ำ

You may be the kind of person who is generous and unselfish in your personal relationships. If so, then you qualify as being *jai kwâang*. Your actions and manner suggest to those around you that you care about those who are less fortunate. You automatically pick up a bar bill or restaurant check, you offer another person a lift in your car, or you are the kind of person who can be friends with your spouse's ex-wife or ex-husband. You offer help or assistance as part of your daily routine and if you do so long enough, you are bound to hear a Thai refer to you as *jai kwâang*.

Jai khOO kwâang khwăang and *náam jai an kwâang khwăang* are other variations of the adjectival *jai kwâang* and refer to the same kind of considerate, thoughtful and generous person, although these two *jai* phrases are more formal and the degree of generosity is emphasized. This refers to the person who is exceptionally broad-hearted as having a heart as broad as a river (*jai pen mÊE náam*). This type of person will make that extra effort beyond what is expected to help someone needing assistance. When there is a fire in a slum, they send food, clothing and building materials to those who are suffering. A wife who adopts an illegitimate child of her husband and raises the child as her own would be seen as having a heart as broad as a river.

Sporting Heart
jai pâm (adj.) ใจป๋า

Someone who spends a lot of money, especially for others, is *jai pâm*. A *jai pâm* person isn't necessarily a show-off. Such a man or woman often takes the form of the leader of the group. The one the others look to for making decisions or expressing opinions. This person establishes his or her position with small gestures. For example, a daughter who spends her five-month savings on her mother's European tour or a husband who buys a five-karat diamond ring for his wife on her birthday is *jai pâm*. Or, when the check for the meal arrives at a table full of friends, a *jai pâm* person picks it up and pays it. It is more common for foreigners to ask for separate checks in a restaurant. Such a practice is the opposite of *jai pâm*.

Goodness

Beautiful Heart
jai ngaam (adj.) ใจงาม
jìt jai ngaam (adj.) จิตใจงาม

A person with a beautiful heart possesses the qualities of a kind-hearted or good-hearted person. This type of person has good virtue, and has a heart that is totally void of malice toward others. These are formal expressions and not frequently used in the vernacular.

Good Heart
jai dii (adj.) ใจดี

Jai dii is one heart quality you want attached to you. One of the first complimentary phrases you may hear as a foreigner—and indeed it is a compliment—is *khun jai dii*, which translates as "You have a good heart." A *jai dii* person is kind and good-tempered. *Jai dii* is also a common response in Thai when you perform a requested or unrequested act of kindness or assistance. The key is that the action you have taken was intended to help another, be it financially or personally. Whatever the nature of the help, your action arose from the goodness of your heart. If a Thai speaker has done something unexpected, something beyond what you have asked, then it is appropriate to refer to that person as *jai dii*. Thai speakers, like most people, would like to have friends and associates they feel are *jai dii*.

In the Thai social system, requesting something from another not only exposes you to rejection but is also a basic violation of *kreeng jai*—or the consideration one owes to others in the social order. An important part of this consideration is not to ask or request your superior, your elder, your employer for something directly. Through indirect means, the need or desire might be communicated, leaving the "higher-ranked" person with full discretion about whether to act or not to act. To act in favor of the person who wants but is constrained from asking is *jai dii*.

Good Heart, Ghost Enters
jai dii phǐi khâw (adj.) ใจดีผีเข้า

A person with a really good heart, one who is always helpful and available to assist others, may be taken advantage of in a society where *kreeng jai* inhibits the asking of favors. If it is known, however, that there is someone of whom one can freely asks favors, that someone may find themselves taken advantage of as people seek them out for assistance. Thus a heart that is too good and helpful finds that "ghosts" will enter it, and their generosity ends. In this case, the ghost is a metaphor for one who is released from the *kreeng jai* inhibitions (meaning there is no fear of rejection or criticism to risk) who is asking the favor.

Grace

Graceful Heart
náam jai nák kii laa (n.) น้ำใจนักกีฬา

A literal translation would be the spirit of an athlete. But, in practice, this is too narrow a definition as the essence of the heart phrase means the acceptance of any failure or defeat with a sense of grace and honor. In the context of sports, "graceful heart" means good sportsmanship, such as where members of a losing team accept defeat and shake hands with the winners. The heart phrase also has many applications outside of sports. Someone who is passed over for a promotion and accepts their fate is said to have *náam jai nák kii laa*. Two competitors are engaged in a heated contest for a contract; after the winner is announced the head of the losing company shakes hands with the head of the winning company.

Kindness

Kind Heart
jai aa rii (adj.) ใจอารี
jai òop ÔOm aa rii (adj.) ใจโอบอ้อมอารี

Jai aa rii or *jai òop ÔOm aa rii* refers to a person who is kind and generous, always ready to lend a hand to those in need. A child who picks up an injured bird or a sick puppy from the street and keeps it in her care until the animal is strong is *jai aa rii*. Similarly, an elderly monk who takes in orphan children, gives them food and shelter, and sends them to school is *jai òop ÔOm aa rii*. The central qualities in this *jai* are kindness, compassion and great generosity.

Soft Heart

jai ÒOn (adj.) ใจอ่อน

You place your personal relationships higher than your self-interest. You have a soft heart and always end up helping your friends, family, children—that makes you *jai ÒOn*. You easily give to others what they ask for, you are likely to be prone to pity, and by your nature compelled to do things against your own or your loved one's best interests. Feeding a biscuit to a puppy because you fear he's hungry and begs in such a cute way is irresistible to you as a *jai ÒOn* person.

Unlike *jai dii*, which may apply to an isolated act of kindness, *jai ÒOn* is more the general pattern of behavior over a long period of time. There is also a negative side to possessing a "soft heart." It can mean that such a person can be easily taken advantage of. The soft-hearted person may satisfy the needs of others without looking after his or her own needs. One wishes this heart status for one's spouse, boss, friends and associates. At the same time, in a tough, protracted negotiation for a joint venture, for example, someone with this kind of "soft heart" may end up with terms that will be detrimental to them.

Token of Appreciation Heart

sĭn náam jai (n.) สินน้ำใจ

This is a slightly different phrasing of *náam jai,* "water heart." The phrase carries the idea of remuneration—a gift or cash—which is given to another as a token of appreciation. *Sĭn* translates as money or property. For example, you may show your appreciation for an act of kindness or a display of loyalty by giving another person a hilltribe antique silver bracelet. Your secretary had a baby girl and you go to the hospital with flowers and a gift. These gifts are a token of appreciation (*sĭn náam jai*) on your part to express your appreciation. It can also have a negative meaning in the context of official corruption. A person may expect under-the-table money as *sĭn náam jai* before performing an official act (which is his duty). The line between a token of appreciation and a bribe isn't always a bright line, as some people may feel obliged to give *sĭn náam jai*, and some, in a position of power to do so, may demand it be paid before an act is performed.

Nobility

Merit-minded Heart

jai bun (adj.) ใจบุญ
jai bun sŭn thaan (adj.) ใจบุญสุนทาน

"Merit-minded heart" applies to the kind of person who rises at the crack of dawn to make offerings of food to monks. Or when a *jai bun* person sees someone in distress or in need, he or she will try to give assistance and comfort. The *jai* phrase is traced to the Buddhist belief that if you make merit, *tham bun*, in this life, you will be born to a better life next time around. If you give money to a child beggar or feed the soi dogs, then many Thais might think you are *jai bun*. Someone is dying in hospital because they can't get a blood match, and you volunteer to donate your blood. By such actions, you are making merit. This expression is an illustration of the relationship between Buddhism and the heart in a phrase that is intended as a high compliment. *Jai bun sŭn thaan* is another expression of the same meaning but carries the dimension of the class system. The word *thaan* in the phrase means giving. Those who give to others in a lower station of life (as the British were fond of saying) have *jai bun sŭn thaan*—a heart prone to giving.

Monk Heart

jai phrá (adj.) ใจพระ

This is another *jai* phrase connected with Buddhism. A person with extraordinary kindness and compassion is a candidate for the description of "monk heart." If you are the kind of person who never hurts another's feelings and forgives someone who has done a terrible wrong to you in the past, then you are *jai phrá*. The phrase refers to an ideal person who has saintly qualities and a limitless capacity for forgiveness. In a world of grasping, greed and self-interest, few such people exist outside of temples. Therefore, this is a rare heart phrase to use or to hear others use. Some monks teach that you must respect your parents because they are the only people in the world who possess the quality of *jai phrá* (at least when it concerns their children).

Noble Heart
jai sǔung (adj.) ใจสูง
jìt jai sǔung (adj.) จิตใจสูง
jìt jai sǔung sòng (adj.) จิตใจสูงส่ง

Like *jai ngaam*, "beautiful heart," *jai sǔung* describes a person of good virtue, who is by nature a noble person—a "noble heart." The noble-hearted person displays his or her acts of nobility in a number of ways. He or she aspires to the higher goodness, lives by the higher moral standards and rarely lowers him or herself to the level of petty malice or destructive (but emotionally gratifying) acts. For example, a *jai sǔung* maid, while doing the laundry, finds a thousand-baht note forgotten in the pocket of some trousers and returns it to her employer. A drunk, former friend of yours shouts a tirade of abuse against you in a party, causing huge embarrassment. But being *jai sǔung*, you try to suppress your anger and ignore him.

Purity

Pristine Heart
jìt jai phÒOng phÊEw (adj.) จิตใจผ่องแผ้ว
jìt jai phÒOng sǎi (adj.) จิตใจผ่องใส

A happy, cheerful person is said to be *jìt jai phÒOng phÊEw* or *jìt jai phÒOng sǎi*. This is another way to describe someone whose heart and mind are pure, pristine, untainted by impure thoughts. This is the person you want to meet. They are always up, in a good mood, witty, having no sense of frustration or disappointment and no signs of the residue from the ordinary damage of family life. It also has a religious overtone connected with the clarity of mind. Monks and followers of the dharma who practice meditation can reach this state of being.

Pure Heart
jai bOO rí sùt (adj.) ใจบริสุทธิ์

The phrase *jai bOO rí sùt* applies to the sort of person who has childlike innocence or has retained his or her childlike innocence into adult life. Such an individual has not become cynical or hardened by the bumps in the road of life. The essence of being a child—sincere, curious, trusting, loving, combined with a purity of feeling and perception—has survived through childhood and continues to exist and shape his or her view of the world. If these attributes are true of you, then you might hear a Thai speaker refer to you as having *jai bOO rì sùt*.

Sincerity

True Heart
jing jai (adj.) จริงใจ

The person with a "true heart" is someone who possesses sincere intention and expresses his or her true feelings of love, care or consideration. If you possess a true heart, you are *jing jai*; you do not hide your emotional state behind a veil of deceit. You do not resort to using guile to obtain an advantage. You have no time or patience for masks or deception in your words or behavior. People always know where they stand with you. Great value is placed on plain, straight speaking and actions. The reward for meeting this high standard is to be known as someone who has a true heart. True to others, true to yourself.

True Essence of the Heart
náam săi jai jing (n.) น้ำใสใจจริง

The literal translation of this delightful phrase is "clear water, true heart." When you hear these words uttered about yourself, it is likely that you have gone out of your way to help someone without any thought of payment or reward. You did what you did out of some genuine or true feeling of giving rather than as a commercial or mercenary act. For you the smile of gratitude is the currency in which you are paid; and when you hear the words *náam săi jai jing* put yourself down as having received a million-dollar emotional pay day.

Strength

Strong Heart

jai khêm khĚng (adj.) ใจเข้มแข็ง

When you believe strongly in yourself or in your abilities to overcome adversity then you are *jai khêm khĚng*. If you are a soldier on the front line and you have been given the order to advance against the enemy, having a "strong heart" or *jai khêm khĚng* provides you with the confidence to face the danger. The heart phrase captures a feeling of strength and conviction in yourself. Without such confidence coming from the heart, a person is made timid and may lack the confidence to take those risks necessary to succeed.

Diamond Heart

jai phét (adj.) ใจเพชร

The person who possesses a "diamond heart" is an epitome of strength. Although this heart phrase is sometimes used to describe a hard-hearted person, its definition isn't necessarily negative. The key elements are strength, strong-minded and unyielding resolution, and a fighting spirit. An example is a young Thai woman who stands up to the abuse of authority and fights for her rights despite the overwhelming odds against her winning. In this David and Goliath confrontation, people admire David for his strength of character in standing his ground against the giant. When it is used negatively, the *jai phét* personality is capable of committing hard-hearted acts of cruelty. A mother, for example, who abandons her infant may be called *jai phét*. The father who disinherits his son because the son decides to forgo business school in order to study painting is *jai phét*. While the unusual strength of the character enables the person to overcome difficult challenges, the "diamond heart" can also be unfeeling.

Hard Heart

jai khĚng (adj.) ใจแข็ง

Opinions differ on whether you have cursed or complimented another when using this phrase. Having a "hard heart" can be good or bad depending on the circumstances presented. For example, if an external enemy is attacking your city you want soldiers who can fight the battle and defend the city. Thus *jai khĚng* is a good quality in a warrior. For a number of Thais, however, this heart quality also has a negative implication: a person who is *jai khĚng* can also be unbending, inflexible, uncompromising and unmoved by the fate of others. If you are a *jai khĚng* kind of person, appeals made by other people to your kindness, decency, or understanding roll off you emotionally like water off the back of a duck. You aren't moved by such appeals, and consider them irrelevant and unimportant in a life where it is dog-eat-dog.

Hot Heart

jai rÓOn (adj.)

ใจร้อน

4
the worst of the human condition

Matters of the heart have a dark, stormy side. *Heart Talk* is rich in a vocabulary to describe bad conduct and behavior and character flaws. The negative human condition in this chapter involves a number of heart expressions for undesirable, objectionable qualities, from minor to major. These qualities range from arrogance, cowardliness, impatience, self-centeredness, and weak-mindedness, to deception and treachery, selfishness, vengefulness, and cruelty.

As in Chapter 3, it is convenient to divide the *jai* phrases into two sections: (i) conduct and behavior and (ii) character traits. Many of these phrases, especially those under character traits, are considered condemnations and are generally not used directly with another person, as they convey a sense of rejection, criticism or insult.

In any language it is always a question of degree and context whether a critical statement is intended to injure or is intended in jest. More than the phrases or words themselves come into play. Facial expression, gestures, the relationship of the parties, the context of the conversation are all relevant in assessing whether a heart phrase crosses the threshold of humor and becomes nasty. In extreme cases, it can be an oral declaration of war. Using these phrases is a little like playing with fire: one can get burnt easily.

While Thai speakers in general have a great capacity for humor and are masters of the fine art of joking, few people of any nationality could be reasonably expected to hear harsh, negative and judgmental phrases from another and maintain their smile. In many cases, such phrases would stay inside one's private thoughts, or at the very least they would be used out of the earshot of the person to whom the phrase is being applied.

CONDUCT & BEHAVIOR

Arrogance

Emboldened Heart
dâay jai (adj.) ได้ใจ

The essence of this heart phrase is a heightened sense of self-confidence or self-pride. It is used to describe someone who communicates through action and words that they think they are better than other people. There is a mild sense of arrogance at work. When people constantly tell someone that they possess special talents, skills or attractiveness, then that someone may develop a *dâay jai* tendency. An "emboldened heart" often follows upon the heels of success. The gambler has won a jackpot and feels emboldened to keep on betting. The motorcycle driver who darts in and out of traffic at high speed, narrowly avoiding a head-on collision, and keeps driving at high speed. Such people feel they have luck on their side and they can do no wrong.

Hubris Heart
lam phOOng jai (v.) ลำพองใจ
húek hŏoem jai (v.) ฮึกเหิมใจ
khúek khá nOOng jai (v.) คึกคะนองใจ
thá yaan jai (v.) ทะยานใจ

These heart phrases apply to a person who behaves in an arrogant, impetuous or high-spirited fashion. The phrases are stronger than *dâay jai*. The added component is a degree of recklessness. Someone who has obtained a measure of success, such as a financial windfall, and brags about and/or displays their success in a reckless manner, may hear one of these heart phrases used to describe them. The bragging and boasting about a killing in the stock market, along with acts of arrogant behavior, show the person is feeling *lam phOOng jai* or *húek hŏoem jai*. Some people act recklessly and are driven by the excitement of the moment, and their actions demonstrate that they do not think about the consequences. These heart phrases are a way to describe such overconfident and reckless behavior.

Reckless Heart

yâam jai (v.) ย่ามใจ

Yâam jai is another *jai* phrase for arrogance and overconfidence. The phrase describes someone who acts in reckless manners due to confidence of past successes. A company greedy for profits may short-change the security and safety standards, resulting in needless accidents and injuries; such an employer is *yâam jai*. A thief who breaks into a house during the daytime because he has done so successfully in other houses in the same neighborhood is *yâam jai*.

Complacency

Careless Heart

chá lâa jai (v.) ชะล่าใจ

This is a popular heart expression to describe complacency. There is an initial burst of interest, but after a while there is no sustained effort to pursue that interest. It also applies to a person who should be aware of the danger, but fails to take into account the consequences of such danger. In other words, you are complacent and careless. When you tell your girlfriend you love her, promise her marriage, and then take no action, you will be thought of as acting with a "careless heart." You act *chá lâa jai* when your lips create intentions that you cannot or will not fulfill when the time for action comes. Carelessness is not limited to expressions of love. You may live in a neighborhood you feel is safe, and never lock your doors. And you leave your keys in the ignition of your car. Not locking your front door even in the best of neighborhoods, or keeping your key in the ignition of your parked car, are examples of acts of carelessness.

Idle Heart

nîng nOOn jai (v.) นิ่งนอนใจ

This *jai* phrase has an overlap with *chá lâa jai*: It suggests an attitude of inaction. When a reporter asks a minister about an investigation into corruption, he might reply, "*Pŏm mâi dâay nîng nOOn jai*. I have everything under control. A committee is looking into it. All is well. Do not worry too much." What is conveyed is that the minister is not motionless; he's always planning, thinking and acting. Someone who is *nîng nOOn jai* is stuck in neutral. Not going forward or backward, just standing still—idle. John wants to go to Chiang Mai but his friend Ron wants to go to Phuket. Ron stays silent and can't make up his mind whether to follow his friend John to Chiang Mai. John says he's going on the morning train. Ron doesn't say or do anything. Ron is *nîng nOOn jai*.

Cruelty

Vicious Heart

thaa run jìt jai (v.) ทารุณจิตใจ

The person who is condemned of having a "vicious heart" has committed an act of emotional violence and cruelty, either by words or conduct. For example, a husband is *thaa run jìt jai* of his minor wife by verbally abusing her. He may also be beating her up, but the emphasis is on the emotional damage he has caused that is immense. The feeling of hurt and pain evoked in the minor wife as she is being struck by him can also be described as *thaa run jìt jai*. In the case of the London underground bombings, one could say that the terrorists were *thaa run jìt jai* of the passengers through their actions. Those who later learned of the bombings would feel that the terrorists were *thaa run jìt jai* of the public.

Deception

False Promise Heart

khÓ kà laa hâi măa dii jai (v.) เคาะกะลาให้หมาดีใจ

The literal translation is that by tapping the top half of a coconut shell you will make the dog happy. Someone makes a promise to do or give something to another but when the time arrives for performance, the promise-maker does not deliver. The promise was false. There will not be a positive outcome or a reward. This is a good heart phrase to remember when dealing with a company, an individual or a government officer. The person across the desk promises with a smiling face and all the assurance in the world that he or she will guarantee to have your phone installed, your computer repaired, your newspaper delivered to your new address or your application for a permit or license processed not later than Friday morning. When Friday morning rolls around, however, these promises are not kept. Such a person possesses a "false promise heart." A man treats a woman very well, with many gifts. She has a boyfriend but doesn't disclose this information. She accepts all of the gifts under a false impression, playing up that the guy has a chance, but she knows that she is playing him along. After the guy finds out the truth, he may use this phrase to describe the woman.

Quick Hand, Swift Heart

muue wai jai rew (adj.) มือไวใจเร็ว

The person who has a "quick hand, swift heart" is often a small-time thief. A pickpocket on a bus, on the BTS, or in a busy shopping mall. Such a person has the ability to take away something quickly without the owner of the property being aware of the taking. The heart phrase can also apply to someone who takes advantage of another with great speed and dexterity. For instance, Vinai is Lek's boss at the office and every time he walks past her desk he quickly touches her shoulder or hair and then walks away before she has time to react.

Obsession

Preoccupied Heart
jai mòk mûn (adj.) ใจหมกมุ่น

"Preoccupied heart" describes a person who is obsessed with something or someone, and is compulsive in his or her actions to obtain the object of the obsession. A person may be totally absorbed by his or her work and forget to eat and sleep until the project is finished. The Thai expression for being obsessed with work is *jai mòk mûn yùu kàp ngaan*. It also applies to a teenager obsessed with sex, a child addicted to computer games or a revengeful minor wife trying to sabotage the major wife. Those with a "preoccupied heart" become totally involved in work, relationship or object of desire, and can't or won't want to eat or sleep. In other words, the rest of the things in their life become irrelevant. The self-absorption is the key attribute. Such a heart is fully occupied and everything but that thing or person is squeezed out of their line of vision.

Self-Centeredness

Egocentric Heart
am phooe jai (n.) อำเภอใจ
chÔOp tham taam am phooe jai (adj.) ชอบทำตามอำเภอใจ

Am phooe jai literally translates as "home district heart." The phrase *chÔOp tham taam am phooe jai* may be roughly put in English as "prone to follow one's own home district heart," in other words, being self-centered or egocentric. This expression of "home district heart" has its etymology in Thailand's history of local administration. Thailand is divided for a number of purposes into a hierarchy of provinces, districts, sub-districts and villages. The usage comes from former times (about sixty years ago, when districts were formally recognized as entities under Thai law), when a trader living in a district in Surin province traveled to Bangkok to sell bamboo baskets. The fact that the trader had freedom to movement to go anywhere in the Kingdom of Thailand translated during this time as *taam am phooe jai*. It was the merchants' right of movement to sell their wares. This usage has evolved and now means to do whatever freely as you wish (normally with disregard to others).

So, in the modern usage the "home district heart" has become an "egocentric heart." A person who behaves in this manner will do whatever whenever she or he pleases without a concern or consideration of the consequences of the action and its impact on others. The person may or may not be selfish but certainly self-centered. For example, Noi shares an apartment with two other friends. One day Noi is hit by an inspiration to renovate the apartment, so she just goes out to buy new wallpaper and proceeds to redecorate the living room and rearrange the furniture. Noi *tham taam am phooe jai* and it does not occur to her, or she does not care, whether or not her roommates will like the new wallpaper and the furniture rearrangement. If Noi often exhibits this type of conduct, her roommates will say she *chÔOp tham taam am phooe jai* or has a tendency to do things her own way—she is egocentric.

Self-centered Heart
aw tÈE jai (adj.) เอาแต่ใจ
aw tÈE jai ton (adj.) เอาแต่ใจตน
aw tÈE jai tuaa eeng (adj.) เอาแต่ใจตัวเอง

A person who acts in a self-centered, egocentric fashion may be described as *aw tÈE jai*. This kind of person does what he or she pleases and thinks the world revolves around him or her. The person is insensitive to the needs and desires of others and puts his or her wishes first. The infractions may range from minor ones, such as a midnight raid on the fridge when he or she eats the last piece of cake and drinks the last cola, to the more serious incidents, such as using the rent money for gambling or to buy a new watch. Joy has a passion for Italian food and always insists on dining at an Italian restaurant when she goes out with her friends. If one of the friends suggests that they go to a Thai, Chinese or French restaurant, Joy throws a fit. Joy is like a spoiled child who is accustomed to getting her way.

Surrender

Defeated Heart
thÒOt jai (v.) ถอดใจ
phÉE jai (v.) แพ้ใจ

These two *jai* phrases are used in circumstances where you have a task or responsibility to accomplish a particular goal but you have lost the will to finish the job. You walk away from a half-finished project or quit before the end of the game. To *thÒOt jai* or *phÉE jai* is to withdraw your heart, admit defeat and walk away. The person who has a "defeated heart" usually feels no hope of winning or reaching the goal. The tennis player who has lost too many points loses his confidence and his will to fight. His heart has left the game but his body is still there. He makes more and more unforced errors. The spectators will say he has already *thÒOt jai*. Lek is four years into her Ph.D. program but hasn't worked on her thesis for over two years. She avoids the work. She puts it out of her mind. Her friend tells her not to *thÒOt jai* and encourages her to keep working on the degree. *PhÉE jai* is used in the same way.

Uncaring Behavior

Inattentive Heart
mâi aw jai sài (v.) ไม่เอาใจใส่

This *jai* phrase describes someone who is not attentive or caring. There are many ways to show a lack of caring. One way is pure indifference or passivity in the presence of another. The person who ignores you, pays no attention to you, and gives you the signal she or he wants nothing to do with you, is sending a message, the rough translation of which is: you don't exist in her or his eyes, heart or life. And this message of neglect and complete lack of interest spins out from the heart: *mâi aw jai sài.* The parent who is uninterested or inattentive in his or her child's welfare is a parent who *mâi aw jai sài* the child. The student who neglects to do homework or pay attention in school is said to *mâi aw jai sài* his or her studies.

Vengefulness

Vengeful Heart
khÉEn jai (v.) แค้นใจ
phùuk jai jèp (v.) ผูกใจเจ็บ
jai aa khâat (adj.) ใจอาฆาต
jai aa khâat mâat râay (adj.) ใจอาฆาตมาดร้าย

A person with a "vengeful heart" does not forgive and forget but habors the grudge and waits for the opportunity for revenge. Perhaps the pain she or he has suffered is so great that it is not possible to put it aside and move on with life. So, this person is likely to be obsessed about giving it back, having the real or metaphorical knife ready for the payback time. Needless to say, this is not a good behavior and conduct. The feeling of *khÉEn jai* and *phùuk jai jèp* can kill the person from the inside. The result is a negative, moody, or vicious and scheming person. *Jai aa khâat* and *jai aa khâat mâat râay* are the adjective forms of "vengeful heart."

CHARACTER TRAITS

Cowardice

The main attribute of the coward is an action or inaction resulting from being afraid. There are degrees of fear, and the heart phrases gauge the relative lack of courage when a person is faced with the unknown or an obstacle in the pathway of life. Some may be afraid of their own shadow, or mistake a shadow for a ghost. Sometimes these heart phrases can be taunts said with the intention of making someone do something that is foolhardy or reckless.

Cowardly Heart
jai mâi klâa (adj.) ใจไม่กล้า
jai khlàat (adj.) ใจขลาด

These phrases say that you don't have the courage of your convictions or are afraid of new, uncertain situations. Perhaps a job has been offered but requires a person to relocate to another country. The person is fearful—*jai mâi klâa*—of leaving

Thailand and turns down the offer. A colleague may say that he or she has a "cowardly heart." You talk about taking the two-month overland trek in Nepal, but at the last moment call it off. A week before the wedding you go into hiding because you are afraid of going through with the marriage. Or maybe someone is pushing you around in the office or at home and, rather than standing your ground, you give in, and acquire the reputation of being *jai khlàat*—your heart is not brave.

Timid Heart

jai sÒ (adj.) ใจเสาะ

This is a wonderfully expressive *jai* phrase, describing a number of different states of the classic fight or flight choice. Someone is walking down a strange soi and finds large, fierce dogs coming straight for them. If they are *jai sÒ*, they are likely to turn and run away. Not infrequently a news report appears in the *Bangkok Post* or *The Nation* about the driver of a bus or a truck, or for that matter just about any driver, who, having caused an accident, immediately flees the scene of the accident. For the native Thai speakers the person who is running away from the scene of action or any challenge is *jai sÒ*. A kick-boxer who is scared upon seeing his menacing opponent and wants to turn back from the fight is *jai sÒ*. The person backing out of the Nepal trek in the above example is also *jai sÒ*.

Silver Fish Heart

jai plaa siw (adj.) ใจปลาซิว

This adjective, like *jai sÒ*, "timid heart," is a label attached to someone who is easily scared. Although in the case of *jai plaa siw* your cowardice makes you comparable to a frightened, tiny silver fish. The small silver fish is thought to be easily frightened, and is considered by Thais to be a cowardly fish. So to be placed heart-wise in the same league as a fingerling fish is far from a compliment, though it can be used in jest amongst close friends. In

general, "silver fish heart" refers to someone who lack stand up to another person (a bigger fish) or to face d who feels overwhelmed and incapable of dealing wit problem. The boss demands that you work over the weekend and you are afraid to tell him that it is your son's birthday and you are committed to taking the family on an outing. In such a case, your wife might refer to you as *jai plaa siw*.

Cruelty

Brutal Heart
jai ráay (adj.) ใจร้าย

This is a commonly used *jai* phrase that covers conduct ranging from meanness to cruelty. At one end of the scale, a person may have made a stupid, silly mistake; he or she may have not taken into account another's feelings or desire. Normally, however, *jai ráay* is used for a person who has acted with cruel disregard for others. This kind of person might kick a dog or sell his own daughter into prostitution. Or she might be the kind of mother who throws her daughter out into the street because of a minor argument. The phrase applies to those in the hotel business who lock all fire-escape doors to prevent guests from skipping out on their bill, even though they know that when a fire starts many people may die. Such people are *jai ráay*. *Khon jai ráay* is a person who possesses a cruel, "brutal heart."

Cruel Heart
jai hòot hêaam (adj.) ใจโหดเหี้ยม
jai am má hìt (adj.) ใจอำมหิต

This phrase refers to someone who has a cruel or very mean nature and has the capacity to commit acts of cruelty. A robber who also kills his victims and terrorists who kill innocent women and children are *jai hòot hêaam* or *jai am má hìt*. Mass murderers, serial killers and sadistic torturers are further examples. Thais are unlikely to use this term in the presence of the person who is being judged as having a "cruel heart" for obvious reasons.

Impatience

Hot Heart
jai rÓOn (adj.) ใจร้อน

Jai rÓOn applies to a person who has an impatient predisposition. Such a person may react negatively to standing in a post office queue, or waiting in traffic on Sukhumvit Road. In the extreme case, it may be that one boxer bites off the ear of another. Or a lover takes revenge by slicing off a body part associated with manhood. There are shadings to this phrase which are usually far less negative in nature. A *jai rÓOn* person generally has a temperament which demands that tasks and assignments are done quickly, and insists on rapid reaction and response from others. In other words, a *jai rÓOn* person is an impatient person. In the Thai cultural context, the impatience and the lack of an easy-going nature, especially if this results in demands being placed on others, may lead the Thais to judge the person as hot-hearted—never a positive quality.

Impatient Heart
jai rew (adj.) ใจเร็ว
jai rew dùaan dâay (adj.) ใจเร็วด่วนได้

The phrase *jai rew dùaan dâay* is an idiom, and like *jai rew*, emphasizes the motivation to receive a quick result. A *jai rew dùaan dâay* decision usually ends in failure or has long-term adverse consequences. A person who chronically makes such decisions violates one of the unwritten Thai social rules: Always appear to have a cool heart. The person with an "impatient heart" may be greedy as well as impatient in nature. This person makes quick decisions, focusing only on the immediate gain and ignores the long-term benefits. Lek owns a small business and hires people to help her run it. After a couple of months, though, Lek is unhappy with the profits earned in the business and dismisses several workers in the factory. As a result, productivity sinks and the business eventually fails. Lek is *jai rew dùaan dâay*.

This expression is also used in another context, usually by adults, to describe young people engaging in premarital sex. When young students fall in love and give in to their mutual attraction and have sex together, their parents will use this expression to reprimand them, suggesting they are irresponsible and don't have self-control over their lives.

Moodiness

Moody Heart
ngùt ngìt jai (adj.) หงุดหงิดใจ
khîi ngùt ngìt jai (adj.) ขี้หงุดหงิดใจ

Ngùt ngìt jai is a state of emotion—moody. Anyone can feel moody when something has not gone the way they had wished, but usually having a bad mood is a temporary state; when time has passed or the matter that bothered the moody person has subsided or resolved itself, then the moodiness should disappear. However, there are people who are prone to feeling *ngùt ngìt jai*. These people are characterized by Thais as *khîi ngùt ngìt (jai)*.

The Thai word *khîi* in this context translates as "excessive." The literal translation is "excrement." This is a commonly used (and heard) heart phrase. It describes someone who by their nature is moody, easily annoyed or irritable. Like most people, Thais do not like someone with this personality trait. A *khîi ngùt ngìt* person is difficult to be around or maintain as a friend. The "moody heart" person is easily upset with small, minor things. People, kids, dogs all get on their nerves. Such a personality type is not widely favored because it comes with complaints about treatment or decisions made by others.

Passivity

Passive Heart
jai chùeaay (adj.) ใจเฉื่อย

This describes a person operating on automatic-pilot mode, sluggish, slowed down into slow motion. Nothing much is going on inside or around that person except for the flicker of life put on hold. It is a non-reflective mental state of being. If you are being lazy, hanging around the house or idling in a shopping center, a restaurant or a bar, doing nothing, staring off into the middle distance, then someone may say you are being *jai chùeaay*. This heart comment, though not a serious condemnation, is often negative. This is because a *jai chùeaay* person is usually viewed as lazy—someone who takes no initiative. Such a person may be well-suited only for a career of unemployment and welfare checks.

Selfishness

Resources such as time and money are scarce. There is competition for what is available. In the midst of such competition some people are more generous and giving than others. Those individuals who, in the pursuit of their happiness, ignore the happiness or interest of others might be rightly called selfish. The *jai* phrases in this category reflect a self-centered state of being and suggest that in Thailand selfishness is a highly personal emotional offence.

Narrow Heart
jai khÊEp (adj.) ใจแคบ
jai khOO kháp khÊEp (adj.) ใจคอคับแคบ

This is expression to convey to others that someone's action is or has been selfish or narrow-minded. The "narrow heart" or *jai khÊEp* person lacks generosity and is unwilling to do even a small gesture to help others even though the cost of doing so is very small. It is the absence of empathy for the plight of others, and for the consequences of his or her actions on other people's lives. Such a person thinks solely of his or her own pleasure or desire. If you expect the person with *jai khÊEp* to take you into account, or to consider your feelings, then you will be in for disappointment. For example, a friend is in need. Perhaps she or he is out of money to buy a bus ticket to visit an ailing mother upcountry and, rather than offer the money, this person refuses. Such a person lacks *náam jai*, "water heart," and is someone with a mean spirit. The person can also be described as *jai khOO kháp khÊEp*.

Salty Heart

jai khem (adj.) ใจเค็ม

The expression fits a miser. Such a person counts every last satang and begrudges anyone who expects him to pick up a bill at the restaurant. This person's hero is Ebenezer Scrooge in Charles Dickens's *A Christmas Carol*—though he wouldn't like the end of that novel, when Scrooge discovers the virtue of *náam jai*. A person with a *jai khem* heart never leaves a tip at a restaurant, he never helps a neighbor who has a problem, and he never gives to charity. If he runs a restaurant, he spends his idle time figuring out ways to pad a customer's bill. He lacks *náam jai*. Thais avoid such people (as do most other nationalities); their personality never makes others feel comfortable, or brings a sense of fun or laughter. They inevitably take advantage of others and put themselves first.

Selfish Heart

khàat náam jai (v.) ขาดน้ำใจ

Thai culture values and rewards a person who has *náam jai*, "water heart," or who is generous and responsive to the needs of others. When someone is lacking in *náam jai* and doesn't have a generous nature, he or she is described as *khàat náam jai*. The underlying personality is self-centered and selfish. Such a person will not stop his or her car to let an elderly person cross the street, or refuses to permit a member of staff to attend the funeral of a relative. Thai people don't like those who possess this quality; but, then, who does?

Showing Off

Over-Generous Heart
jai too (adj.) ใจโต
jai yài jai too (adj.) ใจใหญ่ใจโต
nâa yài jai too (adj.) หน้าใหญ่ใจโต
jai tòoep (adj.) ใจเติบ

If a Thai speaker has used one of these *jai* phrases with you, it is likely that you have shown an act of generosity that is considered excessive (and which was not well-received). These phrases are used to describe the classic show-off or newly rich person in action. These people need to show others that they have money to throw around. *Jai too* translates to "big heart." The phrase is often used along with *nâa yài*, "big face," So the person who exhibits this *jai* quality often does it to gain a big face and recognition of having a big heart. A son of a rich and powerful politician leads his gang of six friends into RCA and picks up every bill. There is an element of vulgarity in his conduct. The display is less about being generous to his friends but to demonstrate his power over them. Such a person has crossed the line of being generous to being a show-off. Others who come in contact with such a person are not genuinely impressed by such behavior though they may benefit from it. In the traditional sense, the excessive generosity is usually beyond the person's means.

Treachery & Deceit

Face of Deer, Heart of Tiger
nâa núeaa jai sŭeaa (adj.)
หน้าเนื้อใจเสือ

This is an ancient Thai proverb similar to the English saying: "a wolf in sheep's clothing." While this *jai* phrase is still used, you do not go around saying this heart phrase to another Thai speaker unless your life insurance is fully paid. The person with the face of a deer appears harmless, but in fact he or she has the heart of a tiger and, as you know, a tiger is carnivorous, silently trailing you until the precise moment when it jumps and tears out your throat. Tigers wait for the right opportunity for the kill. A person who is *nâa núeaa jai sŭeaa* smiles as he lures his "kill" into range before going for the throat. The doctor who invites his wife to dinner, conveying kindly intentions, but later murders her and disposes of her body as a short cut to a messy divorce, is *nâa núeaa jai sŭeaa.* The English translation makes it sound harmless, childlike. If you try this one on a Thai stranger, the chances are you will get yourself a quick kick-boxing lesson.

Priest with a Smile

nák bun jai bàap (adj.) นักบุญใจบาป

A person claims to be a learned spiritual person but in reality this is only a superficial show obscuring his true nature: someone who hides a cruel, mean-spirited heart. The person may be a well-respected member of the community and no one suspects the truth about him. His secret activities are considered morally reprehensible by civilized society. Behind the kind and reassuring smile lurks a person capable of unspeakable acts of cruelty or sinful actions. A "priest with a smile" may do many good things for people in his community and gain their loyalty and respect but he's really a gangster who kills anyone who threatens his business interests. There is a large element of surface deception involved, combined with an evil plan to cause damage or death.

Straight Face, Crooked Heart

nâa sûue jai khót (adj.) หน้าซื่อใจคด

jai khót (adj.) ใจคด

This *jai* phrase is the perfect description for treachery and deceit. The *nâa sûue jai khót* person wears a mask of deception. Normally, the mask presented to others suggests that the person wearing it is good, honorable, decent and reliable, when in fact he or she is seeking to pull a scam. Such a person lacks a code of honor and will, at the drop of a hat, cheat or take advantage of others. The theme of maliciousness underscores this phrase. An example is a well-dressed, well-spoken person who stops a tourist who has been in Thailand for only three days, and strikes up a friendly conversation. The tourist immediately trusts and likes the new friend who suggests they visit a jewelry shop. The con artist offers to take the tourist to this special shop where the tourist will be given the chance to buy world-class gems that can be resold in his or her country for a three-hundred-fold profit. In fact, the gems are of little value and the tourist will lose his or her money. The classic street scam works because the con man is a person with a "straight face, crooked heart."

Unkindness & Selfishness

You may come across the cruel, the bad and the hard people in all walks of life, and in readiness for when you do, in this section you are likely to discover a heart phrase to precisely describe such a person. Normally, this kind of phrases would be used about a person in his or her absence. Using one of these terms in a serious, angry manner may well result in a confrontation. One of the cultural rules in Thailand is to avoid confrontation with others. Thus, when you hear such a phrase being used by Thai speakers, it is usually spoken in a smiling, non-confrontational manner.

Black Heart

jai dam (adj.) ใจดำ

This *jai* phrase is criticism hurled at you in circumstances where you fully understand another person's problem or setback and yet, despite your knowledge of the urgent need for help, you turn your back and walk away. A Thai friend requests a loan to pay for the hospital expenses of her mother and you refuse even though you could easily afford to make the loan. The friend may retort that you have a "black heart." The closest English word to describe the kind of person who bears the label *jai dam* is pitiless. The person without pity doesn't have empathy for the hardships and travails endured by others. Sometimes *jai dam* is used as a substitute word to describe someone's selfish behavior.

Bland Heart
jai jùuet (adj.) ใจจืด

Jai jùuet combines the word "heart" with the word *jùuet* which is often used to describe the tastelessness or blandness of food. The Thais pride themselves on spiced sauces, soups and food. A bland dish is often pushed away uneaten. In matters of the heart, if you hear someone referring to you as *jai jùuet*, your fate may be the same as the bland food—you will be left untouched and alone. The reason is that others perceive that you have no feelings, no *náam jai*. It is as if on your emotional menu the main course of sympathy was left off. And without a steady diet of sympathy, life, like tasteless food, is a meal you might wish to forgo. This term is less strong than *jai dam*. An example of *jai jùuet* occurs on the skytrain when a passenger sees a heavily pregnant woman standing and doesn't offer to give up his seat to her.

Black and Bland Heart
jai jùuet jai dam (adj.) ใจจืดใจดำ

This *jai* phrase combines the qualities of "blandness" and "blackness" to describe an unkind and selfish person, or an action that bears such negative qualities. Your heart is coarse and unopen to the feelings of others. You lack *náam jai*, the fundamental quality of sympathy and empathy and this cuts you off from others. If you have done something that has made someone feel that you were *jai jùuet jai dam* to them, they will long remember this act. Your dealings with them will be forever colored by your failure to show kindness and sympathy. All is not lost, though, as acts of sympathy and generosity can, over time, restore one's reputation as a good person.

Pitiless Heart
jai máay sâi rá kam (adj.)
ใจไม้ไส้ระกำ

The literal translation is wooden heart, black gut. The phrase belongs in the same league as "black heart" in the sense of being indifferent to others' plight. It also connotes a stronger condemnation. A person who is accused of being *jai máay sâi rá kam*, while being pitiless, can also have a nasty, hard heart, and no mercy. A person with this characteristic trait is capable of brutal acts of violence. The Thais may use such a phrase to describe someone who intentionally causes pain or harm to other people and appears to suffer no feelings of remorse or guilt.

Unfeeling Heart
jai krà dâang (adj.) ใจกระด้าง

A person may feel the absence of love for someone else who, finding his or her own love unrequited, will experience *jai krà dâang*. The person on the receiving end of the "unfeeling heart" label is likely to be someone who withholds emotional involvement. An unfeeling person does not care about what happens to others, or is unmoved by it. This may be evidence of a hard-hearted person. Don't expect to move or touch him or her emotionally.

Unreliability

Changeable Heart
jai ruaan ree (adj.) ใจรวนเร
jìt jai ruaan ree (adj.) จิตใจรวนเร
jai khOO ruaan ree (adj.) ใจคอรวนเร

A person who is *jai ruaan ree* flips flops. One day she wants to marry you, the next day she wants to leave you. This is Hamlet's famous "to be or not to be" scene. Well, make up your mind, Hamlet. But he wouldn't be Hamlet if he could. "Changeable heart" is another way of saying someone is inconsistent, indecisive and uncertain. The other *jai* phrases under this heading are used in the same way as *jai ruaan ree*. This expression also applies to someone who can't make up their mind. A student who goes through multiple-choice answers chooses one choice, then decides to choose another, and finally comes back to the original choice. The student is *jìt jai ruaan ree*. A person who is *jai khOO ruaan ree* is someone who is habitually indecisive and changes his or her mind easily.

Fickle Heart

jai loo lee (adj.) ใจโลเล

If you have a "fickle heart" then it is difficult for you to make up your mind about a relationship, job, shopping, or the brand of toothpaste you want to use. You love her tonight but tomorrow is another day, and you might have changed your mind overnight. There is an element of lack of commitment or an inability to make a decision and to keep steadfast with the outcome of what has been decided.

Weak-Mindedness

The person who is weak-minded is easily manipulated. This category captures the personality of someone who is sluggish and who will without much difficulty be led down the garden path. Through innocence, lack of intelligence or weak-mindedness, such a person is not on his guard against others who may seek to take advantage.

Easy Heart

jai ngâay (adj.) ใจง่าย

Traditionally, "easy heart" applies to a woman who is loose or promiscuous (although it can also apply to both genders). A woman who sleeps with her boyfriend in the first week or month of meeting (let alone on the first date) is labeled *jai ngâay*. The essence of the meaning is in the gullibility of the person with an "easy heart"; such a person can be seduced without a great effort. In the modern context, the easy-hearted person may also go out with many different partners and sheds them like an old shirt.

But *jai ngâay* has another, wider meaning that describes a person who is easily convinced or influenced by others; someone who has little capacity to reflect about a course of action and finds it easier to follow the lead of another. In this meaning, it is used in the same sense as *jai baw* "light heart" to describe the characteristic of a person who is easily taken in by others.

People who are taken in by populist government policies can also be described as *jai ngâay*. Thais use the phrase to tease each other. You ask a Thai friend if she would like to go to dinner with you and a group of friends and she replies, "Yes, I accept. I am a *jai ngâay* type. So why not?" It would be a grave mistake, however, for you to first suggest that someone is *jai ngâay* or use this expression outside of your close circle of friends as you may be misunderstood in ways you would rather avoid. Women in particular will find the comment extremely insulting.

Light Heart

jai baw (adj.) ใจเบา

This is a *jai* phrase for a person who is gullible and credulous or who changes his mind at a drop of a hat. In the first sense, it refers to someone who will trust just about anything you tell him but who should know that not everyone can be trusted. The moon is made of green cheese and inter-city khlongs are suitable for bathing and drinking. If you trust this easily, then your have a "light heart": *jai baw*. This is Thai for a sucker, someone easily taken in and led by another, often against his best interest. In the second sense, it refers to someone who has no strong conviction of his own, is gullible and easily changes his stand without questioning the validity of the argument. In the political context, it is said by the Bangkok middle class that the great masses who believe the official government line without any questioning are *jai baw*.

Beautiful to the Eye, Beautiful to the Heart

jà rooen taa jà rooen jai (adj.)

เจริญตาเจริญใจ

5
compliments and insults

Bestowing a compliment or hurling an insult in the Thai language draws on a rich source of heart metaphors. The heart phrases—whether in the verb, adjective or noun form—are expressions of the speaker's own feeling about another. A number of heart phrases in Chapter 3 The Best of the Human Condition can be and are often used as compliments of a person's qualities, conduct and behavior, and character, while those in Chapter 4 The Worst of the Human Condition, especially the phrases that belong in the character traits category, are linguistic instruments of insults.

In this way, the heart phrases for compliments in this chapter are additions to those in Chapter 3. Most are compliments for beauty (of people, things or performances) and expressions of appreciation of qualities of people or things that impress the speaker's heart. The phrases for insults are also additions to those in Chapter 4, but in this chapter they are extreme condemnations, and have stronger emotive punch than those in Chapter 4.

COMPLIMENTS

If you wish to pay a Thai speaker a compliment the chances are you will find an appropriate expression in *Heart Talk*. Some of the warmest Thai expressions are compliments about how a speaker feels about another person; a person is *jai dii* (has a "good heart") *jai mêet taa* (has a "compassionate heart"), *jing jai* (has a "true heart"), or *mii náam jai* (has a "water heart"). The phrases for compliments below are not so much about human character but qualities and beauty that impress.

A word of caution: do not overuse the heart compliments. Thais are sensitive and fully aware of those who attempt to use their language in order to falsely flatter them. If you have chosen a phrase that does not ring true to a Thai speaker, you may hear the return phrase *pàak wǎan* or "sweet mouth." This means you are sugar-coating your words and that you are not expressing genuine feelings. Your integrity is on the line when you pay a heart compliment, especially to someone you have not known for a long period of time. As in all languages, it also is important to distinguish between flattery and genuine compliment.

Beautiful to the Eye, Beautiful to the Heart
jà rooen taa jà rooen jai (adj.)
เจริญตาเจริญใจ

Something or someone that is aesthetically pleasing is *jà rooen taa jà rooen jai*. The beauty is first perceived through the eye and simultaneously experienced with the heart. The aesthetic is in beauty, whether a butterfly or a full moon, brings this condition of the heart into full bloom. Beauty, as the saying goes, is in the eye of the beholder. What is aesthetically pleasing varies from one person to the next.

Captivating to the Heart
jàp jai (adj.) จับใจ
nâa jàp jai (adj.) น่าจับใจ

A good story or tale captivates the reader or listener. A girl writes a heart-felt article for Mother's Day about what a wonderful mother she has. The article is published in the newspaper. Those who read the story are impressed or captivated by the truth of the young writer's emotions. The readers of this beautiful article may describe it as *jàp jai* or *nâa jàp jai*—the readers' hearts are touched, captivated, arrested. Someone relates in vivid detail his or her exploits in finding rare relics in the jungles of Burma and, in so doing, has the entire table captivated, listening to the story. The readers or listeners in the above examples would feel that the newspaper article and story about Burma were *nâa jàp jai*. Another example is the beautiful warm smile on a young woman's face—such a smile is *nâa jàp jai* and will captivate those who witness it.

Eat the Heart

kin jai (v.) กินใจ

The meaning of the phrase *kin jai* is similar to that of *jàp jai*. The girl's beautiful story about her mother can also be said to *kin jai* the audience. The difference is that this phrase is a verb, while *jàp jai* is an adjective. To *kin jai* is to impress. What impresses can be an act or words of another person, a story in a film or book, a lovely song or a beautiful piece of art. What is impressive may speak volumes about the individual so impressed. Wise words of advice from a sage or someone you respect may *kin jai* and continue to do so long after the words were spoken. You have seen *Casablanca* fifteen times and are still taken in by Bogart's performance as the character named Rick, the bar owner. In this sense, the girl's beautiful story (and her action to express her love of her mother), the wise words of the sage and Bogart's "Rick" all "eat your heart."

Fragrant Heart

hǑOm chûuen jai (adj.) หอมชื่นใจ

Conversations in Thailand can center around what is a good or bad smell. What (and who) smells bad is the subject of debate. But there is no debate about the directness of voicing disapproval of bad smells. The same directness applies to good smells. The fragrance of flowers, the skin of a baby or perfume, to mention only three examples, is an experience that makes the heart feel better. The admirer of such good smell would say *hǑOm chûuen jai*. This compliment doesn't apply to food, however. The sense of smell is very important to Thais. An expression of love or intimacy often involves referring to the good smell of the other person. The ps and nose against the cheek is an example of Thai ...ng. Thai people smooch instead of kissing their loved ones. In this act of intimacy, the words spoken by the smoocher will also be *hŎOm chûuen jai*.

Impressed Heart
prà tháp jai (v.) ประทับใจ
nâa prà tháp jai (adj.) น่าประทับใจ
phim jai (v.) พิมพ์ใจ

If you want to compliment a Thai about Thailand you can say you feel *prà tháp jai* or impressed with Thai food, Thai hospitality, the beaches of Koh Samui, the Grand Palace, or the ancient culture of art and dance. Many tourists, who return year after year to Thailand, feel a sense of *prà tháp jai* about the kindness and smiles found in abundance throughout the Kingdom. The thing that impresses you is *nâa prà tháp jai*. So, another way to compliment will be to say the hospitality, the beaches or the culture is *nâa prà tháp jai*. Impressive acts or character of a person such as devotion, kindness, courage or wisdom can also be *nậa prà tháp jai*. Thais are playful with their language and often will have more than one *jai* phrase that can be used in the same circumstances. *Phim jai*, literally "to print on the heart," is a good example. It gives some variation and relief from using the more common *prà tháp jai*.

Imprinted on the Eye, Imprinted on the Heart
tìt taa trueng jai (v.) ติดตาตรึงใจ
trueng taa trueng jai (v.) ตรึงตาตรึงใจ

You encounter an incredible beauty, be it of a person, a scenery, or an experience. Your eye and your heart are attracted to that beauty, so much so that the beauty is imprinted on your eye and your heart. Something that is *jà rooen taa jà rooen jai*, "beautiful to the eye, beautiful to the heart," may impress you only for a short duration, but something that manages to *tìt taa trueng jai* or *trueng taa trueng jai* has a long lasting impression on your heart. The beauty or beautiful feeling remains with you long after the first encounter. While it may be used as a direct compliment, this is an expression which you would more likely relate to others about that beautiful face that is etched in your mind or the breathtaking beauty of the sunset you and your sweetheart watched together during your last holiday.

Satisfactory to the Heart
pen thîi phOO jai (adj.) เป็นที่พอใจ
pen thîi nâa phOO jai (adj.) เป็นที่น่าพอใจ

The essence is a judgment made about the performance or quality of a person or a thing. An employee's performance may be *pen thîi phOO jai* (satisfactory) for his or her boss. This translates into a state of satisfaction concerning his or her working relationship with the employer. The same phrase can also be used in the context of various people in your life: friends, relatives, co-workers, or spouses. You are satisfied with them (or not). One can also experience the same feeling with a project, job, or new car.

Strike the Heart
doon jai (v.) โดนใจ
thùuk jai (v.) ถูกใจ

Doon jai has become a popular slang expression used by teenagers to describe an event, an object, words or another person that has some essence that hits home. The expression now enjoys acceptance among the wider public. You may hear another person insightfully describe the political or economic situation and feel that their analysis is accurate, true and revealing, and the comment strikes your heart, *doon jai*. It is like hitting the bull's eye with a dart. The latest fashion, new music or *Harry Potter* novel may *doon jai* a teenager. The phrase *thùuk jai* is a more conventional expression of the same meaning.

Trustworthy Heart
pen khon (thîi) wái jai dâay (adj.) เป็นคน(ที่)ไว้ใจได้
pen khon (thîi) chûeaa jai dâay (adj.) เป็นคน(ที่)เชื่อใจได้

To trust is to *wái jai* in Thai. Someone who is trustworthy is described in Thai as *pen khon thîi wái* (or *chûeaa*) *jai dâay*. When dealing with strangers of someone you don't know well, if this is a comment you hear about the person whose character you are not sure of, then this is a stamp of approval. Generally, this is a kind of compliment that is not said in the presence of the person in question.

Flattering Heart
phûut aw jai (v.) พูดเอาใจ

This verbal phrase is not a compliment but a response to a compliment. If someone describes you as or asks whether you *phûut aw jai*, after you have given a compliment, it means they feel you are flattering them (usually this comment is given in jest). The seriousness of the compliment is being put to a test. Are you speaking from your heart or does your heart have an ulterior motive? Do you want something from the person you are giving the compliment to? Or are you just saying what you believe the other person wishes to hear rather than saying what you believe to be true? Is this another act of *pàak wăan* or "sweet mouth?" So, "flattering heart" describes the heart of the person giving the compliment. It is now up to the complimenter to admit or refute that his or her heart is a "flattering heart."

INSULTS

You want to pick a fight in Thai? The oral weapon is an attack on the other person's heart. However, while *Heart Talk* provides a rich arsenal of phrases for emotional warfare, using the heart phrases in this section with Thai speakers is definitely not recommended. These heart phrases are reserved for the truly wicked, evildoers and psychotic villains who are capable of inflicting enormous pain and destruction to others. These are the beasts, cruel and heartless individuals, who are susceptible to the lowest of human impulses and act with utter disregard for the feelings and well-being of others. These are the people whose activies may involve rape, murder and mayhem.

As linguistic weapons, these heart phrases should be used with extreme caution. They are not "joking around" phrases but fighting words when addressed to a Thai speaker. Even the most tolerant and patient Thai would be provoked to anger and violence, if he or she is described with one of these phrases. They are unambiguous personal insults; some rank as character assassination *par excellence*.

More often than not, these following phrases are used as a commentary of criminals in the newspapers or someone not present in the discussion. If one of them is used in the presence of the person in question, then the discussion has undoubtedly turned into a verbal warfare. Unless you are very experienced in flight or an expert on Thai culture and inter-personal relationships, it is better to find another phrase or, better still, another language when you wish to resort to outright, direct criticism.

Animal Heart

jai sàt (adj.) ใจสัตว์

"Animal heart" is an adjective. It is something one possesses as a personality attribute. A *jai sàt* person has no human morals, and behaves like an animal. A murderer would be thought to possess *jai sàt*. The infamous Chinese cannibal "*Si Ui*" who ate Thai children after World War II is the quintessential *jai sàt* of Thai folklore. If uttered against another person, *jai sàt* is a horrible insult and the utterance guarantees that the verbal battle will lead to physical blows being exchanged.

Base Heart

jai tàm (adj.) ใจต่ำ

jìt jai tàm (adj.) จิตใจต่ำ

These two phrases of "base heart" describe the nature of the person or a particular opportunistic act. The person who is *jai tàm* or *jìt jai tàm* always thinks about life or others in a negative or obscene or hurtful way. His or her mind tends toward focusing on base instincts. This person has a degenerate mind, never sees the good in another, and views life as a jungle where only the most terrible beasts can survive. The *jai* word is often used for someone who loves pornography or other things considered depraved by society. This kind of heart is difficult to heal or change; it goes to the nature of the person and his or her view of life and others. Thais wish to avoid people with these qualities. The person with a "base heart" is also an opportunist and unburdened by moral or ethical principles that stop most people from taking full advantage of others. Examples are: (i) a person walks past an unattended vendor's fruits stall and, seeing the fruits looking so tempting, steals the fruits from the stall, and (ii) a pickpocket gropes a woman on a bus or the BTS.

Cruel Heart

jai hêaam (adj.) ใจเหี้ยม
jai hòot hêaam (adj.) ใจโหดเหี้ยม
jai am má hìt (adj.) ใจอำมหิต
jai dam am má hìt (adj.) ใจดำอำมหิต

Someone with this heart quality is unusually cruel and merciless, capable of brutal acts of violence that are diabolical and incomprehensible to an average human being. Such a person is a heavy hitter of death and destruction; he or she uses violence like everyday cologne. Pol Pot, the infamous leader of the Khmer Rouge, provided a local example in neighboring Cambodia. A hardened criminal who killed an innocent child or an evil employer who brutally abused a child servant, or the father who regularly beats his wife and children are also candidates for the label of "cruel heart." All the *jai* phrases above are interchangeable.

Depraved Heart

jai tàm cháa (adj.) ใจต่ำช้า
jai tàm saam (adj.) ใจต่ำทราม

This is the stronger version of "base heart." Someone with a "depraved heart" is guided by base instincts and is ready to sink down the ladder of humanity by the lowest of animalistic impulses. Touched with the brush of evil, they possess a cruel streak that warps their nature and are capable of depraved and wanton acts of cruelty. Being *jai tàm cháa* or *jai tàm saam* is about as bad as one can get and still be considered a member of the human race. These are people who may have thrown their daughters out in the street or sold them into prostitution, landmined Sukhumvit Road, and barbecued local soi dogs. A father who rapes his own daughter or a group of men who rape a woman are also appropriately condemned as *jai tàm cháa* or *jai tàm saam.*

Despicable Heart

jai leew (adj.) ใจเลว
jai leew saam (adj.) ใจเลวทราม

"Despicable heart" belongs in the same class as "depraved heart." It is yet another insult that describes the quality of the lowest instinct that lurks in the heart of humanity. Although it may not rank among the top few of the worst condemnations reserved for mass murderers, baby killers and those who killed their own parents. This is not the kind of heart you want in anyone you know. A person deserving of this description is capable of carrying out contemptible acts that will cause injury, fear and even death to others. Such a bad person is felt to have an evil heart, a heart without feeling for the plight of others. Don't expect those with "despicable heart" to feel anything approaching remorse for their evil acts; it isn't in their nature.

Devil in One's Heart

maan hŭaa jai (n.) มารหัวใจ

A "devil in one's heart" or *maan hŭaa jai* is someone who destroys the love existing between people. This is the classic soap-opera love triangle where a couple, husband and wife or boyfriend and girlfriend, find their counterpart in the relationship has entered into a loving, caring relationship with a third person. The effect is to alienate the affections of the deceived person. The outsider to the relationship, who knowingly intervenes to cause the break-up of an existing relationship, is a *maan hŭaa jai.* Another example, from a non-romantic context, is a woman who expects that her mother's last will give her all of the land and money. Later, the daughter discovers that the father has two children with a minor wife and the mother decides to include them in the will. After the mother's death, the daughter discovers that her two half-brothers have inherited property from her mother. The daughter feels that the half-brothers have taken property from her and calls them *maan hŭaa jai*.

Dog Heart

jai mǎa (adj.) ใจหมา

It is one thing to love dogs but it is quite another to suggest to a Thai that she or he has a dog's heart. This is light years away from being a compliment. It is slang that covers the same territory as "depraved heart" and "despicable heart." To call someone a "dog heart" means they are mean and evil, lacking in honor and human decency. A person crosses the street and is hit by a motorcycle and the driver doesn't stop to help the injured person but runs away. An unstable person stands on a balcony and is contemplating jumping to her death; a man in the crowd shouts for her to jump. He's *jai mǎa*.

Evil Heart

jai chûaa (adj.) ใจชั่ว

jai chûaa ráay (adj.) ใจชั่วร้าย

jìt jai chûaa ráay (adj.) จิตใจชั่วร้าย

If you call someone *jai chûaa*, it means you are attacking another person as a wicked, evil or mean individual. This is a grave insult in the Thai language. Thais would avoid using this *jai* phrase directly with another. This is a *jai* phrase befitting loathsome villains in movies. An act of drug or human trafficking and corruption is *chûaa*. This strong condemnation which, if used with the wrong person, may provoke a violent response or earn you a trip to a local hospital. The other two phrases, *jai chûaa ráay* and *jìt jai chûaa ráay* are variations of the same insult with an emphasis on the bad, mean and evil quality of the person and the heart. *Ráay* is synonymous with *chûaa*.

Heart of Stone

jai hǐn (adj.) ใจหิน

Only the most unfeeling of hearts can be said to be made of stone. A person who shows no mercy and feels no compassion for the hurt, injury or suffering of others has a heart of stone. Acts of violence or cruelty can be carried out by those with *jai hǐn* as they lack any concept of sympathy for others. The lack of empathy for others makes them inhuman, possessing a heart not of flesh and blood but one carved from stone. During a time of war, a *jai hǐn* person would make a perfect killing machine; during a time of peace he walks among others without a sense of human sympathy. "Heart of stone" belongs in the same class as "cruel heart" and "savage heart."

Monster Heart

jai yák (adj.) ใจยักษ์
jai maan (adj.) ใจมาร
jai yák jai maan (adj.) ใจยักษ์ใจมาร

A *yák* means an ogre or a monster in Thai, and a *maan* is a devil. So, branding someone as having the heart of a monster or a devil is to say clearly that the person is without humanity and without normal feelings. The monster heart metaphor carries an extremely negative image. In this context, an ogre (which is the literal Thai translation) is looked upon as a mean, cruel and brutal monster-like figure of a child's nightmares. The devil's heart needs no explanation. Like "cruel heart" and "savage heart," these heart phrases are used to express revulsion about those who show little true feeling about the well-being of others. The mother who abandons her newly born child is commonly referred to as *jai yák*. *Jai maan* and *jai yák jai maan* can be substituted for *jai yák*.

Perverted Heart

jai saam (adj.) ใจทราม

"Perverted heart" is of the same class and character as *jai tàm*—a very bad person who tends toward evil, mean and perverse acts. Such a person may exploit child labour in a factory, or force children into prostitution or pornography. It is used interchangeably with *jai tàm* and the two words can be combined as *jai tàm saam*.

This heart phrase is normally applied to a person who indulges in perverted activity. Perversion in this case has an immoral quality attached. The man who fondles women on a bus or the BTS is *jai saam*, and if he is caught by the authorities he might well spend some time learning heart phrases inside a Thai jail. The heart phrase can apply to both genders. A woman, who takes pleasure in abusing her child or student with perverse punishment, would also be said to have a "perverted heart."

Savage Heart
jai thá min (adj.) ใจทมิฬ
jai thá min hǐn châat (adj.)
ใจทมิฬหินชาติ

A person who possesses a "savage heart" has a great capacity for brutality. Included in this category would be those who commit international war crimes such as genocide. Such people often resort to the murder of innocent women and children in a civil war. On a more limited scale of action, *jai thá min* may be used to describe a professional gunman who kills others for money. It is also suitable for describing a terrorist who puts a bomb in a public place, killing many innocent people. *Jai thá min hǐn châat* combines savagery with the hardness of the stone (*hǐn*), indicating an unusual hardness of this "savage heart." The latter expression is poetic and found in Thai literature.

Wicked Heart
jai bàap (adj.) ใจบาป
jai bàap yàap cháa (adj.)
ใจบาปหยาบช้า

A parent who murders his or her own child is *jai bàap*. Someone who kills a monk and a student who kills his own teacher or parent are further examples. Such a person lacks any sense of right and wrong, of moral and immoral. *Bàap* means sin in Thai, so, while the condemnation points to the evil and wickedness of the person who has committed such reprehensible acts, "wicked heart" also connotes the lack of spirituality and sinfulness of the acts. The examples show the ultimate betrayal of loyalty and trust—the murder of family members by another member of the family. The modifier of *yàap cháa* indicates and further emphasizes that the sin is horrible.

Gold Chain Around One's Heart

sôo thOOng khlÓOng jai (n.)

โซ่ทองคล้องใจ

6
heart talk in relationships

Understanding and correctly using heart phrases is essential in order to express feelings people experience in their relationships. Feelings of appreciation, empathy, trust, respect, deception, suspicion, betrayal, and pain are among the themes found in many of the heart phrases contained in this chapter.

The personal relationship may be between: (i) husband and wife; (ii) boyfriend and girlfriend; (iii) parent and child; and (iv) friends. Within the confines of such relationships, heart phrases provide a rich vocabulary for lovers and friends to register the full scale of their feelings—from tenderness to fury. As you study the heart phrases you will better appreciate the universal emotional preoccupations embedded in the fabric of most relationships. What makes Thai heart phrases special is the wide range of expressions that we might associate with the feelings found in a love relationship.

The Thai language arguably has the largest number of heart phrases in any language. Each is rich in texture and nuance, allowing the speaker to express with precision his or her feelings within most relationships. The heart phrases, for purposes of convenience, have been divided into twenty-three general categories. The emotional landscape in a relationship draws those involved into a variety of mental conditions ranging from trust to betrayal, appreciation to pain and trust feelings. Among Thai speakers, the art of learning and using these heart phrases is to discover a safe passage through the emotional minefields of a relationship.

Appreciation

Feelings of joy and tenderness are woven in Thai into a number of heart phrases. This section contains the verbal valentines that lovers, friends and parents use all year round to express their positive, joyful, happy feelings, to convey a sense of appreciation and well-being that another person is part of their life.

Appreciative/Grateful Heart

súeng jai (adj.) ซึ้งใจ

sâap súeng jai (adj.) ซาบซึ้งใจ

When someone has assisted you in completing a job or a project, then you feel deeply grateful and appreciative for their assistance. You feel *sâap súeng jai* toward that person. The heart expression covers a broad range of situation in which you are on the receiving end of helpfulness and for which you are grateful. Maybe you are lost in Bangkok and someone helps you find the place you are looking for on a map. Or you are at a phone booth and don't have the right change, and someone gives you the proper coins. You've been evicted from your condo, and Tom, your friend, gives you a place to stay for a month. You will feel *súeng jai* toward Tom. Or your favorite love song may express your own feeling so well that you feel *súeng jai* about the song. In Thai, in other words, you appreciate acts of kindness from your heart.

Joyful Heart

chûuen jai (adj.) ชื่นใจ

This is a commonly used *jai* phrase as an expression of satisfaction, relief or joy. When you feel joy in your heart, you experience *chûuen jai*. How that joy enters the heart speaks volumes about the person. It normally involves the small touching gestures in a relationship. A man gives a woman flowers and a kiss on her birthday and she feels *chûuen jai*. You receive a compliment from your boss at work, or your child comes back from school and gives you a report card with many A's, you feel *chûuen jai*. When you are hot and thirsty, a glass of cold water makes you feel *chûuen jai*.

Betrayal

There are a variety of heart phrases to articulate feelings of betrayal, dishonesty, deception and disloyalty. Someone in the relationship has breached the bond of trust and acted out of self-interest, in a selfish fashion and often to the detriment of the other who has given their trust. These heart phrases are used in intimate personal relationship where, the partners expect to receive and to give loyalty and to be faithful. This ideal does not always prevail in reality. The man who loves two women, or the woman who loves two men is not *jai diiaw*, "one heart." When loyalty or faithfulness is questioned or disappears, the following phrases often come into play.

Betraying Heart
aw jai ÒOk hàang (v.) เอาใจออกห่าง
aw jai ÒOk hàak (v.) เอาใจออกหาก

This *jai* phrase is used when you gradually shift your loyalty from one person to another. You work in an office with Daeng and have a close, personal relationship. Then Lek starts to work in the office and over a period of weeks you begin to transfer your attention and affection to Lek. You spend less time with Daeng and start to avoid her. Daeng suspects that you have a "betraying heart." While *aw jai ÒOk hàang* usually occurs over a period of time, it can also happen quickly. You walk into a crowded room with your lover and see the most beautiful woman you've ever laid eyes on crossing the room and giving you a seductive smile. Instead of moving on, ignoring this opportunity, you mentally start planning an escape into the night with this beautiful stranger. In effect, you are moving your heart away from your lover, i.e. *aw jai ÒOk hàang*. In the underworld of gangsters, the heart phrase also applies to a gang member who is disloyal to the gang by giving evidence to the police. In circumstances of double-dealing, the person who betrays another is rightly labeled as possessing a "betraying heart." *Aw jai ÒOk hàak* is an old usage of the same expression.

Pierce the eye, Pierce the Heart
tam taa tam jai (v.) ตำตาตำใจ
Cut the Eye, Cut the Heart
bàat taa bàat jai (v.) บาดตาบาดใจ
bàat jai (v.) บาดใจ

The essence of *tam taa tam jai* and *bàat taa bàat jai* is that the person who has been betrayed is a witness to the act of betrayal. Thus the act of disloyalty pierces the eye and also pierces the heart. The emotions registered would include loathing, anger, pain and shock. The sight of your spouse or lover unreservedly flirting with another man or woman will pierce or cut your eye and your heart. The child who sees his father walking arm in arm with a woman who is not her mother, would also find the sight *tam taa tam jai* or *bàat taa bàat jai*.

Stabbed Heart
thîm thEEng jai (v.) ทิ่มแทงใจ

The essence of this *jai* phrase is that someone has been stabbed by the betrayal of a beloved. For instance, the boyfriend arrives back in Bangkok after six months abroad and discovers that his girlfriend has sold the five-baht gold chain and diamond ring he bought for her. To add insult to injury, he learns that she has used the money to buy a new motorcycle for her secret boyfriend, Somchai, a motorcycle taxi driver. The acts of selling the jewelry and buying the motorcycle for the secret boyfriend would *thîm thEEng jai* her returning boyfriend.

Character of the Heart

Condition of the Heart
sà phâap jìt jai (n.) สภาพจิตใจ

This heart phrase describes the emotional state of being at the moment or at any given moment. In relationships, it is important to be aware of the condition of the heart of others. The "condition of the heart" (*sà phâap jìt jai*) of those you care about may be positive or negative, and may shift over time from one state to another. They may be feeling dejected, depressed or sad;

or happy, hopeful or excited. The communication of the condition of the heart may be made through words, gestures or acts by the person wishing to describe the emotional state of being. The parents or teachers, for instance, who are attentive in "reading" the condition of the heart of their children and students, will be able to provide them with appropriate comfort in times of need and to celebrate with them during times of joy.

Core Spirit of the Heart
hŭaa jìt hŭaa jai (n.) หัวจิตหัวใจ

Hŭaa jìt hŭaa jai is a synonym for *hŭaa òk hŭaa jai* and used in similar circumstances. The focus is on the emotional and mental state of the person. The concept of *jìt* refers to the mental condition of the person in question. When someone commits an incomprehensible act of violence or brutality, it leaves others to question how any human being could do something this terrible. A mother who kills her two-year-old daughter would leave most people asking what is the mother's heart made of that she could murder her small, helpless daughter. Most people would agree that the mother *mâi mii hŭaa jìt hŭaa jai* or the mother doesn't have a heart. The *jai* phrase is often used in the context where it is clear that the person described has done something terrible and outside the bounds of what society finds acceptable.

In a second usage, the phrase is used to describe an emotional state of utter bereavement. A husband who loses his wife and is beside himself with grief, shuts out the rest of the world and has no energy or inclination to do anything but cry. While in this state his friends might describe him as *mâi mii hŭaa jìt hŭaa jai*. This means he has lost his spirit to do anything else during this period of grief.

Emotional State of Heart
hŭaa òk hŭaa jai (n.) หัวอกหัวใจ

This heart phrase is often used in a complaint or protect against someone's (real or perceived) lack of compassion or sensitivity. Steve loves golf and spends every weekend on the golf course with his friends. His wife feels that he is insensitive to her and his family. When she complains to him, Steve's dismissive and uncaring personality triggers her to say that he *mâi hěn hŭaa òk hŭaa jai* of his wife and his family. In another example, when a person does not come to the rescue of someone hurt in a car crash, but drives past without stopping, others would say such a person *mâi mii hŭaa òk hŭaa jai*.

Heart
jai khOO (n.) ใจคอ

There are two main uses for *jai khOO*. The first is in the context of a person's personality or natural disposition. The second meaning is related to a person's emotional reactions to another person or an event. In the first sense, the cause of your bad mood speaks volumes about your personality and character. Someone by nature may be *jai khOO kháp khÊEp* or narrow-minded (such a person usually has a hard time parting with his or her money or refuses to listen to the opinions of others). Another person, on the other hand, is helpful and generous, and is open to the views of others. Such a person is said to be *jai khOO kwâang khwăang*; his or her heart is as wide as a big river.

True Nature of the Heart
ní săi jai khOO (n.) นิสัยใจคอ
náam săi jai khOO (n.) น้ำใสใจคอ

In any relationship, the true nature or the real character of a person always manifests sooner or later. These phrases are ways to describe a person's personality or true character. The word *ní săi* means habit. People have habitual ways of dealing with others and we think of this as representing their nature. What is habit might be described as either strength or weakness. These phrases are neutral in terms of good or bad character traits. It depends on the circumstances, as the *jai* phrase relates to the inner nature of the person acting. You might have a neighbor who is fussy and petty.

Her actions supply many examples of a personality that is fussy and petty. Over time this builds in your mind into a convincing case that the neighbor has negative personal characteristics. You soon learn to avoid her.

There is always some additional qualification used with these phrases. In the first example you would say that the neighbor is *ní sǎi jai khOO jûu jîi*—she is fussy and petty. But a person who is thoughtful to his mother, always looking after her, bringing her food and flowers, would be *ní sǎi jai khOO dii*. Lek is on an Internet dating site and receives an email invitation from a total stranger. She asks her best friend Nong whether she should accept, and Nong shakes her head and warns Lek that she doesn't know the *ní sǎi jai khOO* of the man who has given the invitation. He might be good, but he might be bad. *Náam sǎi jai khOO* has a similar meaning but is an older phrase and has fallen out of use.

Confused Heart

jai sàp sǒn (adj.) ใจสับสน

The literal translation is "confused heart." The core meaning refers to the state of mind of a person being described as opposed to a characteristic trait of that person. The confusion may be a temporary or permanent state. This *jai* phrase is often used in circumstances where a person must make a choice and doesn't know what to choose. Such a person doesn't know what to do next or which end is up. It may be that the beautiful woman can't decide between two suitors, or a student can't decide whether to go to Australia or to Canada for university.

Crooked Heart

jai khót (adj.) ใจคด

A crook is someone who can't be fully trusted. Crooks live outside the bounds of rules that most people abide by and believe are important. A man or woman who is disloyal to their partner is, in many ways, also placing themselves outside of the normal expectations of what is permissible in a relationship. The nature of such a person, a relationship "outlaw," is *jai khót*. This translates as a person with some serious emotional breakage, damage that has never been repaired. The "crooked heart" is deceiving the other about his or her true feelings. For example, when the husband is away on the business trip the wife is out with another man, and when the husband returns she says that she stayed at home missing her husband. She is *jai khót*. It is also used in the business context of an employer telling his staff that the company is doing poorly and there are no profits, meaning there will be no annual bonus. In reality the company is profitable, and the employer isn't telling the truth in order to avoid paying a bonus. The employer in this case is *jai khót*.

Maximum Effort Heart
jai tem rÓOy (adj.) ใจเต็มร้อย

If you possess a "maximum effort heart" you give your full energy, concentration and spirit to an activity, friendship or romantic relationship. You completely commit your efforts to making the activity, friendship or romance a success. Such an attitude makes for a good employee, student, friend, lover or teammate. When a member of a football team is interviewed and asked about the upcoming match, he is likely to say that he and his team members are ready to give the maximum effort to win the match, in other words, they are *jai tem rÓOy*.

Convenience

Convenient Heart
sà dùaak jai (adj.) สะดวกใจ

When you want to ask someone to do something that may inconvenience them, it is polite to ask whether the request is convenient for them. Specifically, whether they are *sà dùaak jai* with the request. The employer may ask an employee to work overtime, and ask him or her whether he or she feels *sà dùaak jai* working on the weekend. When you invite a friend to a party, you might ask whether they are *sà dùaak jai* about attending a function where most of the people do not speak Thai. Is it, in other words, convenient—will they feel comfortable—attending this party with non-Thai speakers?

Convenient Heart

thà nàt jai (adj.) ถนัดใจ
sà nàt jai (adj.) สนัดใจ

The meaning overlaps with the phrase *sà dùaak jai*. You are soliciting whether a request for someone to do or not to do something is convenient. It is also used to mean that you seize an opportunity to do something that you want to do. Two people have an argument. One person wishes to win the argument and waits for a convenient moment, when the other person is off-guard, and then takes advantage. In a boxing match, one fighter waits to find an opening to punch the other in the head and knock him out. At the moment the fighter is distracted by someone in the audience, the opponent takes that opportunity to hit him hard. You fight with the feeling of *thà nàt jai*: looking for the chance to deliver home the knock-out punch.

Problem-free Heart

khlÔOng jai (adj.) คล่องใจ

When you ask a friend to do a favor, such as driving you to the airport, and she does this willingly, without complaint, then you feel problem-free about her. You feel that you are not placing a burden on your friend. In the past you have driven her to the airport so her taking you there isn't unfair. You have an old-model personal computer, then you buy the latest and fastest new computer; once you start using the new machine and you see how much more productive you are, then you will also feel *khlÔOng jai*. The central aspect of *khlÔOng jai* is that your decision can be made smoothly and easily. There are no obstacles or problems standing in the way of what you wish to do or wish to happen.

Difficult Relationships

Relationships are troubled when another person's conduct or personality makes it difficult to maintain a smooth and cordial exchange of views, or to maintain respect and admiration. In Chapter 4, we looked at negative aspects of behavior and character traits. Several basic *jai* phrases have been selected to illustrate how people with negative behavior have difficulty forming and keeping a relationship alive. There is a convenient method for conveying the essence of another person by use of the following heart phrases. It is important to remember that these are merely illustrative of a vast number of potential character traits possessed by friends, lovers, colleagues and others with whom one has formed a relationship.

Difficult Heart
aw jai yâak (adj.) เอาใจยาก

This *jai* phrase is used to describe a person who is difficult to please. This type of person is never satisfied with the room temperature, the food is too spicy or too bland, the wine too sweet or too dry. It doesn't mean that you can't ever please such a person but it can be a long, difficult and trying job to keep him or her pleased. A boss may also be viewed as *aw jai yâak*, fussy, if the work from the employee is always criticized as being not according to instructions or filled with mistakes.

Disobliging Heart
khàt jai (v.) ขัดใจ

There are two meanings of this phrase, which are: (i) to refuse to oblige another's wish, and (ii) to be displeased or on bad terms with another. In the first sense, a naughty, stubborn child often *khàt jai* his mother—he never does what she asks. In the second sense, Nid and Noi are friends and they got into a little spat, so they now feel *khàt jai* with one another. But since they are good friends that will pass. The phrase is also used to describe displeasure with another's action. For example, Lek feels *khàt jai* that her driver is late to pick her up.

Bad Mouth, Good Heart
pàak ráay jai dii (adj.) ปากร้ายใจดี

Someone who uses cutting or insulting language (such as the vernacular of the fish market vendor) may have a heart of gold inside. The roughness or crudity of expression may not necessarily mean the speaker has a bad heart. For instance, in the Thai language there are crude ways to refer to oneself and others: *kuu* as oneself and *mueng* as another. This is gangster talk. The person using such crude language may have a good heart and help people in the community by donating time and money. This heart phrase is a perceptive insight into the willingness of Thai speakers to forgive rough or crude language so long as the speaker is of good heart.

Intractable Heart
lǔeaa jai (adj., adv.) เหลือใจ

Lǔeaa jai describes the feeling when a person can no longer bear a situation when another behaves in an exasperating way. When a naughty child refuses to read or do his homework despite repeated instruction from his mother, the mother is likely to feel *lǔeaa jai*. She has reached her limit, and simply leaves the room and abandons the child to his own devices. *Lǔeaa jai* can also be used in a positive sense. A policeman chases a robber down a back soi, he falls, stumbles, but continues running after the bad guy. Those watching the scene might say the policeman's actions are *lǔeaa jai*.

The negative sense of the word is when another's behavior makes one exasperated as he or she simply refuses to desist from a certain annoying action and becomes a nuisance. A persistent tele-marketer is a good example of someone who is *lŭeaa jai*. Even after you tell the caller that you are not interested in his or her product, the annoying caller still persists with the pitch. In the presence of someone who is *lŭeaa jai*, you will be tested on your ability to remain calm and cool in your heart.

Distant Eye, Distant Heart
klai taa klai jai (adj.) ไกลตาไกลใจ

If you stay away from Thailand (or any place, for that matter) for too long, those you have developed a relationship with and who have been left behind are likely, over time, to start to forget about you. Memories about others fade over time. So if you are far from another's eye, then her or his heart may also be far from you. The phrase is like the English saying: "out of sight, out of mind." In the Thai phrase *klai taa klai jai* it is the heart and not the mind that is far away. In a romantic relationship, *klai taa klai jai* is less than a desirable state. In other words, long-distance relationships can be difficult to sustain.

Frustrated Heart
àt ân jai (v.) อัดอั้นใจ
àt ân tan jai (v.) อัดอั้นตันใจ

These *jai* phrases describe the bottled-up feelings that cannot be expressed to another, or circumstances do not permit the expression. The condition is one of frustration. You have something on your mind but you feel you can't tell the other person what you want or fear. Your friend wants to take a job in another city but you feel the move will be bad for her. She has her heart set on the move and you feel unable to express your reservations about her decision. Another example is in a company. An employee is given a big pile of documents and told to finish the work by the end of the day. The employee can't tell her friends to help her because they are overworked too. A person is in debt and the creditor gives a seven-day deadline and threatens that if no payment is made then something bad will happen to her. There is no one she can turn to for help. In these examples, the person is frustrated, rendered speechless by circumstances, in the sense there is no one available to help or to be confided in.

Master of the Heart

pen jâw hŭaa jai (v.) เป็นเจ้าหัวใจ

"Master of the heart" is a common *jai* phrase. It arises in the context of power struggles within the home, family and office. It describes a person who is (or attempts to be) in control of someone else. A person who uses control and authority to limit another's freedom may well hear this accusation. This is a bad-news heart message. If someone complains about someone *pen jâw hŭaa jai*, it means another person has been pushing wants, demands or desires onto them. Sending out messages such as: change your hair style, change your clothes, shoes or the way you walk and talk. The "master of the heart" is a dictator and lacks respect for the freedom of others. If you are on the wrong side of a control freak, this is the heart phrase you are screaming to get out of his or her sight. It can also have a positive meaning. It may be used by a woman to refer to the man who she feels is so important that occupies her heart, and is the master of her heart—or vice versa.

Weary Heart

lá hèaa jai (adj.) ละเหี่ยใจ

In a chronically bad relationship, you are always in conflict and argument with the other person, and this makes you *lá hèaa jai*. *Phŭaa meaa lá hèaa jai* is a Thai saying for a husband and wife who have been at one another's throats for a long time. The underlying feeling of *lá hèaa jai* is the emotional exhaustion from the conflict and lack of understanding. In a culture that places high value on unity and harmony, this is not a desirable relationship.

Fear

Afraid Heart
wàn jai (v.) หวั่นใจ
phrân jai (v.) พรั่นใจ

These *jai* phrases translate as fear, the kind of fear within. There may be good reasons for such fear or it can be irrational. It may also be the fear of taking an emotional risk with another. Something holds you back emotionally. What causes fear in such circumstances depends on your upbringing, life experience (good and bad), and personality. Some hearts bond more easily than others. Thus few generalizations hold true in describing "afraid heart." Yet, you can be certain that a person feels 100 per cent *wàn jai* if he or she suspects another person seeking a relationship is *lǎay jai* (having many hearts). Such a person is afraid of exposing his or her heart when it is certain to be broken. The person will hold back until the bond can be made with a sense of trust and commitment. These *jai* phrases aren't confined to fears arising from relationships. You may fear a terrorist attack or that the stock market will crash or that someone from the government will arrive at your door at three in the morning.

Fear of Retribution Heart
wuaa sǎn lǎng khàat hěn kaa bin phàat kÔO tòk jai (proverb)
วัวสันหลังขาด เห็นกาบินผาดก็ตกใจ

The literal translation is: The cow with a torn out spine is frightened when seeing a crow fly past quickly. The essence, as the heart phrase is dread of retribution. Someone has done something wrong and consequently feels that the person they harmed will seek justice for the wrong suffered. The harm may have been a crime or other activities that cause the person to feel guilt. For instance, an employee may have lied to his or her boss about the loss of an important contract, so when a co-worker mentions the word "contract," the employee becomes jumpy for fear that his lie and failure will be exposed. The employee is the cow with a torn-out spine.

Grudge & Resentment

Astringent and Bitter Heart

jai fàat jai khŏm (adj.) ใจฝาดใจขม

This heart expression is not widely used. When a woman has broken her lover's heart, the lover will likely feel *jai fàat jai khŏm*, an astringent and bitter feeling inside. It results from heartbreak that follows the break-up of a marriage or relationship. Now that the couple is estranged they feel *jai fàat jai khŏm*. This causes a feeling of bitterness. The heart phrase is slightly dated and now you would be more likely to hear the expression *khŏm khŭen jai*.

Bitter Heart

khŏm khùuen jai (v.) ขมขื่นใจ
rá thom khŏm khùuen jai (v.) ระทมขมขื่นใจ

When your heart is filled with bitterness, you can use this *jai* phrase. You are in a situation in which you can neither control nor change. You have a helpless feeling because you don't have any real alternative. You discover that your husband keeps a mistress and you bring up the subject with him but he's unable to break the relationship. You hate the situation yet can't do anything to change it. You can't leave your husband, but also feel great pain. Your wife tells you that she's a lesbian and is in love with another woman. You have children together and don't want to divorce your wife. You decide to maintain the existing domestic set-up but each day you have this bitterness in your heart.

Cut Heart

bàat măang jai (v.) บาดหมางใจ
rá khaang jai (v.) ระคางใจ

When you have a quarrel with a friend and a week later see him or her on the street, you may feel *bàat măang jai*. You may wish to avoid those you have had a conflict or quarrel with. Seeing your former lover coming down the street, you may duck around a corner to avoid talking with her or him. A person feels *bàat măang jai* about dealing with an old flame and wishes to escape the feelings he or she evokes by making a retreat in the opposite direction. The essence of *bàat măang jai* and *rá khaang jai* is a feeling of being upset and of wishing to avoid confrontation with the person who causes this feeling. Sometimes the two phrases are combined: *bàat măang rá khaang jai*.

Estranged Heart
khùn khÔOng mŎOng jai (v.)
ขุ่นข้องหมองใจ
phìt phÔOng mŎOng jai (v.)
ผิดพ้องหมองใจ
mŎOng jai (adj.) หมองใจ

These expressions that translate as "estranged heart" are often used in the context of a conflict in a close relationship. Long-term friends or siblings, or husband and wife are examples of such a close relationship. A person discovers that his close friend has cheated him in a land transaction by selling the land at an inflated price; he feels *mŎOng jai* towards his friend. The man who bought the land trusted his long-term friend and never expected him to cheat. The wife feels *khùn khÔOng mŎOng jai* with her husband because he has said something that suggests he still loves his ex-wife. *Phìt phÔOng mŎOng jai* is used in the same way but is a rather old-fashioned expression. There is a sense of betrayal and tension felt by at least one party in the relationship when these phrases are used.

Grudge Heart
phìt jai (v.) ผิดใจ
phìt jai kan (v.) ผิดใจกัน
măang jai (v.) หมางใจ

You have had a run-in with someone at the office and feel angry or sore as a result of the encounter. It is normally a trivial event that causes the feeling of a grudge. But the feelings are stronger and more active than *bàat măang jai* and *rá khaang jai*. The grudge may have been caused by an argument, or someone has double-crossed or betrayed you, or the feeling may result from a lingering sense of being wronged. The bottom line is that someone has accumulated a grudge against another. Two neighbors who have known each other for years share a common fence. Daeng picks a mango and eats it. Her neighbor comes out and says, "That is my mango! You shouldn't take it." This makes Daeng's feelings for the neighbor suddenly change. She feels *phìt jai*. And thereafter she will avoid the neighbor. This is a low-grade grudge and unhappiness. Such a feeling is written across the actions and words of a person harboring "grudge heart." When two people have a grude against each other they can be described as *phìt jai kan*. *Măang jai* is used similarly.

Rancorous Heart

nĚEng jai (v.) แหนงใจ

You have just finished a heated quarrel with your spouse, child or friend and the emotion after the fight ends can be described as *nĚEng jai*. The aftermath has left you feeling a little angry, a little upset, a little annoyed and suspicious of the other person. Unresolved doubts remain lingering in the heart. Here are a few examples of how such doubts may enter the heart. You may have battled with your spouse over the issue of how best to discipline your child when the child comes home late from school, and you don't share the same point of view. You may have fought without satisfactory resolution with your child over the amount of time he or she spends watching television, talking on the telephone with friends, or surfing on the Internet, and both of you are left feeling *nĚEng jai*. You may have quarreled with a friend over her failure to repay you the money she has owed you for the last three months and are suspicious of her renewed promise to pay you tomorrow. Another *jai* word that is also appropriate in these circumstances is *khlEEng jai,* "doubting heart."

Resentful Heart

jèp jai (v.) เจ็บใจ

jèp krà dOOng jai (v.) เจ็บกระดองใจ

The essence of *jèp jai* is a range of experience that causes pain to the heart. Some of the hurts may be small.

Others may loom large and cause a lifelong scar. For example, when the husband or wife finds that their spouse has a lover he or she will be *jèp jai*. If the resentment is profound and extreme, the expression is *jèp krà dOOng jai*—the hurt is felt through the shell of the heart—the person is in an extreme, highly volatile state. The feeling may precede violent action. The husband or wife may try to kill the offending spouse and/or the lover. These phrases have been known to come packaged with fists and weapons.

Heart Connection

Know Another's Heart

rúu jai (v.) รู้ใจ

When you know another person's habits, taste, desires, fears and dreams you achieve a personal intimacy that translates as *rúu jai*. You know another person's heart. This is not a heart phrase to be said lightly as idle pillow talk. For a Thai speaker, it is one thing to "measure another's heart" or *wát jai,* but to truly know another's heart is a quantum leap in knowledge. In your life you may know only a few hearts: your own (if you are lucky), that of your father and mother (if you have had a Thai upbringing the chances are great this will be true). If someone asks if you have a *khon rúu jai*, this is a polite way of asking you whether you have a lover.

Read Another's Heart

àan jai (v.) อ่านใจ

When another person has suffered an emotional setback, you seek the true cause of the upset. If it is a close friend or a family member, the person with the ability to read another's heart may know, without being told, the cause of the suffering or misery. The ability to read another person's heart arises from a combination of observation, knowledge of his or her family and background, and attempts to keep current with the hopes, dreams and fears of that person. By reading another's heart, you have a good idea of what the person wants or what he or she will do. With strangers it is more difficult to read their hearts because they are not part of our lives. Nonetheless, if a mother is crying beside the body of her child, even though she is a stranger, most people will be able to read the grief in her heart.

Remind One's Heart

tueaan jai (v.) เตือนใจ

There is an element of nostalgia in this heart phrase. A person may give you a photo or a ring belonging to your parents, spouse or an old school friend. The item is a memento for you to remember the other person. When you look at the photo you will miss your wife or sweetheart. It also applies to the ghastly photos on Thai cigarette packages showing smokers in a number of gruesome states of physical collapse brought about by smoking. The idea is to have a constant reminder of the deadly effect of smoking. *Tueaan jai,* then, is used whenever one—whoever that might be—wishes to present a reminder to others of something viewed as important, whether it is the memory of a relationship or a warning about health.

Same Heart

jai diiaw kan (adj.) ใจเดียวกัน
jai trong kan (adj.) ใจตรงกัน

Jai diiaw kan is state of being that ideally you should share with your spouse or lover—harmony and compatibility. These heart phrases may generate positive, good feelings of enjoying a shared view of life with another. There is an absence of conflict over choices to be made. You are in complete union with another person. You like the same movies, food, friends and holidays. You both drink fresh-squeezed orange juice and put strawberry jam on your wholewheat toast while listening to contemporary jazz. You both have the same favorite color, and prefer a hard mattress to a soft one. At the same time, it is possible to experience *jai diiaw kan* with a total stranger. For example, you may wish to have an aisle seat on a flight from Bangkok to New York City but a stranger wants it too. Through a mistake, the seat is double-booked. Your desire for the same seat creates a state of competition, and this common desire or hunger for the same object causes one's heart to feel the hard edge of the "same heart." *Jai trong kan* has the same meaning as *jai diiaw kan* and can be used in the same context. In addition, *jai trong kan* can also be used to express mutual attraction.

Sit in Another's Heart
nâng nai hŭaa jai (v.) นั่งในหัวใจ

The heart phrase comes from a Thai proverb: To sit in another's heart is to have knowledge of another's mind and soul. Thus it is putting oneself in the place of another in order to know how the person thinks and feels. With such understanding it becomes easier to anticipate the other person's wants, desires and moods. The essence of this heart phrase is that one has intimate (insider's) knowledge of another's mental landscape and knows how to follow the paths to happiness and avoid the drop into despair and disappointment. Parents may use this phrase to instruct their children to be sensitive in their relationship with nature, family or friends and to have empathy for others' situations.

Straight to the Heart
trong hŭaa jai (adj.) ตรงหัวใจ
thEEng jai (v.) แทงใจ

Literally this means (a shot) going straight through the heart. The shot could be an action of another person or the person himself that so squarely strikes your heart (in a good way). Someone says or does something that *thEEng jai* or *trong hŭaa jai* for you. Or it could be love at first sight—the Cupid has shot an arrow straight into your heart.

Touch One to the Quick
jîi hŭaa jai (v.) จี้หัวใจ

This *jai* phrase is less often used than *thùuk jai*. In this emotional state you may have "goosebumps" from a moving experience. It is likely that another person has done something to stir such feelings in you. You witness a special act of kindness, tenderness, goodness or valor; something unexpected has touched you emotionally. Perhaps you were at the cinema and a scene in the film made you feel sad or happy. If so, then you are touched or *thùuk jîi hŭaa jai*. Perhaps you received flowers on your birthday from someone special. The feeling can be either uplifting or sad. Either way what happened is described as *jîi hŭaa jai*. The pronunciation here requires some practice; *jîi* is pronounced like the Gee in the Bee Gees, a group which plays the kind of music that might *jîi hŭaa jai* some people.

Understand with Sympathetic Heart

khâw òk khâw jai (v.) เข้าอกเข้าใจ

The phrase means to understand the emotional state of another person. The closest English expression is "I feel your pain"—you *khâw òk khâw jai* the other person or what he or she is going through. Using this phrase allows you to show your feelings of sympathy in the face of another person's suffering or unhappiness.

Hypocrisy

Mouth Not Straight with Heart

pàak kàp jai mâi trong kan (v.)
ปากกับใจไม่ตรงกัน

pàak yàang jai yàang (v.)
ปากอย่างใจอย่าง

These two *jai* phrases are idioms that cover the situation when a person says one thing but thinks or feels something different. The words don't match the heart, in other words, the classic doublespeak: saying what you don't feel. These are powerful *jai* phrases to describe the hypocrite. A man tells his lover that she is the only person in the world for him, and the next day she sees him walking down the street with his arm wrapped around another woman. The lover will feel that this man is *pàak kàp jai mâi trong kan*.

In another example, when Som tells Noi that her dress is beautiful, but in Som's heart she feels the dress is so ugly it wouldn't be worn by a witch to a Halloween party. Som can be described as *pàak yàang jai yàang*. When an employer praises an employee for inferior work, which the employee knows is inferior, then later complains in an executive meeting that this employee is not doing good work, the employee feels that the employer's act is *pàak kàp jai mâi trong kan*.

In a culture where saying "no" is difficult for many people, and saying "yes" is thought to please others and avoid confrontation, these heart phrases can be used to register the hypocrisy of a "yes" which is not really a "yes" but a "no." Also these phrases can be used to test another's sincerity and true intentions, by playfully asking whether the person is *pàak kàp jai trong kan* (the words match the heart) or not. Any time, in other words, that the mouth is out of alignment with the heart—the possibilities are legion—these are good heart phrases to remember.

Sweet Words But Want to Slit the Throat Heart

pàak praa săi (náam) jai chûeaat khOO (v.)
ปากปราศรัย(น้ำ)ใจเชือดคอ

This Thai idiom is another heart phrase for hypocrisy. *Pàak praa săi (náam) jai chûeaat khOO* means someone is speaking well or using polite words and language but the intentions behind the words are evil or bad. The hidden motive is an unexpressed wish that is not well intended; it may not be the literal wish to slit the throat of the other person, but it is safe to say that she or he isn't an object of the speaker's affection. The employee is disciplined in front of his or her colleagues and meekly admits the mistake, but inside his or her heart is the desire to run a knife across the throat of the employer. Another example: Suporn's aunt is dying and Suporn is the principal beneficiary under her aunt's will. The aunt is a selfish, arrogant, bitter woman. When Suporn visits the aunt in the hospital she speaks sweetly to the dying woman while at the same time wishing the aunt would die.

Mistakes

Mistaken Heart
thà lăm jai (v.) ถลำใจ

When you have unwittingly placed your heart in the wrong place or person, you can be said to *thà lăm jai*. The classic case is when you realize that someone has made a mistake in loving or trusting another. This is a heart condition of more than average pain or regret. One feels cheated, let down, betrayed. These are strong emotions. For instance, Somchai knows that Lek, who works in his office, is unattainable. She is beautiful, young, well educated and from a high society family. Somchai is only a junior clerk with an ordinary education and family name. But Somchai has already *thà lăm jai* and is in love with her.

A second example is a company driver who is discovered to have cheated on his expense account. The employer had placed faith and trust in the honesty of the driver. The employer has *thà lăm jai* with his driver; that is, the employer's heart is mistaken about the driver, making him regret that he trusted him.

In the political scene, political parties often form alliances and the leaders are seen shaking hands and smiling before the cameras and they proclaim that they are brothers and trust each other forever. This can be a mistaken trust. Later, when the alliance splits apart, even though the leaders promised they would never abandon each other, they do so. One of the politicians may claim that the other's treachery comes as a shock and that he is sad about having trusted the other leader. The mistake of trusting the betraying politician is said to be *thà lăm jai*.

The Stumble that Breaks the Heart
thà lăm lông chák ngâay thà lăm jai chák yâak (proverb)
ถลำล่องชักง่าย ถลำใจชักยาก

This is a Thai proverb which translates as: If we take a misstep, it is possible to recover without much difficulty, but if we misstep with our heart, then it is much more difficult to step back without falling down. When the parents discover their daughter is attracted to a man who is already married, the mother will likely use this proverb as a warning that if the daughter allows herself to enter an illicit affair with him, she will break her heart.

Pain & Hurt Feelings

A person suffering wounds from the slings and arrows of a relationship will likely resort to one of these heart phrases. In the Thai language many heart phrases have evolved to express feelings of hurt, pain and sorrow. This is the heart vocabulary for injuries and harms that arise in personal relationships. One person has emotionally battered, let down, disappointed another. Like broken dreams, broken hearts are part of the human condition. These *jai* phrases often occur along with tears. The circumstances are such that the feelings are often raw, open, and difficult for a person to bear.

Bruised Heart
chám jai (v.) ช้ำใจ

Someone says or does something that causes you to experience emotional pain. This feeling is *chám jai*—your heart is bruised and it's painful. The degree of pain is directly related to the seriousness of the wrong felt. Sometimes it might be a minor slight—the husband is rude to his wife, and the wife feels *chám jai*. If the husband left his wife for another woman she would also feel *chám jai*—but the magnitude of pain is likely to be far greater.

Hurt Feeling Heart
krà thueaan jai (v.) กระเทือนใจ
sà thueaan jai (v.) สะเทือนใจ

In the context of relationships, these two heart phrases apply to the classic case when your feelings have been hurt by actions or words. Someone you care about may have said harsh words that caused you to have hurt feeling—to feel *krà thueaan jai* or *sà thueaan jai*. Hurt feelings can also translate, in some instances (but not all), as a loss of face. For example, Lek learns that someone she thought was a close friend has started a false rumor about her state of health. Upon learning of this betrayal, Lek would experience a "hurt feeling heart." When a student is caught red-handed in the act of cheating during an examination and exposed before the entire class, the loss of face may be sufficient to cause the student to kill himself by jumping off a building. Also, the story of such a death or a similar tragic story of suffering and hardship can make readers feel *sà thueaan jai*; that is, deeply moved or sad. Reading a story about poor children upcountry who don't have shoes or enough food to eat will also cause one to feel *sà thueaan jai*.

Hurt Heart
sà lĚEng jai (v.) แสลงใจ

This *jai* phrase applies in emotional circumstances where someone feels they have been cut to the core by another person or event. When Lek sees her former boyfriend walking in Emporium with a beautiful young girlfriend, this sight hurts her heart and she feels *sà lĚEng jai*. A mother constantly compares her daughter to the neighbor's daughter, telling her own child that she is less beautiful and talented. The daughter sees her mother loves the neighbor's daughter more than she loves her, and this makes her feel *sà lĚEng jai*. In a company Daeng sees that Lek has received a large bonus and feels that this should have been shared between both of them, she will feel *sà lĚEng jai*.

Hurting Heart
chÔOk chám rá kam jai (v.)
ชอกช้ำระกำใจ

This *jai* phrase is another variation on the theme of broken hearts. The degree of misery is of a higher intensity. On a misery scale of one to ten, this heart phrase ranks about 8.9. The heart phrase is used for the major moments of sadness and misery in one's life. In the context of heartache and heartbreak, this is the phrase to use. A husband who leaves his wife for another woman (or man) would cause her to feel *chÔOk chám rá kam jai*.

Deeply Hurt Heart
jèp chám náam jai (v.) เจ็บช้ำน้ำใจ
ráaw raan jai (v.) ร้าวรานใจ

This is another of the "big hurt" category of heart phrases. You will have suffered a major emotional blow before you use the *jai* phrase "deeply hurt heart." You feel *jèp chám náam jai* when you've done nothing wrong to warrant the words or deeds of another. The essence of the hurt is that you are suffering as a result of action or inaction even though you don't deserve this negative outcome. For instance, Lek is a university student and is informed by her teacher that she has failed her final year and will not graduate with her class. She asks her friend Charles to help her with English. Charles not only fails to assist her, but also says he is not surprised that she failed because she is really dense, and no amount of tutoring would help. Charles' harsh words make Lek feel *jèp chám náam jai*. In another example, a wayward son who refuses to work and has gangster friends, is told by his father to get a job and change his life or he will be disowned. The son, upon hearing his father's verdict, would feel *jèp chám náam jai*. In the context of a long-term relationship, the woman who leaves her husband for a richer, more handsome and younger man, will likely find that her abandoned husband feels *jèp chám náam jai*.

Sometimes the hurt and pain from the unfortunate turn of event in the relationship refuses to go away and one finds oneself in an enduring state of broken heart. The heart has been cracked, broken and refuses to heal. In this state of deep hurt, one feels *ráaw raan jai*. The husband whose wife left him for a younger, richer and more handsome husband may have a tough time recovering. He may feel *ráaw raan jai*.

Love Sick Hea

pen khâi jai (v.) เป็นไข้ใจ

You are love sick. When you are in the process of breaking up with your lover and both of you realize that the relationship has come to an end it is likely that you will feel *pen khâi jai*. Your heart feels sick because the love you had cherished has vanished. There is a second, non-romantic sense for the phrase. A person may have had his or her heart set on a particular career or job, and what was sought after failed to materialize. Feeling the loss of such a dream is another reason to experience a "love sick heart," which translates into the loss of something important and ideal. In this case an opportunity for a career or job.

Resentful Heart

jèp jai (v.) เจ็บใจ

rúu sùek jèp jai (v.) รู้สึกเจ็บใจ

When you feel rejected by a lover, a friend or an employee, you are liable to feel *jèp jai*. That is, when you don't get what your heart desires, then the feeling of *jèp jai* arises. The feeling is one of resentment, frustration and anger. Words or deeds cause you to feel *jèp jai*. This heart phrase can be the siren and flashing red light of an emotional emergency vehicle. People who feel *jèp jai* feel flares of real pain, and they are often under considerable emotional distress. "Resentful heart" may be translated into action; it can become the prelude to a serious emotional scene and, in some cases, physical confrontation. When someone says that you made them feel *jèp jai*, it is time to exit and wait for the cool-down period to arrive when you can reconcile.

Sad Heart

sâw jai (adj.) เศร้าใจ

When the machinery of joy and hope breaks down, the phrase *sâw jai* may come in handy. Some experience is causing you to suffer from a broken-heart condition. The "sad heart" person is miserable, feeling emotional pain and sorrow. The situations include: (i) you've been dumped by your girlfriend or boyfriend; (ii) has disappointed you by their words or deeds; (iii) you finished watching a sad movie in which a child dies in a grisly murder; and (iv) you heard news that some innocent people suffered a great misfortune such as a building has collapsed, killing a hundred people, or a hotel fire has caused many deaths.

Throbbing-pain Heart

pùaat jai (v.) ปวดใจ

This *jai* phrase is "throbbing-pain heart." It is the equivalent of a headache or stubbing your big toe against the bed in the middle of the night, but the pain is in the heart rather than in the head or the toe. You see your ex-wife with her new husband and child and the sight causes you a kind of throbbing pain in your heart.

Wounded Heart

phlĚE jai (n.) แผลใจ

mii phlĚE nai jai (v.) มีแผลในใจ

This means a wound to the heart that is never forgotten. The cause of that wound remains with the person for life. The heart carries a scar. Such a scar often comes from the experience of a bad relationship or misadventure, for example, a car crash. A child who watches his parents arguing and in a state of constant conflict may have *phlĚE jai*. When he grows up he will never forget this trauma and he promises himself that he will never fight in front of his children. Mostly the phrase is used in a romantic context where the woman or man with the wound in the heart seeks another person to heal it.

Wretched Heart

trOOm jai (v.) ตรอมใจ

To experience *trOOm jai* is to enter into a state of profound unhappiness and despair. The essence of *trOOm jai* is that the duration of the pain and grief is long; it may last for a lifetime. For instance, consider a couple married for two years, who are very much in love. One day on the way to the office, the husband is killed in a road accident. The widow, in these circumstances, would experience *trOOm jai*. The grief is so large that she feels she will die. The scale of misery for the "wretched heart" condition is immense. Hence, this heart phrase is confined to extreme circumstances, where the person is totally overwhelmed by a profound sense of sadness and grief.

Console Another's Heart
plÒOp jai (v.) ปลอบใจ

When someone you love or care about is experiencing emotional pain or distress, you seek to give comfort. The comfort you offer comes from your heart, and the act of comforting another is *plÒOp jai*. You "console another's heart" by lending a sympathetic ear, giving the suffering person emotional support and guidance. The emphasis is on the aspect of helping the person to deal with the emotional pain or a setback and to lift his or her spirit. For example, you may *plÒOp jai* a friend who has been abandoned by his wife, saying that he should look at the bright side; he's free to date again.

Pleasing Others

There are a number of heart expressions that convey the desire to allow others to have their way. Whether this is viewed as an act of pleasing or spoiling depends on the nature of the relationship between the person granting permission and the person receiving it, as well as the context in which it occurs. The heart phrases arise also in circumstances where there is a conflict of desire and one person yields to the wishes of the other.

Follow Another's Heart
taam jai (v.) ตามใจ

You want to permit someone to have their own way, allow them to make a choice or decision, for example, to choose a movie, a restaurant, or a holiday destination. At the same time, you are giving up your own choice over the matter and following along with the wishes of another. You *taam jai* the other person. The phrase is also used to express to another person that he or she can do whatever in his or her own way. The literal translation is "follow as you like your own heart" (*taam jai*), or "you go ahead and do what you think is right." Also, it can mean that you are spoiling or indulging another person.

As One's Heart Wishes
yàang jai (adj.) อย่างใจ
pheaang jai (v.) เพียงใจ

The emphasis of this expression is squarely on a person obtaining what she or he wished for and not on the granting of another's wishes. Though there is a connection, as you can give someone something that they really wish for. That is, you can make another's wish or desire come true. Perhaps your wife has always wished for a house. You build the house for her exactly the way she likes it (*yàang jai*). There are many examples of things wished for: a new house, a new computer game, or traveling to Canada. You may want to grant such a wish for another. The essence is in getting (or granting) exactly what the person wishes for.

Please Another's Heart
aw jai (v.) เอาใจ
aw òk aw jai (v.) เอาอกเอาใจ

This describes the act of a person who makes a special effort to bring home a small gift to his wife and child. It might be a special sweet or flowers or the latest video. By making these gestures, he gives a constant reminder of his affection for them. It also has the added benefit of ensuring the recipient's affection to the gift giver. Small gestures such as allowing another family member to watch a reality show on TV when you would rather watch the news. While in a restaurant, ordering the sea bass on the menu because you know that this is your friend's favorite dish. *Aw jai* is a common heart expression. In a company, when an employee wants a promotion or a bonus, she may bring the boss water or sweets. Here there is an ulterior motive to get a benefit from the pleasing behavior. And the idea of gift-giving as a form of *aw jai* is a part of the Thai tradition.

The second phrase *aw òk aw jai* carries the same meaning as *aw jai* but usually involves more extraordinary efforts to please another person. It is more than the small courtesy shown to another. There is more feeling and commitment behind the use of this *jai* phrase. The person displaying *aw òk aw jai* behavior often has his or her own motive: it might be love, loyalty or a promotion to a better position in the company.

Respecting Others

Mind and Spirit Heart
jìt jai (n.) จิตใจ

The essence of *jìt jai*, as a general heart phrase is a mental state when one is thinking or feeling. It is what is going on inside your head or heart from moment to moment. You are always in one state of *jìt jai* or another in the sense that we draw our identity, dignity and humanity from our mental image formed by those around us.

Life, Mind and Spirit Heart
chii wít jìt jai (n.) ชีวิตจิตใจ

Chii wít jìt jai focuses more on the worldly aspect of living or existence. In practical usage, *chii wít jìt jai* covers the notion that other people have value and are entitled to be treated with due regard. *Chii wít jìt jai* is violated when one's employer treats one as a machine rather than as a human being, because every human being possesses *chii wít jìt jai*. An extreme example is the case of a factory where the employees are held as virtual slaves. The employees suffering from mistreatment feel that they have been robbed of their *jìt jai* or *chii wít jìt jai*. These heart phrases are broad enough to encompass the treatment of animals, when the person abusing or beating an animal is said to ignore the animal's *jìt jai*. All creatures in the *jìt jai* universe are entitled to respect and life and fair treatment.

Different Heart
tàang jìt tàang jai (adj.) ต่างจิตต่างใจ

She likes red but he likes blue and they agree to differ. Diverse minds often translate as diverse hearts. You say to your friend after a period of argument which fails to change her mind, *tàang jìt tàang jai*. An impasse has been reached. Two (or more) people disagree about a subject but agree to disagree without changing the other's mind. Each side agrees to disagree and to move on. In theory, this is accepted without hard feelings.

Understanding Heart
jai khǎw jai raw (n.) ใจเขาใจเรา

This heart phrase applies when empathy for others is suggested. You attempt to understand another person as you understand yourself. "Understanding heart" is a popular expression taught to Thai children and is not difficult for them to comprehend. The emotional terrain is similar to that occupied by *hěn jai*, "see another's heart." In the context of friendship, it is a call for sympathy and understanding.

This heart phrase is the equivalent of the "Golden Rule of Hearts." If you wish to be treated equally and fairly then you must give such treatment to others. Thus the boss who has a rule that his staff must work until 8.00 p.m., but he leaves the office at 5.00 p.m., would be in violation of this golden rule of hearts because his rule applying to others does not apply to himself.

Revealing the Heart

Open One's Heart
pòoet jai (v.) เปิดใจ

When two people are close enough to disclose their most secret, hidden feelings to each other, then they *poòet jai* to one another. They open their hearts to each other. It may also apply outside an intimate relationship, to an entertainer, such as a singer, who has created a bond with his or her audience by opening his or her heart to them. *Pòoet jai* is probably the best translation for the English phrase: "Let's have a heart-to-heart talk."

Drill into Another's Heart
jÒ jai (v.) เจาะใจ

The metaphor is to "drill" into another's heart in order to unearth the rich ore of secrets locked inside. The name of a popular Thai TV show is *jÒ jai*. The participants on this show are asked to reveal something about themselves that they haven't exposed to anyone else. *JÒ jai* is used as a verb in the context of extracting the revealing information. It is an informal cross-examination of another's secret past and present. Among the most popular TV shows these days are those that *jÒ jai* TV and movie stars and other famous celebrities. A TV host will *jÒ jai* a politician about his secret affair and challenge him to *plueaay jai*, to reveal all to the audience.

Reveal One's Heart
plueaay jai (v.) เปลือยใจ

You reveal your thoughts or mind without any effort to filter or conceal emotions or feelings. This is no ordinary conduct. It is not natural to bare your soul to everyone, although this happens more often on the Internet when people can hide behind a false identity. It also happens in the world of Hollywood where stars give vivid details about the break-up of their marriages.

An act of *plueaay jai* may be direct and honest communication between a couple to resolve a conflict. In that case, you feel no need to censor your words in order to please the other. For most people, this doesn't come naturally. Most people are less forthcoming. Others must drag out their true feelings or secrets, as in the cases associated with *jÒ jai*. People reveal themselves when they feel comfortable and friendly towards others; and when someone reveals details about their own life, it is easier to reveal details in return. This openness then leads to more and deeper revelations.

Revenge

Revengeful Heart
khÉEn jai (v.) แค้นใจ

Revenge happens for many different reasons. The anger does not go away and revenge is the only way to exact retribution for the wrong. Saying sorry won't repair the wrong. In the public arena, in the heat of politics, one faction of the ruling political party may feel *khÉEn jai* for the dumping of one of their members from the cabinet. The faction leader takes revenge by withdrawing his support and having his faction vote with the opposition to cause the government to fall. Someone who cheats, fails to pay their debts or causes disgrace to another's name, may awake one morning to find a severed dog's head inside the family compound or their car spray-painted or otherwise damaged. This dog's severed head is a testament to a "revengeful heart." Other times this feeling of revenge may be unrealized (as there is no opportunity or the person lacks the courage to carry through with the planned revenge) and the feeling stays locked, festering in the heart.

Vindictive Heart
phùuk jai jèp (v.) ผูกใจเจ็บ

If you intend to cause harm or injury to another as the result of a past wrong done to you or someone close to you, the forming of the intention is *phùuk jai jèp*. Panit's husband is unfaithful and she discovers evidence of his infidelity. She decides to take revenge on the other woman (and not the husband). Her feeling of wishing to carry out this act of revenge is *phùuk jai jèp*. Another illustration comes from politics. If a person has been given money by an election candidate to distribute to voters, but keeps the money himself, and that candidate loses the election then discovers the theft, the candidate may form the intention to cause harm to the dishonest canvasser (though the dishonesty of the canvasser must be viewed with some irony given his or her mission). The planning of this revenge is *phùuk jai jèp*.

Vengeful Heart
jai aa khâat (adj.) ใจอาฆาต
jai aa khâat mâat ráay (adj.) ใจอาฆาตมาดร้าย

These *jai* phrases are normally used by a third person to describe someone who is dead set on revenge. This is usually a life-or-death situation. It is unlikely that you would hear this *jai* phrase from a Thai speaker standing next to you at the bar. "Vengeful heart" is an-eye-for-an-eye, a tooth-for-a-tooth kind of heart talk. It describes someone who is unforgiving and will never forget the pain or insult, and in the end will take revenge. A verbal warning often precedes an act of revenge (but not always). In a business context, when a close friend betrays you in the company and you are fired, then you won't stop until you find a way to make his life miserable and repay him for the injury you've suffered.

While the avoidance of confrontation is a cardinal article of behavior amongst Thais, when a certain threshold is crossed the thirst for revenge may be great as is evidenced by the phrase *jai aa khâat mâat ráay*. Anyone described as *aa khâat mâat ráay* is someone to fear and avoid: and if the revenge is directed toward another, then that person may soon be on his or her way to the next life.

Satisfaction

Satisfy Another's Heart
tham hâi phOO jai (v.) ทำให้พอใจ

In this case, one is the agent who is giving the feeling of satisfaction to another person. A child is in a bad mood and begins to cry because the mother won't buy her sweets. The mother relents, buys the sweets and gives them to the child. The mother has, in other words, *tham* her child *hâi phOO jai*. The same applies in the grown-up world when someone wants something and the absence of this object makes them unhappy; one looks to another to provide this missing object. In an advertising company, the creative director assigns a new account to Somchai who knows this is an important international client. He works hard on the product concept to *tham* his boss *hâi phOO jai*.

Show a Dissatisfied Heart
sà dEEng kì rí yaa mâi phOO jai (v.) แสดงกิริยาไม่พอใจ

Non-verbal acts, such as a long sigh, the slamming of a door, the stomping of feet, are signals of displeasure. To demonstrate any of such behavior is to *sà dEEng kì rí yaa mâi phOO jai.* A husband shows up at three in the morning drunk and disheveled, and the wife gives him the quiet treatment, the cold shoulder, or stares at him with obvious disapproval. Your son comes home with a report card filled with F marks and you respond with a disapproving frown. Your best friend flirts with your wife and you hint with a withering glance that he may soon have a reason for plastic surgery on his nose. If these things happened, chances are a person's heart will experience displeasure with the conduct of another and respond in an indirect, often non-verbal fashion. Facial expression and body language are the methods of showing (*sà dEEng*) that you are displeased (*mâi phOO jai*).

Secrecy

Concealed Heart

am phraang jai (v.) อำพรางใจ

In Thailand, listening to Thai music, one hears *am phraang jai* in Thai torch songs. This feeling is the opposite of *pòoet jai* or "open one's heart." The person with a "concealed heart" has likely invented a fantasy relationship with another. There is no disclosure to the object of this fantasy. The secret is kept locked inside. You may be in love with the beautiful secretary in the office but you are too shy to ask her name. Yet inside your heart you may have invented an entire relationship with her. Not that you would ever disclose this secret life. You keep your feelings locked deep inside your heart. The phrase is not limited to a secret fantasy life. You may have feelings of envy, dislike or annoyance toward a member of your social group but you don't show these feelings openly.

Hidden Deep in the Heart

nai jai (adj.) ในใจ

lúek lúek nai jai (adj.) ลึกๆในใจ

The secret feelings buried inside a person's heart may be anger, jealousy or revenge. Such secrets may well be from a past relationship. The woman has left her lover of many years and, though she finds a new lover, the secret of her prior love burns deep inside her heart. This is a secret that she cannot reveal or express to her new lover. This is particularly poignant if the reason for the departure was death or something other than hostility. The secret of that lost love remains locked in the heart forever no matter what love comes afterwards. "Hidden deep in the heart" is an adjectival phrase that can be applied to many situations. Your neighbor makes a special display of welcoming you to her house but deep in her heart she wishes that you hadn't come around. Someone else listens to you speaking English, after having said that she understands the language perfectly, but deep down she wishes that you would switch to the Thai language.

Secret Crush in the Heart

ÈEp mii jai (v.) แอบมีใจ

The best use of this *jai* phrase is for the unexpressed amorous feelings that you may have for another person. At the office, you may have a romantic interest in your co-worker. But even though you have these feelings you will not let the other person know how you truly feel. Indeed, you may go out of your way to mask those feelings.

Secret Stress in the Heart

hŭaa jai kèp kòt (adj.) หัวใจเก็บกด

You may experience any number of negative emotions, such as anger, frustration, depression, disappointment, but rather than expressing them openly you bury them deep inside. This *jai* phrase is akin to the English notion of the stiff upper lip. Not complaining about setbacks in life but getting on with it. Lek has studied very hard during her term at university. She is serious and doesn't go out on the party circuit with her less serious friends even though she is frequently invited to join them. Lek is sad because she cannot participate in the fun times with her friends. She wants to talk openly to her friends about her feelings, about her conflict with her desire to study for an examination, but she keeps this conflict inside herself, smiles at her friends and says she cannot go because she has a headache.

A child may be uncommonly reserved and non-communicative in school. Her teacher tries to draw her out but the child says very little in reply. The teacher finds out from the child's friends that her mother is seriously ill and the father is an unemployed, drunk, abusive man. Someone with a "secret stress in the heart" is typically quiet and withdrawn. No one can keep things bottled up forever. Eventually such a person may explode with anger. The heart undergoing a great deal of secret stress is a ticking time bomb.

Thoughts inside the Heart
khwaam nai jai (n.) ความในใจ

This *jai* phrase describes thoughts that you keep to yourself. As unexpressed or undisclosed thoughts they remain a secret to those around you. While undisclosed or unexpressed, *khwaam nai jai* isn't necessarily connected to deceit or lies. It is neutral in this respect and only means that you wish to keep your thoughts to yourself. When you decide to open your thoughts to another, you also open your heart by revealing the true thoughts inside.

Sincerity

The exploration of feelings in a relationship is often about the degree of sincerity of the people involved. Each person wants to feel that another person is sincere in his or her words and actions and there is no deception or hidden agenda involved. Conversely, everyone wishes that others close to them will believe and trust them. These heart phrases provide a variety of expressions that provide a way to ask about the sincerity of another.

True Heart
jai jing (n.) ใจจริง

A woman cooks to please her boyfriend but her food is horrible. He eats the food and smiles but in his "true heart" he wants to tell her, "Darling, please stop cooking. This food is terrible and it is killing me." But he keeps those feelings to himself. *Jai jing* are the private true feelings that aren't expressed. The maid tells her employer that she loves dogs, but when she's alone with the dogs she beats them. In her heart, she really hates the creatures. There is a thin, gray line at work with *jai jing*. It is not always expressed but at the same time you can't say that it is always hidden.

A person works for a company where the work hours are 8.00 a.m. to 5.00 p.m. but the owner expects his employees to work until 6.30 p.m. and on weekends, yet doesn't offer to pay overtime. The employees may feel the fundamental unfairness of such a system but they won't feel comfortable expressing those feelings to the employer, and more likely than not will leave that company and hope the next employer demonstrates a greater degree of fairness in the workplace. The feeling (unexpressed) of the unfairness is the true feeling or *jai jing*. A clever lover or friend will seek ways to allow the other to express those secret feelings. Indeed the prime minister installed a complaint box outside Government House as a way of allowing those with these hidden feelings to express them.

Show Truth in One's Heart

sà dEEng khwaam jing jai (v.)

แสดงความจริงใจ

To show the truth in one's heart is to *sà dEEng khwaam jing jai*. The feeling inside one's heart is coupled with a tangible act of *sà dEEng khwaam jing jai*. The taxi driver finds a handbag left on the back seat. He finds the passenger's ID and phones Jor Sor 100 (the radio station that monitors traffic problems in Bangkok), and asks for help to find the woman. His action is an example of *sà dEEng khwaam jing jai*. When a maid finds a thousand-baht note in her boss's dirty laundry and returns the money to him, she is definitely *sà dEEng khwaam jing jai*.

Dead in Earnest

jing jai yàang nÊEw nÊE (adj.)

จริงใจอย่างแน่วแน่

When you feel totally involved or immersed in an activity or in your relationship with another person, you feel *jing jai yàang nÊEw nÊE* or absolutely sincere. All other distractions fall away, and the full weight of your concentration is directed at the activity or toward the other person. This is a good feeling of being "dead in earnest."

With Sincere He
dûaay náam săi jai jing (adv.)
ด้วยน้ำใสใจจริง

This *jai* phrase expresses the feeling of giving something to another without any expectation of receiving a benefit in return for the gift. Another person may help a friend in his or her work or studies. It is done out of the goodness of one's heart and not for selfish reasons. The person rendering the good deed would not accept money for his or her action. The taxi driver returns the lost mobile phone and refuses to accept a reward for his actions, and says, "I keep your phone with a feeling of giving it back without any reward. I have done this *dûaay náam săi jai jing*." The intention of the person to forsake a reward, even while performing a good deed, comes from an earnest heart. *Dûaay náam săi jai jing* describes the altruistic intention of such a person.

Suspicion

Doubting Heart
khlEEng jai (v.) แคลงใจ
krìng jai (v.) กริ่งใจ

These two heart phrases occur more frequently in written Thai. Occasionally, when spoken, they sppear when there is a question of breach of trust. Usually another person is the object of distrust or mistrust because of his or her actions or spoken words. It is similar in this way to *mâi wái jai*, which translates as "I do not trust you," or "I have doubts about you."

Mistrustful Heart
rá wEEng jai (v.) ระแวงใจ

A suspecting heart is one with warning signals flashing. You are suspicious and mistrustful about another in a relationship. It can be a spouse, friend, neighbor or colleague. The suspicion arises as a result of a quarrel or conflict. Something has gone emotionally wrong in the relationship. The "mistrustful heart" has doubts about the loyalty of another. For instance, a man arrives in the morning with lipstick on his collar and his wife e evidence; she will likely feel *rá wEEng jai* that he has been with another woman. The warning bell goes off and she becomes wary about his explanation of having been delayed by the traffic on Sukhumvit Road.

The Beloved

Beloved Heart
săay jai (n.) สายใจ

The state of being *săay jai* is mostly felt in the relationship between a mother and child. It describes the strong bonds of love in the relationship. Another meaning is that of a beloved person. A more literal translation of this *jai* phrase would be "chain of the heart." This heart phrase reflects a combination of duty, love and obligation toward a child, and demonstrates that the mother truly cares about his or her well-being. Such a mother feels that her sons and daughters are a permanent and essential feature of her emotional life. She includes them in her thoughts and actions; their feelings matter to her. She may also have *săay jai* feelings about a friend, lover or parents. In the Thai culture, a child is *săay jai* of her parents.

Center of the Heart
klaang jai (n., adj.) กลางใจ

Some people who have been responsible for improving or bettering your life cause you to have a good feeling about them. They are always in your thoughts as an inspiration or guide. They reside in the center of your heart or *klaang jai*. People who are your *klaang jai* could be a special friend, teacher, mentor, monk, father, mother or child. There is an endearing quality about this feeling.

Iris of the Heart
kÊEw taa duaang jai (n.)
แก้วตาดวงใจ

This phrase refers to the person who is the most important thing inside your heart. It is common for Thais to say the most important people in parents' hearts are their children. It is an essential feature of Thai culture that the children occupy the center of what is good, pure, kind, untainted; and motherhood is highly valued and admired by Thai women.

Eye of the Heart
duaang taa duaang jai (n.)
ดวงตาดวงใจ

This *jai* phrase refers to the beloved, the object of your love and affection. The love, admiration and importance of a husband and wife to each other is an example. There is overlap between *duaang taa duaang jai*, "eye of the heart" and *kÊEw taa duaang jai*, "iris of the heart." *KÊEw taa duaang jai* is more appropriate for children and their mother in their relationship. On the other hand, if a child is loved by the whole family—brothers, sisters, uncles, father, mother and grandparents—the child is *duaang taa duaang jai* of the family.

Gold Chain Around the Heart
sôo thOOng khlÓOng jai (n.)
โซ่ทองคล้องใจ

This *jai* phrase expresses the feeling parents often have about their children who are in an orbit around lives. You hold your baby in your arms and you know this feeling of the baby being a circle around your heart. The baby is like a gold chain that strings together the mother and father in a strengthened bond of love, commitment and affection. The feeling is a special emotion that recognizes the closeness of hearts in shared lives. It is a good feeling, a feeling better than gold.

Star of the Heart
duaang jai (n.) ดวงใจ
yÔOt duaang jai (n.) ยอดดวงใจ

The notion of destiny and fate is strong in the Thai culture. There are many Thai expressions which incorporate the Thai word for destiny or fate: *duaang*. But in this case, the word *duaang* means star. A child is *duaang jai*—the star—of his mother and father. This means the child is the most important and loved person for the parents. The phrase can also be applied to romantic relationships. In the traditional sense *duaang jai* also refers to the beloved woman. In the case of romantic relationships, there is the poetic idea of fate or destiny bringing the couple together. Perhaps they had a relationship in a prior life. Both phrases may be used as terms of endearment.

Trust

There are many heart phrases used by Thai speakers that relate to trust in relationships. There are heart phrases for different levels of trust—from firm belief and conviction in another to confidence and closeness between partners to testing of loyalty of another in the relationship.

Trust with One's Heart

wái jai (v.) ไว้ใจ
wái waang jai (v.) ไว้วางใจ

When you trust another with your heart, you are certain of his or her loyalty, integrity or ability to perform the task at hand. You feel you are able to trust the person with your secrets, your confidence, or personal information that is most important to you. You have confidence that the person will not let you down. If you have this feeling about someone, it means you *wái jai* or *wái waang jai* that person—you trust the person with your heart.

Person with Trusted Heart

phûu thîi wái jai (n.) ผู้ที่ไว้ใจ

When you trust someone completely you can speak from your heart to them; then you have *phûu thîi wái jai*. The "person with trusted heart" can be your spouse, mother, child, close friend or loyal employee. For most Thais, the mother is someone they can speak their true heart to. This is your true confidant, the person who you think will always be there for you, never turn away from you in life. It may be difficult for some to include their lovers or spouses in this category.

Have Faith in the Heart

waang jai (v.) วางใจ

This heart phrase describes a state of being which is both positive and sought after. A person who feels *waang jai* achieves this feeling of comfort and ease in the presence of a select group of special people. He or she is able to rely on a few close friends, spouse, or lover, and confide a secret or something very important. When you feel *waang jai*, you feel that by relying on another person you have been released from the general obligation of presenting a certain face (including the strict demands of the *kreeng jai* state) to the outside world and can act freely and speak freely. In this state of personal reliance, you feel that all is in good hand—a secret will be kept in confidence or a task will be accomplished.

For example, a coach may start a player in the test match because he feels *waang jai* in that player's ability. An office manager may assign a project to an employee whose past performance gives her a sense of *waang jai* in the employee's ability to successfully complete the new project. Thai politicians also use this phrase to give the population a feeling of comfort in times of violence, unrest or natural disaster. In these circumstances they are appealing for the population to trust their judgment in how best to handle the problem and not to question them too closely on the details on how the government is dealing with the issues. The success of playing the *waang jai* card often depends on the level of education of those listening to the politicians.

Believe in Another's Heart

chûeaa jai (v.) เชื่อใจ

wái níeaa chûeaa jai (v.) ไว้เนื้อเชื่อใจ

When you have faith in others' intentions, explanations or decisions, then you believe in them. You start with the default belief that your friends, colleagues, spouse and children are acting in good faith and are honest and reliable. Your trust expresses itself through your belief in the sincerity of their hearts. There may be money missing from the petty-cash box, but as the boss you don't suspect any of your employees of taking it because you *chûeaa jai* them. You think there must be some other explanation for the missing cash. The boyfriend has come back at three in the morning, and asks his girlfriend to believe that he was attending a seminar on company law. He is asking her to trust his explanation to have faith in him or *chûeaa jai*.

You may ask another to *chûeaa jai* you, to believe in your integrity or ability. If you are an hour late for an appointment and want the person waiting to believe you were caught in heavy traffic. In Bangkok, this reason is normally taken at face value. But if you show up four hours late with lipstick on your collar and ask your lover to believe you were late because of traffic, it is likely she won't *chûeaa jai* your heart. In the context of trust in a person's ability, for example, if the employer chooses the best employee for an important project then he must feel *wái níeaa chûeaa jai* about the employee chosen. This evidences a stronger feeling of trust than *chûeaa jai* in its simple form.

Convinced Heart

plong jai chûeaa (v.) ปลงใจเชื่อ

Plong jai chûeaa is a slightly different kind of trust. For example, in the case of the missing petty cash in one of the previous examples, it turned out that one of the employees really did take the cash. You are surprised and feel that you *plong jai chûeaa* the employees' integrity. Unfortuantely you now learn that your belief and trust was misplaced for one of them. In this sense, *plong jai chûeaa* can sometimes be blind trust. Many Thai women like to visit fortune-tellers who read their tarot cards or palms in order to predict the future. After a number of the predictions come true, the cynical person starts to believe that the fortune-teller has skills and abilities and his or her next prediction will come true. The person who reaches this feeling of conviction might be described as *plong jai chûeaa*.

Close to One's Heart

sà nìt jai (adj.) สนิทใจ

You feel that you can expose your deepest nature and share your private interior life with another. When you open your heart, the experience creates the feeling associated with "close to one's heart." When you feel close to a friend or lover, you have a sense of *sà nìt jai*. The feelings are warm, intimate, gentle, arising from a true sense of closeness. This heart phrase (commonly used) is often used to describe feelings of close personal intimacy with another. The scope for such feelings of intimacy is not limited to husband and wife or boyfriend and girlfriend, and includes a wide range of relationships such as friends, parents, colleagues, fellow Thai speakers or religious leaders.

Confident Heart

mân jai (v.) มั่นใจ
thŭue jai (v.) ถือใจ

You feel a sense of confidence about yourself, others, or your ability and skill in dealing with a situation that you face. For example, you may feel confident about your abilities as a driver, in a tennis game, in learning a language or in mastering a social skill. Or you may feel confident that another person's skills and abilities can be trusted. You are a long way down the road in any relationship when you feel *mân jai* about another. You only will feel that you are *mân jai* at the point that all misgivings, doubt and mistrust have disappeared. At this point your heart is confident about the other person and you have achieved intimacy. *Thŭue jai* is an old-fashioned phrase for *mân jai*. Hundreds of years ago a Chiang Mai prince leading an elephant charge against an invading army of Burmese might feel *thŭue jai* that he would win the war.

Sure Heart

nÊE jai (v.) แน่ใจ

This is another *jai* phrase for those with self-assurance about themselves and their choices or actions. In a relationship, when you are certain about your feelings toward another, you can say you feel *nÊE jai*. In other contexts, you may use the expression to signal your self-assured decision or opinion, whether it is to purchase a new shirt, to order a new item from the menu, or about the entertainment value of a film. Like *mân jai*, *nÊE jai* refers to an emotional state of confidence about an action and plans for action, as well as to a feeling about another person or object.

One Heart

jai diiaw (adj.) ใจเดียว

This heart phrase is an idiom translating as the one woman's man or the one man's woman. The man or woman who is and remains faithful to their partner has *jai diiaw*. In the "one heart" there is only one room. That is, there is just enough space to accommodate one special person. This *jai* phrase is closely linked to the concept of monogamy. The love and loyalty are reserved for your one and only. At the opposite end of the scale is the "butterfly" who flies from lover to lover as if they were flowers in a field. The butterfly does not have "one heart." Another example would be if Ning's husband dies and she does not seek another husband or partner; she also may be said to possess *jai diiaw*. Having "one heart" is a phrase commonly heard in conversations about romantic relationships.

Trusting Blindly Heart

taay jai (v.) ตายใจ

You trust another's views, decisions, wishes and explanations without question. You believe and trust blindly the other person. Normally, you would have a close relationship with the person you trust blindly. The office worker who arrives home at three in the morning and gives the explanation that he was in a business meeting may seek to draw upon the "trust blindly heart" of his wife. If his wife trusts him, then she is likely to feel *taay jai*. But if he comes home at three in the morning two nights in a row, *taay jai* will likely not be the response. She may also question whether he has "one heart." Your accountant may have done the books for your company over many years. Every filing and report has been done on time. You trust her blindly. One day you discover that she has embezzled company money and disappeared from the country. That is the downside of *taay jai* in business.

Measure Another's Heart
wát jai (v.) วัดใจ
daw jai (v.) เดาใจ

These heart expressions, *wát jai*, "measure the heart," and *daw jai*, "guess the heart," involve the process of sizing up the qualities—spiritual, emotional, moral—possessed by another. When you meet someone, you take measure of (or guess, depending on the metaphor of choice) that person's heart. Similarly, if you are planning to enter into a close personal or business relationship with a Thai person, then he or she may ask about the nature of your heart.

The true test, however, is not in the words but in the actions or deeds that define the nature of your heart. Is your heart true or untrue, big or small, broad or narrow, straight or crooked?—these are a few of the possible metaphors applied to measure another's heart. These *jai* phrases represent an inner voice which tests the motives and good will of another person. In other words, are you a person they can trust? With this expression, you become a "tailor of the heart"—measuring every dimension and asking whether it fits the emotional requirements you feel are important. It also applies to business, sports, or any competitive arena where people test or measure their courage, skill or ability against others.

Test Another's Heart

lOOng jai (v.) ลองใจ

The heart must make choices, and feelings about our obligations and loyalties to others (as well as to ourselves) inform the choices that are made. When there is a question of loyalty or there is a conflict about what is the right thing to do, someone—your spouse, friend, colleaque or boss—many put your heart to a test. They may seek to determine their importance in your heart or whether your heart is in the right place (where they expect). You, whose heart is being tried, feel torn, undecided and possibly hurt if you feel the test is undeserved. When your wife says to you, "You can go out on the town with your friends, or stay home and help me wallpaper the living room," she is testing your feelings about her. She is *lOOng jai* in this testing of your heart.

Keep Secrets to Yourself Heart

cháang săan nguu hàw khâa kàw meaa rák mâi khuaan wái waang jai (proverb)

ช้างสารงูเห่าข้าเก่าเมียรักไม่ควรไว้วางใจ

This old Thai proverb translates literally to mean a man can't trust the elephant, cobra, old servant or beloved wife. While obviously unfair to women, this proverb is still in use. It comes from an old folktale and teaches that one can't trust an elephant even though it has been well fed and housed since it was a baby; it might turn on the owner and step on him when he's not looking. A cobra can be trained, but the true nature of wild animals will not easily disappear. Like the elephant, the cobra could become dangerous and may strike without warning. The old servant who has been looked after may gossip to the neighbors, so one shouldn't tell him secrets. And at the same time, a husband shouldn't tell his wife secrets because she may also use the secrets to betray him later. The wisdom of the story is that it is best to keep secrets to yourself.

Truth

Pierce Another's Secret Heart
phûut thùuk jai dam (v.) พูดถูกใจดำ
(phûut) thEEng jai dam (v.) พูดแทงใจดำ
thEEng jai (v., adj.) แทงใจ

The essence of these *jai* phrases is that you make comments or observations that cut through the core of another person's heart. The word *jai dam* in this case is not the same as "black heart" which refers to a mean or pitiless person, but means the same as "thoughts inside the heart" or the thoughts that one keeps to oneself—one's secret heart. When you "pierce another's secret heart" you can be blunt, direct, straight talking, or you can be indirect and sly. The effect is the same: you hit another person hard. This is an emotional shove.

The comments are offered without necessarily taking into account the impact on the feelings of the other person. Normally, this is a negative characteristic. For example, you have just broken up with your spouse. At a dinner party you are seated next to a person who asks about your ex-spouse. If you have gone through the painful break-up and are trying to forget your personal problems, these comments are hurtful and painful. The person has effectively pierced your secret heart—*thEEng jai* or *thEEng jai dam*. *Phûut thùuk jai dam* is used in the same context, but less frequently.

Vulnerability

Small Heart
jai nÓOy (adj.) ใจน้อย
khîi jai nÓOy (adj.) ขี้ใจน้อย

This is a common *jai* expression among Thai speakers. A person who is *jai nÓOy* is extremely sensitive and may become easily hurt or more readily sad than others. Such a person may read into your actions or words motives, which you neither intended nor wished to be read. The *jai nÓOy* person may suggest that you have made an unfair accusation or insulted him or her. Care must be taken not to speak carelessly with such a person or you run the risk of hurting his or her feelings.

Someone with this nature is easy to anger and offend. They are, in the English sense, thin-skinned and every small barb wounds them deeply. Someone who is *khîi jai nÓOy* might be said to have a chronic condition of touchiness and you are advised that they can be hurt by something which was not intended or was otherwise innocuous in nature. This personality type is often cranky and irritable and occupies the territory of chronic bad moods.

Vulnerable Heart

jai bÒOp baang (adj.) ใจบอบบาง

Someone with a "vulnerable heart" is easily emotionally affected, hurt or upset. Life with such a person is not always smooth. One explanation for a person who is *jai bÒOp baang* is that he or she was raised in an overly protective environment. Another explanation is that the person is vulnerable owing to a difficult emotional period, such as a divorce or loss of a parent, or it may be the nature of the person to have such a delicate constitution that the small bumps and knocks of life register as a major shock. To make such a person happy and content means that one must take care of his or her every wish and desire. If, for whatever reason, one should fail to do what he or she wants, then the results are predictable. The person with the vulnerable heart may sulk or cry.

Awe Heart

kreeng jai (v.) เกรงใจ

kreeng òk kreeng jai (v.) เกรงอกเกรงใจ

7
heart talk in society

In the Thai language, the relationships formed in the larger context of family, friends, business, job and school are reflected in heart phrases. While most of the heart phrases in this chapter are used in the context of relationships and some may also appear in other chapters, Heart Talk in Society reveals more of the public face of the heart. In the West matters of the heart are often viewed as private. In the Thai language the basic social interaction with strangers, government officials, colleagues, friends or business associates has found expression in heart phrases. It is beyond the scope of this small book to analyze fully how the private and public world of heart shapes the network of relationships in Thai culture. The goal of examining how heart phrases are used in society is far more modest. It is enough to provide a starting point to explore the broad outline of how the language of heart describes the nature of Thai society and culture. The heart phrases used in the Thai social context involve and reflect class and hierarchy, the sense of community and solidarity, consensus, and the notion of friendship. Other expressions useful in dealing with others in a group or society are also included in this chapter.

Class & Hierarchy

A heart vocabulary is useful to understand the way people behave with others of different social rank within the Thai class system. In general, the classical Thai hierarchy (which is more like caste than class) retains certain features associated with a feudalistic system. Patrons and benefactors have traditionally exchanged protection for loyalty and other benefits. This is less about friendship, more about power arrangements distributed in such a fashion that there is often little choice but to fit into the existing class system. However, the traditional social structure is gradually changing as calls for political change suggest a restructuring of the old arrangements. The social system is evolving in Thailand and will continue to do so, lessening the old obstacles to social mobility. Being high-born or low-born is of less importance than it was thirty or forty years ago. Access to education has widened the middle class, especially in Bangkok and other urban centers. Hierarchy is more closely connected with wealth, and professional and social position. The last name of a person still lingers as an important class indicator, though, again, education is gradually leveling the importance of this factor.

Awe Heart

kreeng jai (v.) เกรงใจ

kreeng òk kreeng jai (v.) เกรงอกเกรงใจ

There are few *jai* phrases more difficult to translate and explain. And there may be no other heart phrase more important than "awe heart," which is the heart of hearts of the Thai culture and class system. The phrase reflects a rich brew of feelings and emotions—a mingling of reverence, respect, deference, homage and fear—which every Thai person feels toward someone who is their senior, boss, teacher, mother and father, or those in powerful position such as a high-ranking police officer. Anyone who is perceived to be a member of a higher social class is owed *kreeng jai*. In practice, a person with "awe heart" would be inhibited from questioning or criticizing such a person. "Awe heart" also includes social decorum so that children are thought to be well raised when they know who and when to *kreeng jai*.

"Awe heart" remains a core *jai* expression that also accounts for what appears on the surface as an incredible degree of politeness and civility found in exchanges between Thai people. A sense of face is also involved in this phrase. The social rank and class is mapped or, better, encoded in "awe heart." It defines the way that people of various ranks communicate, behave and react with one another. It defines also their expectations about the range of behavior to be received from others.

One of the first songs school children learn is about the importance of *kreeng jai*. To say that someone knows *kreeng jai* is to confer a substantial compliment. That is, depending on your point of view, you can be deemed to be well-mannered, or submissive to authority and to your place in the caste system. It explains the tendency to maintain a smile, to never complain and to never reveal feelings of disappointment or frustration with someone of a higher social rank. The public mask must, in other words, be one of perfect contentment. On the opposite side, to say that someone does not know or practice *kreeng jai* means he or she is being rude or doesn't understand or follow the conventional social decorum. The social system depends on the smooth working of *kreeng jai*; once it is breached, then the whole structure of class and of the relationship between people is called into doubt.

"Awe heart" marks the social boundaries in a highly hierarchical system in which the sense of station and relationship to others is keenly felt and respected. *Kreeng jai* also means a display of consideration between those of unequal social rank, whether in the home or workplace. An employer demonstrates considerate behavior toward an employee or servant, and the employee or servant reciprocates with a display of considerate behavior toward the employer.

This definition merely touches the surface of "awe heart," which is in part the creation of social theater but is also seen by many Thais as essential to the consideration every person should show to each other. Viewed as another way of showing how to be considerate in a social context makes this essential *jai* phrase more accessible and understandable to foreigners.

Humble Heart

jeaam jai (v.) เจียมใจ

A person who knows and accepts his or her station in life is said to be *jeaam jai*. A person who is *jeaam jai* knows his or her place. The person has neither interest nor ambition to break free of the assigned position in order to achieve social mobility. This person is like a Victorian-age English butler who knew when to be silent, when to avert his eyes, and how to behave in front of his employers—which was usually in a servile role. Such a servant, at least on the surface, is happy with his status and has no desire to do another kind of work. A poor man may love a rich woman. He loves her but because of his low status he must remain silent. This is an example of the class and social system in which people are expected to maintain their place. If you think a person is overstepping his social mark, and you wish to put him in his place, you might use the phrase, "*Mâi jeaam jai*." But as a foreigner you might have to be careful because the social class rules don't necessarily apply to you in the same fashion.

Good Heart

jai dii (adj.) ใจดี

At first glance, this *jai* phrase may not seem to reflect a hierarchy, but "good heart" can be understood as a omponent of the *kreeng jai* world of reciprocal social obligations. A person who is *jai dii* is said to possess a kind and generous nature. For example, when a mother takes her children shopping or to see a movie, the children think she is *jai dii*. The boss who gives good bonuses or buys presents for employees is *jai dii*. *Kreeng jai* makes it awkward (even painful) to ask or request something from someone of higher rank. The smiling mask of contentment would have to be dropped. Many are not prepared to make themselves so vulnerable. Thus desires or wishes are often left unexpressed—at least directly—and a high value is placed on a person who has the ability to read such desires and wishes, and grants them without the risky business of a formal request. A person of high social rank who has such ability and acts according to the wishes of those under him or her is *jai dii*.

Suffering Heart
khěn jai (adj.) เข็ญใจ

In times of plenty, those who have feelings of "suffering heart" are found living on the margins of society. The suffering arises from a combination of physical and mental struggles. When the economy as a whole plunges and many people have lost money, land, cars and jobs, the number of people who feel stranded in an impoverished life without the resources to lift themselves out and into a better life increases dramatically. The people who lost everything in the tsunami in the south of Thailand would be *khěn jai*. The emotional tone is one associated with an overwhelming sense of suffering, misery and destitution. The destitute person feels he will never have enough money for a better life. The unpublished poet with no other means of obtaining money also feels *khěn jai*.

Purchase Another's Heart
súue jai (v.) ซื้อใจ

This *jai* phrase applies when you give a benefit in exchange for another's loyalty. In a patronage system it is common for the master to give benefits (money, land, food) to those he wishes to bring inside his circle of power and influence. This often has implications in the political system where powerful and influential people are able to buy the loyalty of others. Those who "sell their hearts" will likely vote for the candidate requested by the "purchaser of the heart." This expression is not limited to the political context. A husband may "purchase" the heart of his wife. He can do this in a variety of ways, by being faithful, loyal, sensitive and patient with his wife, or if he lacks all of these qualities then he must give her a great deal of money.

Thank You Heart
khÒOp jai (v.) ขอบใจ
khÒOp òk khÒOp jai (v.) ขอบอกขอบใจ

These *jai* verbs translate as "thank you" but should be used with caution foreigners as they might create the impression that the foreigners consider themselves in a higher social class. It is better for foreigners to stick with *khÒOp khun* when expressing thanks to a Thai. *KhÒOp jai* implies a superior/inferior social relationship, or one between people of unequal social rank, and is also a sign of age difference. For instance, it might be used by someone senior to express their appreciation to someone who is their junior. It is another example of the way the social system is ordered in Thailand. The lesson is that the simple words "thank you" convey a powerful social message.

The word *òk* in the second *jai* phrase acts as an intensifier. It is often used when an act is beyond the call of duty or friendship. Normally, the phrase appears when talking about the kindness or generosity of a third person. For example, your friend tells you a story about how Daeng's father is ill but Daeng doesn't have money to pay the hospital. Lek lends Daeng 20,000 baht and Daeng *khÒOp òk khÒOp jai* Lek.

In an Instant Heart

bàt jai (adv.) บัดใจ

This is an old term and is now confined to classical literature. Khunnai Ratree requests her maid to bring a glass of water, and the maid quickly complies. She arrives seconds later with a glass of cold water. This is a compliment to the maid's quick reaction. Khunnai Ratree says to her gratefully, "*Aw náam maa hâi bàt jai jing jing*." You rarely hear this *jai* phrase in modern usage.

Spontaneous Heart

than jai (adv.) ทันใจ

This contemporary heart phrase means someone has responded or reacted quickly to a request. It is the absence of delay or excuses, and the performance of exceptional service that is cause for using this phrase. For example, someone phones their travel agent and requests a last-minute booking on a flight to Hong

Kong. The agent phones them back within ten minutes and confirms that they are booked and their ticket is ready for collection. The speed and efficiency of such service is makes the client feel *than jai*.

The essence is the feeling resulting from a response or action that is fast. You want to do something immediately, such as take off for the weekend to Chiang Mai. You take a plane rather than a bus because you want to arrive quickly. A person with a "spontaneous heart" likes quick action. Lek phones a friend and invites her to come around ten minutes later. The person extending the invitation feels that the person who has arrived on such short notice is *than jai*. In the competition between pizza sellers, the fast delivery gives the customer the feeling of *than jai:* they don't have to wait long. In the world of the Internet, sending an email or an SMS message makes the sender feel *than jai* as the message is instantly delivered.

Community & Solidarity

Act with Willing Heart

sà màk jai (v.) สมัครใจ

In the context of community, the idea behind this *jai* phrase is the act of volunteering to do something good and useful for others. The good deed has not been demanded or required by the person on the receiving end. The essence is the person's own free will to contribute to the betterment of the community. The expression is not limited to the context of social activism or community spirit. In the realm of personal relationships, small acts of kindness fall within this heart phrase. Here the person acts from his or her own free will rather than out of being ordered or forced to do something. Thus an employee who places fresh cut flowers on the boss's desk shows that she has acted with a willing heart. Such a person, in Thai culture, has displayed *sà màk jai*. The emphasis is on a willingness to do more than is required, to volunteer time and energy, resulting in making the lives of those around them more pleasant and comfortable.

Appropriate Heart

jai dii kÊE dâay jai ráay kÊE mǎi (proverb) ใจดีแก้ด้ายใจร้ายแก้ไหม

The literal translation is "good heart unties thread, cruel heart unties silk." This heart phrase is another example of a Thai proverb used to describe group or community activity. The rural texture of the phrase should not be thought of as a limitation on more general usage. In essence, this phrase means that work is best given to people who have the capability of performing the task or assignment, and withheld from those who cannot efficiently do the work. Thus the person who is able to untie the thread may be unable to untie the silk. Conversely, the person who is good at untying silk may be inept at untying thread. Within the context of a company, factory, school or sports team, those who allocate the assignments should attempt to take into account the individual strengths and weaknesses of those under their charge. The heart phrase also applies at the political level. A person without any experience or training in economics would make a poor appointment as Finance Minister or the head of the Bank of Thailand. A person appointed to be Minister of Justice who has no legal training would likely be ineffective in carrying out the responsibilities of his or her job.

Cooperative Heart

rûaam jai (v., adj.) ร่วมใจ
sà mǒoe jai (adj.) เสมอใจ

The "cooperative heart" signifies a personal bond or connection with others. The feeling associated with such a connection is a hallmark of solidarity in a group of friends or with the community. The emotional bond arises through a unity of purpose and feeling. Such feelings may arise out of friendship. The emotional state may also arise among co-workers or students who work closely together to finish a common project, such as rebuilding schools in the south of Thailand after the tsunami. Villagers may *rûaam jai* to contribute money to build a temple for their village. The *jai* phrase *sà mǒoe jai* has fallen into disuse.

Glue of the Heart

kaaw jai (v.) กาวใจ

The essence of *kaaw jai* is the bond that keeps people together. A man and woman wish to separate but their child convinces them to stay together. The child is the glue to cement their relationship. The child is *kaaw jai*—"glue of the heart."

Heart Joining Heart

jai prà săan jai (idiom) ใจประสานใจ

This is the title of a well-known Thai song. *Jai prà săan jai* is sung whenever there is a special community event with lots of Thais in attendance. For instance, it is traditional to sing it on New Year's Eve, at the end of a regional sporting event among the Thai participants, and at special occasions at school. The song creates a strong sense of community spirit. The lyrics evoke a number of strong emotions, such as feelings of friendship, solidarity, understanding, love, harmony and unity. The message conveyed by the lyrics is that people belong to a large community who share and are held together by these feelings. It is an inspirational song that many Thais know by heart, but few foreigners are aware of *jai prà săan jai*.

Mobilize the Heart

plùk jai (v.) ปลุกใจ
ráw jai (v.) เร้าใจ

The main idea is to mobilize or rally others. An employer may *plùk jai* or *ráw jai* her employees in a pep talk in order to increase their productivity. It can also appear in a political context where someone with radical views about the fairness of the government, or social or political systems wishes to rally support for their cause. Such a person might announce his or her own version of Utopia for the masses, and expect them to wake up to the rallying call for change in the way things are structured. *Plùk jai* can be (but is not limited to) the wake-up call issued by a revolutionary.

Power of the Heart

phá lang jai (n.) พลังใจ

When a large group of people or indeed the entire community unite, there arises the powerful sense of community and solidarity. The community members feel the power in their hearts, expressed in Thai as *phá lang jai. Phá lang jai* describes a feeling in the heart that comes from being part of a collective action designed to help others. For example, the relief workers during the tsunami, who spent many days rendering assistance to the injured and the families of those who were missing, feel this sense of power in the heart.

String of Hearts together

rÓOy jai (v.) ร้อยใจ

With the problems of unrest in the south of Thailand, millions of Thai-made paper birds were dropped by airplane over the southern provinces as a gesture of peace. By making the paper birds millions of people *rÓOy jai* in harmony with the goals of the larger community. There is an important element of feeling that some common good is being advanced. On Father's Day or Mother's Day (which fall on the king's birthday and the queen's birthday respectively), Thai people go to Sanam Luang to *rÓOy jai* or to string their hearts together—to come together as a community—so as to celebrate this holiday.

United Heart

náam nùeng jai diiaw kan (n.)
น้ำหนึ่งใจเดียวกัน

This heart phrase is used to describe people who are working together in unity and harmony. "United heart" is used among friends, colleagues or members of the same sports team. The defining element is the ability of these people to feel unity and a shared sense of common purpose. Managers or senior executives of companies, as well as coaches, have the responsibility for creating this feeling of hearts in harmony, and the more they succeed, the better the performance of those working for them is likely to be.

Confederate Heart
phûu rûaam jai (n.) ผู้ร่วมใจ

When a person has been in a relationship for some time it is natural for him or her to develop a close, intimate bond with that other person. Using an Internet metaphor, such a person is special and the emotional frequency has a wider bandwidth. Less is held back. There is no problem logging on to the other person's emotional wavelength. More feelings are transmitted faster and more accurately. They are a confederate in life; a confederate of the heart—*phûu rûaam jai*. The heart phrase is an expression of a high degree of bonding between two people or in a group of people. You may have many friends and relationships but it is rare that you will have many confederate hearts.

Consensus

Agreeing Heart
yin yOOm phrÓOm jai (v.) ยินยอมพร้อมใจ

Consensus building is the essence of this heart phrase. The agreement or consensus to be reached may be among friends as to which restaurant or movie to go to for an evening of relaxation. *Yin yOOm phrÓOm jai* occupies an important role within the family unit as well. The family as a unit reaches a decision to sell a plot of land or shares in a family-owned company, or to send a son or daughter abroad for education. In a number of cases, the decision to marry falls within the general consensus of the family. There is a strong impetus to act in concert with the approval or consent of friends and family. Decision-making, in other words, is less individualistic and there are always attempts to take into account the feelings and desires of the group.

Following Heart
khlÓOy jai (v.) คล้อยใจ

When a group of people appear to reach a consensus the emotional force in that community often makes others follow along with the majority so as not to appear to be left out of the collective judgment. In a conference where policy is building around a new product, the CEO asks the members around the table whether they all agree to bringing out the product for an April launch; as people start to raise their hands, a consensus builds until everyone around the table has their hand in the air. A group of friends go to the cinema, and there are four movies playing. The leader of the group wants to see a romantic film and asks the others what they want to see. It is possible that they want to agree with the leader's choice and say they agree that seeing a romantic film is what they want as well. This heart phrase is now rarely used and can be placed in the category of old-fashioned (or out-of-fashion) language.

Reaching Out Heart
nÓOm jai (v.) น้อมใจ

The essence of this *jai* phrase can be summarized as: humility, compromise and reconciliation. A father and son quarrel and don't talk to each other for a week. At the end of the week, the son breaks the silence and speaks with his father. The son feels it is not good to not speak to his father. He works over in his heart that talking to his father is the right course of action. Swallowing your pride, softening your heart through humility and reaching out to reconcile with another is an act of *nÓOm jai*. In this sense, *nÓOm jai* is used as a verb to describe the action of reaching out or moving forward in order to resolve an impasse. The phrase is also used to show respect to the king. On Father's Day in Thailand, which is King Bhumibol's birthday, Thai people light candles and show respect to their king, and this act of respect is *nÓOm jai*.

Consumer Society

Vogue Reaction Heart
tùuen jai (v.) ตื่นใจ
tùuen taa tùuen jai (v.) ตื่นตาตื่นใจ

Your heart races faster when you see the latest fashion or style. The feeling is excitement over witnessing something new or innovative. For the computer nerd, the latest computer game can cause this reaction. For the upcountry farmer, he might feel *tùuen jai* when he sees a new tractor for sale. Or in Siam Square, a young woman who has dyed her hair blonde might draw the reaction of *tùuen jai* from an elderly woman who has just arrived from upcountry. *Tùuen taa tùuen jai* is a more elaborate expression of the same meaning—it is not only the heart that has an excited reaction but also the eye.

Seduce One's Heart
lÔO jai (v., adj.) ล่อใจ

Used as a verb or adjective, "seduce the heart" refers to a person or thing that is making an emotional bribe. This heart phrase can have the softer meaning of tempting another heart with a reward given in return for desired behavior. The context is when you want to provide an incentive to another person to want or desire something (which can be an object or a person). Once you feel the desire for something (perhaps after an effective marketing campaign) you will do what is necessary to acquire it. Beg, borrow or steal to possess the object of desire. You may, at this critical juncture, realize that you have been seduced. You may be helpless to stop the inevitable result: you acquire that which has seduced you. The seduction is not necessarily sexual. For example, it can also be a kind of incentive to make others work harder; the bonus for productive work can *lÔO jai* the employees, who desire the extra cash.

Seduction Machine of the Heart
khrûeaang lÔO jai (n.) เครื่องล่อใจ

This is the noun form of *lÔO jai*. What machinery seduces an individual heart is wide-ranging and varied. The seduction of owning and being seen in the presence of a BMW, Rolex watch, gold and diamonds, an estate in France, an apartment in London is *khrûeaang lÔO jai* for many people. These objects are the "seduction machine of the heart," driving the person who wants to possess such things with a lusty desire to acquire and retain them.

Encouragement

Power of the Heart

kam lang jai (n.) กำลังใจ
mii kam lang jai (v.) มีกำลังใจ
hâi kam lang jai (v.) ให้กำลังใจ

The noun *kam lang jai* suggests a sense of spirit or encouragement to complete a project or task, or to succeed in accomplishing a mission. A politician has *kam lang jai* to win an election. A student has *kam lang jai* to compete in the debating club. The girl who wins a beauty contest and the football player who does well in a game also have *kam lang jai*. Tiger Woods no doubt has such a heart after winning a major golf tournament. After an argument, when one person apologizes then the people involved reconcile, this gives them the feeling of *kam lang jai*. The verb form, which translates as "to feel encouraged," is *mii kam lang jai*.

When you wish to give someone encouragement to perform well, you give them the strength of the heart or *hâi kam lang jai*. When a football team is on the pitch, the crowd shouts their support, giving the team encouragement. When an officer leads his men into battle, he provides them with encouragement and strength to defeat the enemy. Your friend or spouse may be in hospital and you go to their bedside to give them strength.

Send One's Heart

sòng jai (v.) ส่งใจ

You can also "send" your heart to show your support to someone. The phrase "send one's heart" is used in the context of fans or supporters giving their encouragement at sports events, in a beauty contest, or to soldiers on the front line. The idea is to give moral support to others as they reach a crossroad in their lives and when victory or defeat is uncertain. The people responsible for victory need the emotional support of others. It can also be used in personal relationship, for example, a friend or a family member can *sòng jai* to someone they care about who is far away.

Strength of the Heart

rEEng jai (n.) แรงใจ
sòng rEEng jai (v.) ส่งแรงใจ

Support and encouragement from others give rise to *rEEng jai*, "strength of the heart." This noun is very similar to *kam lang jai* and is often used in the same context. The act of supporting members of a football team in a tough match is an example of giving *rEEng jai*. It isn't limited to a community of people such as at a football match. A mother and father can encourage their child by telephoning her and encouraging her to do well in the final examinations. A good employer also knows how to provide emotional support to his employees. Lek is trying a new job as a copy-editor at a publishing house, and the employer, after reviewing her work, gives her *rEEng jai* and encourages her to keep up the good work. The verbal expression *sòng rEEng jai* is used when you want to show support to someone who is not immediately with you. In other words, you can send the support from your heart to others long distance.

Cheer-on Heart

aw jai chûaay (v.) เอาใจช่วย

Friendship is about supporting your friends, urging them on to success or victory. You *aw jai chûaay* your friend to be a winner. It is expected that a friend will show his friendship by rooting for his friend, family, school, club or business to win in a contest. The heart phrase refers to the act of cheering on the sidelines of the contest and of giving encouragement, support and applause. The "cheer-on heart" provides a morale boost through active support and encouragement.

Recovered Heart

jai maa (adj.) ใจมา

This phrase describes the feeling when you receive the support of others through acts of their positive encouragement. A student who is about to sit an examination is given a talk by her teacher or parent that encourages her to believe that she will do well. After such a pep talk the student will feel *jai maa*. The essence is that a person feels lack of confidence but the feeling passes because others have given the necessary support so that she feels able to accomplish a difficult task. You use the phrase when another person is close to defeat, or on the edge of failure, in order to provide the encouragement to keep that person trying to overcome the odds and fighting to victory.

Hugely Recovered Heart
jai maa pen kOOng (adj.) ใจมาเป็นกอง
jai maa pen krà bung (adj.) ใจมาเป็นกระบุง

"Hugely recovered heart" is used to mean that one has recovered from a moment of terror or loss. The recovering-hearted person may have turned into the wrong street, and felt lost, stranded, only to discover, by pure chance, that his or her best friend has arrived in a car. The sight of the sudden arrival of this friend allows him or her to recover from the feeling of terror that comes from being lost, isolated and stranded. One feels heartened and the feeling of courage and resolve suddenly returns. In a football match, the losing team scores an important goal just five minutes before the end of the match, the players on that team will feel *jai maa pen kOOng*. The cheering from their supporters also gives them a feeling of encouragement. Another example is in the event of a major accident. You worry that your companion has serious injuries and may die unless taken to hospital. When you see the ambulance arrive, you have the immediate feeling of relief, or a hugely recovered heart. The second phrase is used in the same way.

Fairness

Just Heart
jai pen tham (adj.) ใจเป็นธรรม
mii jai pen tham (adj.) มีใจเป็นธรรม

It is in the nature of some people to be fair-minded and to seek justice for others. Those with a "just heart" feel upset and concerned when they see other people who are suffering, living in poverty, or helpless in the face of adversity. They sense the unfairness about the way resources, benefits and opportunities are distributed. The lack of justice in such a distribution disturbs their *jai pen tham* nature. The person with a "just heart" has a social conscience and does not wear blinkers when confronted with the unfairness and injustice that goes on around them.

Friendship

Friendship is an important release from formal behavior demanded from the "awe heart" world of those who are older, more powerful, or occupy a higher social rank. In a hierarchical culture like Thailand, friendship can be an equalizing factor. Not surprisingly, the heart phrases honor this freedom of being with one's friends, and by understanding the range of these expressions, some of the emotional expectations of friendship are revealed.

Association of the Heart

khóp kan dûaay jai (v.) คบกันด้วยใจ

Association among people who come from different social ranks or classes is sometimes difficult, though one can be friends with someone who comes from a different background, religion or ethnic group. For example, there are two people, one poor and the other rich, yet despite this difference they form and maintain a friendship. When friendship comes through the heart, the friends are said to *khóp kan dûaay jai*; they share an "association of the heart" which allows them to overcome such differences. The phrase does not describe a surface or pretend association but one that is sincere.

Friend of the Mind, Friend of the Heart
mít trà jìt mít trà jai (n.) มิตรจิตมิตรใจ

When those around you have a friendly disposition, then you will feel that you have *mít trà jìt mít trà jai*. "Friend of the mind, friend of the heart" is a sense of security that arises from the feeling of having people you can count on to be supportive. With these people you feel that a close emotional bond has been created. Such friends preclude a hostile environment and you can let your guard down and relax. This is a long phrase and can be shortened to *mít trà jìt*. This version is more frequently used in the context of commenting on the "friend of the mind, friend of the heart" that your friend has beating in his or her chest. Another context is the upcountry farmer who leaves his field to help you change the blown tire on your car. As he's a complete stranger, his willingness to help qualifies him as having *mít trà jìt mít trà jai*.

Good Friend Heart
phûeaan rûaam jai (n.) เพื่อนร่วมใจ

This *jai* phrase refers to a person who is your close and good friend, someone in whom you can trust and confide. It is also similar to the English idea of soulmate. In a good marriage, the wife feels this about her husband, and he feels it about her. There is no residual fear in the heart when in the presence of *phûeaan rûaam jai*. Instead, there is a sense of relaxation that comes from not worrying about the mask that is worn in public with strangers. One may wish to introduce a friend to a third party with "good friend heart," which is all the explanation necessary to define the nature of the relationship.

Complicit Heart
pen jai (v.) เป็นใจ
rúu hěn pen jai (v.) รู้เห็นเป็นใจ

Not all friendship is for the betterment of society. Criminals have friends who are usually other criminals. The essence is the secret alliance between people who set out to accomplish a mission. It does not have to be a major crime like a bank robbery. For example, the person seated in the back of the car may look the other way as the chauffeur runs a red light or double parks. Or two crooks may be *pen jai* and decide to rob people on a soi. The spin is on a kind of conspiracy between two or more people to deceive, cheat or allow another to do something that is morally suspect or illegal. Thus the "complicit heart" is not always about friendship. It may be passive behavior. One person simply looks the other way, and by doing so indirectly encourages the immoral or illegal act. Used in another context, it may describe a condition or situation such as a bright, sunny day, and you agree with your wife to go on a picnic to the beach. A bullish stock market in the run-up to a general election is *pen jai* for the incumbent government, who takes credit. The person who *rúu hěn pen jai* has knowledge of and agrees to the conspiracy to do something that is usually morally suspect or illegal. While *pen jai* deals with implicit, indirect involvement, *rúu hěn pen jai* is active, knowing participation in the scheme.

Considerate Heart
mii kÈE jai (v.) มีแก่ใจ

Friendship is about rendering assistance when a friend is having a problem or experiencing trouble. When a difficult situation arises, and the problem persists, one friend comes to the assistance of another. The friend is *mii kÈE jai* in helping another in need; she is considerate and thoughtful. She might take care of your child when there is an emergency or provide a ride to the hospital when you fall and injure yourself. This action is the opposite of self-centered, selfish behavior. A person with a "considerate heart" takes another person's feelings of frustration, gloom and doom to heart, and stands ready, willing and able to give support.

Showing Water Heart
sà dEEng náam jai (v.) แสดงน้ำใจ

If you demonstrate consideration to others and offer assistance, then you are said to *sà dEEng náam jai*. A community or society is held together and strengthened when its members are considerate and helpful to one another. The consideration and sympathy offered acts like the glue that holds the community together. Often the act of *sà dEEng náam jai* may be a small gesture. Dropping a few coins in a beggar's bowl. Giving up one's seat on the bus or the BTS for an elderly passenger. There is an element of reciprocity involved as well. One neighbor helps another to harvest rice from his field, and the next month the rice farmer helps his neighbor build a new fence.

Refuge for the Heart
thîi phûeng thaang jai (n.)
ที่พึ่งทางใจ

When you seek spiritual refuge, which is an important aspect of this *jai* phrase, you read the teachings of Buddha. Others find refuge in amulets, spirit houses, or spiritual leaders whose insights into life provide greater understanding as to the meaning of life. The phrase also has a more general application, meaning a person in whom you can trust and confide your personal and spiritual problems. Friends can be *thîi phûeng thaang jai* for one another.

Laughter in the Heart
hǔaa rÓ nai jai (v.) หัวเราะในใจ
khǎm nai jai (v.) ขำในใจ

Friends can be a source of amusement, especially when they do something that makes them appear unintentionally vulnerable and childlike. Observing such an action causes one to feel amused inside. "Laughter in the heart" may arise when a friend is diverted; perhaps he or she is lost in a daydream, and he or she trips and nearly falls. But the observing friend resists laughing out loud—which might cause the person suffering the near pratfall to lose face—though inside the friend is laughing. The feelings associated with "laughter in the heart" can and do occur when someone is alone and remembers something said or done that strikes them as humorous and such a recollection triggers laughter in the heart.

Do It One's Own Way Heart
tham taam jai chÔOp (v.)
ทำตามใจชอบ
tham taam am phooe jai (v.)
ทำตามอำเภอใจ

A person with this heart is not someone who makes a good friend. A person who exhibits such behavior is the ultimate bore and, even worse, does not know *kreeng jai*. His conduct displays flashes of selfishness, insensitivity and absence of concern about the well-being of others. If invited into your house, this kind of person may immediately head for the kitchen, open the fridge and help himself, then pop open a 2,000 baht imported bottle of wine and drink it straight from the bottle as he goes into your sitting room and put on a heavy-metal record with the volume turned up.

The *jai* phrase *tham taam am phooe jai* translates literally as "follow your home district heart." Thailand is divided for a number of purposes into provinces, districts, sub-districts and villages. The phrase uses only the district reference. This usage comes from former times (about sixty years ago, when districts were formally recognized as entities under Thai law), when a trader living in a district in Surin province traveled to Bangkok to sell bamboo baskets. The fact that the trader had freedom of movement to go anywhere in the Kingdom of Thailand translated during this time as *taam am phooe jai*. It was the merchants' right of movement to sell their wares. They weren't limited to selling or trading inside the home district. In more modern times the phrase is much closer to *tham taam jai chÔOp*, with equal emphasis on personal freedom and disregard for others.

Injustice

Shout in the Heart
tà koon nai jai (v.) ตะโกนในใจ

This Thai idiom translates literally as "shout in the heart." The person represses his or her true feelings, which may range from anger to hatred, in circumstances where he or she wishes to avoid a confrontation or the loss of face. While not good for blood pressure it maintains social harmony as people with negative emotions swallow their feelings in order to avoid trouble or being labeled as someone who lacks patience. An example is in an office setting where one person is promoted and another person is passed over; the one who isn't promoted may shout inside his mind (*tà koon nai jai*) that the boss's decision is unfair, but he wants to keep his job so he says nothing. The essence is that a grievance or injustice rises up in a person who feels he or she has been a victim of another's action or inaction.

Justice

Satisfy One's Heart

săa jai (adj.) สาใจ
săa kÈE jai (adj.) สาแก่ใจ

When you know someone who has got their just desserts, then use *săa jai*. They have done something and the time has come to pay their dues. The notion of justice behind this phrase is karmic justice. The English equivalent would be the phrase: "What goes around comes around." *Schadenfreude* is also a close approximation. An employer has promised his secretary a raise, and then later he breaks the promise. A week later the employer loses a big contract with a customer. The secretary may think to herself about the boss: *săa jai*. If she said it to the boss, she might be dismissed. *Săa kÈE jai* is a variation of *săa jai*.

Satisfy Wild Side Heart

sà jai (adj.) สะใจ
sà jai kŏo (adj.) สะใจโก๋

Sà jai has the same meaning and is used in the same way as the *jai* expression above. *Sà jai kŏo* is slang and comes from the underworld or gangster community (likely limited to the junior gangster rank), although it has gained currency outside of those circles and is used by teenagers. A group of gangsters may attack their enemy and beat him up, and afterwards they walk away and say that the fighting was *sà jai kŏo*. A punk rock or a rap concert that arouses the "wild side" of the teenagers' heart may be later described by the fans as *sà jai kŏo*. It is informal street language.

Aching Stomach, Doubtful Heart

jèp thÓOng khÔOng jai (v.)
เจ็บท้องข้องใจ

The ancient usage goes back to a King Ramkhamhaeng edict that anyone who had an aching stomach, doubtful heart could petition the king. It means that an incident or event has happened which has caused you to feel pain. The pain can be either physical or mental. A wife wanting a divorce from her abusive husband or a tenant who is mistreated by the landlord can feel *jèp thÓOng khÔOng jai*. Thus "stomach ache" is a metaphor for every kind of injury. It does not necessarily mean the pain is literally in the stomach. According to the edict, any citizen who felt *jèp thÓOng khÔOng jai* could seek justice from the king. The phrase is now no longer used.

Persuasion

Persuade Another's Heart

juung jai (v.) จูงใจ
chák juung jai (v.) ชักจูงใจ

Juung jai or *chák juung jai* is to persuade someone to do something. You may tug at the heart of the person you wish to convince to do something, or take a certain course of action. The objective of "persuade another's heart" is to compel another person to act according to your desire. The beautiful flower in the market stall persuades someone to buy it. The attractive art cover on a book convinces someone walking by to buy the book. Or the lovely salesgirl in the department store persuades a young man to buy another telephone. One person or object may make another person feel *thùuk chák juung jai* or being on the receiving end of the persuasion.

This *jai* phrase can have a negative meaning, such as the gangster who persuades young kids to sell drugs on the street corner. Billboards are constantly broadcasting messages to persuade people to buy the latest consumer product. Advertising agencies are hired to ensure that the products and services of their clients *chák juung jai* the intended consumers.

When you are emotionally convinced about a thing, an object or a place by reading (a book), watching (a movie) or listening (to an advertisement on the radio), you feel *thùuk chák juung jai.* It can happen face to face, person to person as well. If the story is amusing, then the feelings of *chák juung jai* is humor the person feels. If the story is sad, then it likewise conveys the sense of that person's feeling of sadness. The heart phrase picks up the tone from the experience of the observer or audience, persuading the heart with humor or sadness.

Reconcile One Another's Heart
pràp khwaam khâw jai (v.)
ปรับความเข้าใจ

In the Thai language, one negotiates from and through the heart. Though reconcile may be closer to the true meaning as negotiation implies a room of lawyers arguing out of self-interest. This heart phrase is used as a verb: to *pràp khwaam khâw jai* is to negotiate or reconcile to a new understanding between the parties. There may be a misunderstanding between parties to a business arrangement, and through the process of negotiation such misunderstandings are hopefully eliminated. The *jai* phrase is not limited to commercial deals and applies equally between family members, lovers, friends, colleagues and classmates. Parents may take two brothers who are arguing into a corner and tell them not to come out until they *pràp khwaam khâw jai*.

Soothing Heart
klÒOm jai (v.) กล่อมใจ

This heart phrase refers to an act of soothing another, acting as an emotional caretaker for another who is depressed, troubled or worried. For example, your best friend has received some bad news and you wish to give comfort at the moment of distress. In such circumstances, you wish to *klÒOm jai* or soothe the friend through her emotional trauma. The "soothing heart" understands how to provide comfort and compassion to those who need such comfort at a time of crisis. It can also be used in the context of trying to persuade another person to change his or her mind. A marketing person may describe a condo unit in such a way that eliminates the doubts and worries of the person looking to buy it.

Pride

In Western literature the words pride and proud can carry a negative implication, as in Thomas Campbell's *Pleasures of Hope*: "The proud, the cold untroubled heart of stone, that never mused on sorrow but its own." In the heart phrases that follow, there are several ways to express the high opinion a person has formed of himself or herself. In most instances, the source of pride is in having accomplished something of value or having performed successfully. Pride can also be strongly felt about one's family, village, province or country.

Delighted Heart
plûuem jai (v.) ปลื้มใจ
prìm jai (v.) ปริ่มใจ
plàap plûuem jai (v.) ปลาบปลื้มใจ

When you receive a promotion for your work and you feel proud of yourself, then you may be *plûuem jai*. This is the sense of pride in individual accomplishment that comes from your own personal efforts. You set out to accomplish a task and actually do so. Also, it can be the transitory feeling of pride arising from the praise or flattery given by another. *Plàap plûuem jai* is part of the class system and the senior/ junior pecking order. When the senior confers praise on his or her junior, the junior will feel *plàap plûuem jai*. When a woman is conferred with the honorable title of khunying she will also feel *plàap plûuem jai*.

Proud Heart
phuum jai (v.) ภูมิใจ
phâak phuum jai (v.) ภาคภูมิใจ

You are *phuum jai* or proud when you have accomplished something that makes you feel good or successful. You experience a sense of joy from the accomplishment. You can feel proud about yourself or others; and others may have a sense of pride in you. Parents experience this feeling with a good child. Or a "proud heart" may come from feeling part of a larger organization: a feeling of pride toward one's country, hometown, university or family. *Phâak phuum jai* is a stronger version of *phuum jai*. When some lucky Thai university graduates receive a university diploma from the king, they and their family will feel *phâak phuum jai*. The pride may reflect more than something personal and extend to feelings of heritage (a Chiang Mai person's feeling for Lanna culture and language) or to nationality (being Thai).

Responsibility & The Family

There are exceptions to every rule, but generally the family occupies a central role in the lives of most Thais. There is an abiding sense of obligation to the family within each member. Traditionally, children were raised to feel responsible to their parents throughout their lives. An obligation of such dimensions that it could never be fully paid. Many of the phrases in this section often occur in a family context, although they may be used outside the family as well.

Caring Heart

sài jai (v.) ใส่ใจ

A mother may *sài jai* by reminding her sons and daughters of the importance of an education. By doing so, the mother demonstrates an interest in the future welfare of her children. In other relationships, the caring heart is a demonstration of one person's wish to guide another person's future, whether a child, lover, spouse or friend, in a positive, helpful way. Such a person wishes for what is best for them and encourages others in their lives. His or her action and involvement in the process of encouragement, guidance and direction is an act of *sài jai*.

Attentive Heart
aw jai sài (v.) เอาใจใส่

This is another heart phrase with the same basic meaning as *sài jai*—paying attention and concentrating on a task, a relationship, a project at work, a sporting event. Also, it can be used to demonstrate your interest in the welfare and happiness of others when you advise them on the best course of action in accomplishing what will be in their best interest. A husband may *aw jai sài* his wife, or conversely the wife may *aw jai sài* her husband. When the person giving the advice occupies a higher social rank or is senior in age, then the one receiving it is more likely to pay close attention and concentrate on what is being said.

See with the Heart, Listen with the Ear
aw jai duu hŭu sài (v.) เอาใจดูหูใส่

This Thai idiom is used to concentrate the eye and the ear; the heart is used to focus both. A monk will use this phrase as a Buddhist teaching to concentrate on what one is doing. Pay attention to the task at hand. Don't have your mind somewhere else. If you are reading a book don't at the same time watch TV and listen to the radio. You often see Bangkok drivers eating and talking on a mobile phone as they are racing down Sukhumvit Road. If you could ever catch one of these people, you might want to remind them of this phrase. Some Thais feel that only "old" people or monks use this expression. Young people think it is a bit too preachy.

Lessons for the Heart
sŎOn jai (adj.) สอนใจ

This *jai* phrase refers to the proverbs or sayings that provide examples of right conduct or doing good deeds. It literally translates as "that which teaches the heart." It also has a practical application. A man drinks too much and then causes an accident. His action is a lesson for him that he shouldn't drink and drive. A woman dates a thoughtless and impatient man, and after she breaks up with him she learns the lesson that thoughtfulness and patience are essential in a relationship. Many fables have this element of a moral story or lesson. If you learn from your own mistakes and those of others, you have mastered the lessons in life.

Center Heart

jai klaang (n.) ใจกลาง

The heart phrase is, among other things, descriptive of the location of a building or street. For example, some would say that Siam Square is *jai klaang* in Bangkok, in the heart of town. Others might vote for Silom Road. "Center heart" also has another meaning, for the feelings one may have about the importance of another person in one's life. The mother or father might be thought of as *jai klaang* for a child. Parents occupy a central place in the hearts of their children.

Geographic Center Heart

jai mueaang (n.) ใจเมือง

jai klaang mueaang (n.) ใจกลางเมือง

Jai klaang is the center of a city. *Jai mueaang* is the center of a country. London is *jai mueaang* or the capital of England. Ottawa is the capital of Canada and Washington, D.C. the capital of the United States. The center of a city is called *jai klaang mueaang*. Victory Monument is *jai klaang mueaang* in Bangkok. While *jai klaang* is common in everyday speech, *jai mueaang* is mainly confined to textbooks.

Heavy Heart

nàk jai (v.) หนักใจ

When someone feels responsible for and worries about their children, parents, spouse or lover, they feel *nàk jai* toward that person. They may have a son who does not live a good and respectable life; he refuses to work, hangs out at nightclubs with questionable friends, and otherwise has a lifestyle far below their expectations. Then they will likely experience at first-hand a "heavy heart."

Relieved Heart
baw jai (adj.) เบาใจ
baw òk baw jai (adj.) เบาอกเบาใจ

The essence is the sense of relief when circumstances cause a worry to disappear. Lek has passed her driving test and when told by the examining official of the success, Lek is likely to feel a sense of relief. An employee finishes her report by the required deadline. The doctor came out of the operating room and tells the patient's family that the patient will be all right. All these provide a sense of *baw jai*. The daughter of a close-knit family wishes to study abroad but they are worried until a relative in Canada offers to give a room to the daughter. The news that the daughter will stay with relatives in Canada causes the mother and father to feel *baw jai*.

Interested Heart
sŏn jai (v.) สนใจ
sŏn jai yai dii (v.) สนใจใยดี

Sŏn jai is a common verb in Thai, meaning to be interested in another person, thing, or activity. The level of interest may be low or high depending on the context. A vendor may use the term as an indirect way of selling goods. Sometimes the heart phrase is used to determine whether a person has a preference. Other times, the heart phrase may be posed in question form: Are you interested in going to the movies? Are you interested in an article written about the stock market? In Thai culture it is a grave insult to say that the parents aren't *sŏn jai* about their children or that the government is indifferent to the needs of upcountry farmers. A variation is *sŏn jai yai dii*, meaning attentive and caring about others. This variation is, however, often used in negative form. Parents who don't care about their children may be criticized as "*mâi sŏn jai yai dii*" about their children.

Stay Alert Heart
yàa nîng nOOn jai (v.) อย่านิ่งนอนใจ

This is a prescription or warning to you not to let your heart go to sleep in the middle of a serious situation. In other words, you must maintain a state of awareness or vigilance. In the south of Thailand, where there have been troubles, local or national officials might employ this *jai* phrase should they feel that others are not taking the problems seriously. A teacher may also use this phrase as a warning to students who are getting behind in their studies, telling them to begin immediately to read the required lessons and not to delay for other activities such as going out with friends.

Kicked Below the Belt Heart

klÒOng duaang jai (n.)

กล่องดวงใจ

8
body talk

A number of heart phrases are not directly connected with emotions or the metaphysics of emotions; such expressions describe a physical condition. The descriptions are of the functions (malfunctions) of the body, and in Thai these have a special *jai* vocabulary. An emotionally stressful situation may bring on the physical conditions described below. The *jai* phrases in this chapter communicate the nature of how the body reacts to stress, disease, surprise, nerves, excitement or fear. One can select among the heart phrases in this chapter a variety of descriptions for body smell and heart attacks, and for breathing, fainting and trembling. The language that expresses the physical act of dying and the feelings associated with dying are also found in this chapter. Physical acts are often used as metaphors as well. Where appropriate the metaphors have been included in the definition.

Attributes

Center of the Palm
Palmful Amount
jai muue (n.) ใจมือ

Jai muue has two different meanings. The first refers to the center of the palm of your hand. The second meaning is an ancient unit of measurement. Four standard palmfuls (*jai muue*) equal one fistful (*kam muue*). This measurement was used for rice or salt when there was no other way of measuring the units to be sold. Most young Thais would likely have no idea about the meaning of this *jai* phrase.

Heart

hŭaa jai (n.) หัวใจ

Moving from the heart as the center of feelings, we now enter the physical realm of the heart—*hŭaa jai*. This is the organ known as the heart, located inside a person's chest cavity and assigned the task of pumping blood twenty-four hours a day to the rest of the body. It also has a metaphoric use which is the subject of this book. One example of the metaphoric use of this phrase is when a woman is rejected by her lover who seems not to show any emotion; she may say that he doesn't have a *hŭaa jai—mâi mii hŭaa jai*—he doesn't have a heart. It doubles, therefore, as an expression for people who have no feelings about others.

Nice Breasts

nâa òk nâa jai (n.) หน้าอกหน้าใจ

This is not a reference to heart *per se* but to a woman's breasts, and is a slightly rude reference as well. The expression has a definite sexual spin. A doctor would not use this term, for example. While women may use this phrase among themselves, they would not view the phrase as a compliment if used by someone outside this circle of friends. A woman with beautiful breasts walking past a construction site might receive catcalls as well as comments on her *nâa òk nâa jai*, which would cause her embarrassment if not anger.

Breathing

Breathing, passing out and smells are covered by a number of heart expressions.

Breath

lom hăay jai (n.) ลมหายใจ

This heart phrase relates to one's actual breath. The air that goes in and out of the nostrils and into the lungs is *lom hăay jai*. It can also be used as a metaphor. For example, during the courting period a man may say to a woman that she is his *lom hăay jai* or his very breath for living.

Breathe
hăay jai (v.) หายใจ

The verb *hăay jai* is the Thai expression for the act of breathing. There are also romantic notions which are variations of this phrase. A person may say to her lover that she misses him *thúk lom hăay jai*, meaning she thinks of him with every breath taken, or thinks of him all the time.

Inhale
hăay jai khâw (v.) หายใจเข้า

Hăay jai khâw means to breath in or to inhale. It is a technical term found in medical textbooks, or a phrase that a patient who goes to a hospital with a respiratory condition might expect to hear from a Thai doctor using a stethoscope as he or she performs a physical examination. In a popular Thai song the young woman uses *hăay jai khâw* to express her deep, abiding love for her boyfriend. It's another way of saying she misses her lover. The act of missing is like the act of breathing. It is there at every moment. She inhales him into her heart—or if she really wants to express her love she can also use the phrase *hăay jai khâw hăay jai ÒOk pen thooe*. The metaphors of inhaling and exhaling are ways to express the desperation that only love can cause.

Exhale
hăay jai ÒOk (v.) หายใจออก

When you breathe out or exhale air from your lungs, you *hăay jai ÒOk*. The expression is also a technical term mostly confined to a doctor's examination room.

Breathe Freely
hăay jai khlÔOng (v.) หายใจคล่อง

This is ordinary, normal, unobstructed breathing. If you suffer from a bad head cold, then you cannot *hăay jai khlÔOng*. It is also a metaphor for being able to breathe easily when everything is going according to plan. When there are no serious problems or obstacles in daily life, this is the normal condition. As a metaphor it can be applied when the particularly strict boss leaves the premises and the employees suddenly erupt into song and dance, playing and running around because they have a wonderful sense of freedom. One would say the employees feel *hăay jai khlÔOng*, or are enjoying their personal freedom.

Breathe Through the Mouth
hăay jai thaang pàak (v.)
หายใจทางปาก

Someone who is a mouth-breather might hear someone using this heart phrase to describe their way of breathing through their mouth rather than their nose.

Cannot Breathe
hăay jai mâi ÒOk (v.) หายใจไม่ออก

If you cannot breathe, you will feel *hăay jai mâi ÒOk.* This is obviously a feeling you will not experience for very long before either passing out or dying. It is also the stuffy feeling of spending a night in a hot, closed room without a fan or air conditioning. An hour in the back of a tuk-tuk on Sukhumvit Road during a traffic jam can produce the same condition. It can also be used to describe the claustrophobic feeling that can creep into a relationship with a spouse, lover, friend or fellow worker. In this sense, it is a call for some isolation and privacy.

Have Difficulty Breathing
hăay jai mâi sà dùaak (v.)
หายใจไม่สะดวก

When you smell a foul or rotten odor, or when you have a heavy head cold, then you feel *hăay jai mâi sà dùaak*. This is the opposite of *hăay jai khlÔOng*, or breathing freely. As a metaphor it is used in circumstances where personal freedom has been taken away. When the boss is in residence, he hates loud music and talking so the employees may whisper to each other that they feel *hăay jai mâi sà dùaak,* as one of them very much wants to turn up the radio.

Have Butterflies in One's Stomach
hăay jai mâi thûaa thÓOng (v.)
หายใจไม่ทั่วท้อง

This state of being means some excitement or nervous feeling makes it hard to breathe, and in the literal sense, it means you cannot breathe throughout your stomach (*mâi thûaa thÓOng*). It is similar to the English expression "to have butterflies" in your stomach. Your friend has set you up for a blind date. As you walk closer to the restaurant where you will meet your blind date, your breathing rate rapidly increases. The rapid breathing is like hyperventilation. In another example, the boss of a company brings everyone into the conference room where he will read the names of those employees to be laid off. During the period of waiting, the employees in the room will feel *hăay jai mâi thûaa thÓOng*.

Hold One's Breath
klân jai (v.) กลั้นใจ
ân jai (v.) อั้นใจ

It is a boiling-hot mid-summer day and you walk past a polluted khlong, which is giving off a rich variety of foul, pungent odors. As you pass along the khlong, a little wind blows the stench across your path, causing you to *klân jai*—to hold your breath. This heart phrase applies generally to some bad smell and the natural reflex action of holding your breath in reaction to it.

The phrase also applies to overcoming feelings of sadness or fear. Another example of *klân jai* is in circumstances of controlling one's feelings. You may have received bad news about a friend's accident and, rather than breaking into tears, you don't display to others the emotions you are experiencing. The act of holding this feeling inside is *klân jai*. If your wife makes you go to the opera and you hate opera but go along to please her, you again hold your breath and please your wife. *Ân jai* is used in this second meaning.

Panting Heart
sà thÓOn jai (v.) สะท้อนใจ

At the end of the marathon many of the runners are winded after the long run and their breathing is closer to panting than normal breathing. The panting is in *sà thÓOn jai* Thai. It also describes that caught-in-the-throat cry of a small child who is overly tired, hungry and listless.

Tight Heart
nÊEn nâa òk nâa jai (adv.)
แน่นหน้าอกหน้าใจ

Some of the runners in the above example may feel short of breath. Maybe they can't catch their breath. They may be out of shape but press themselves to finish a ten-mile charity marathon in Lumpini Park, and as they pull to a stop they feel tight-hearted or *nÊEn nâa òk nâa jai*. It is possible that they are about to experience a heart attack. Also, if a woman's bra is too tight she may confide to her friend that the tight-fitting bra makes her feel *nÊEn nâa òk nâa jai*.

Fragrant Heart
hǑOm chûuen jai (adj.) หอมชื่นใจ

When you smell a good smell, an appropriate expression is *hǑOm chûuen jai*. The good smell may be the fragrance of flowers, the skin of a baby, perfume or the cheek of your lover. The fragrant you received through your nose makes your heart feel better. The expression usually applies to pleasant aroma in the environment or relationship but not food.

Dying

When someone is about to die these are some of the heart phrases they might hear being whispered in Thai by those around them. There are a number of *jai* phrases that describe the moments preceding death. Also included here are other heart phrases for heart problems and heart attacks.

Heart Stops Beating
hŭaa jai yùt tên (v.) หัวใจหยุดเต้น

This is a phrase to use for the moment a person stops breathing. *Hŭaa jai yùt tên* means that the heart stops beating. The phrase marks the last moment of the person's life.

Breathe One's Last Breath
khàat jai (v.) ขาดใจ

Khàat jai translates as "breathe one's last breath." It has a poetic ring in English translation. It means the last dying breath before a person dies. The emphasis is on the physical act of taking that last breath before death. This phrase appears in Thai newspaper accounts of victims dying at the scene of an accident, and also in romantic literature. A hero in a novel may say to the heroine that without her close presence in his life he will feel *khàat jai*. It is a way to dramatize (perhaps overly so) one's undying love for another.

Finished Heart
sîn jai (v.) สิ้นใจ

Sîn jai is a verb for the act of taking one last breath before dying. It is a euphemism like "passing away," used as a polite substitute for saying someone has died. The phrase may mask a bad feeling mixed with fear and horror and sadness. The feeling is generated from the realization that a person's life is being extinguished. But a religious person, such as a monk, feels *sîn jai* might have a good feeling. Unlike *khàat jai*, which is the physical act of taking the last breath before death, *sîn jai* is the phrase used to avoid using more direct words such as die, death or dying.

Have a Heart Attack
hŭaa jai waay (v., n.) หัวใจวาย
hŭaa jai jà waay (v., adj.) หัวใจจะวาย

Hŭaa jai waay is the Thai expression for the basic garden-variety heart attack. If it is used as a noun, then the person is already dead. If it is used as a verb, then the person spoken about is suffering from a heart attack. A person who complains of experiencing *hŭaa jai waay* will likely be understood to be asking for an emergency trip to the hospital.

Hŭaa jai jà waay is used as a metaphor (as opposed to referring to an actual heart attack). When a woman sees a very handsome man, she may say to her friend that she feels *hŭaa jai jà waay*—the sight of the handsome man causes her to feel as if she was on the verge of a heart attack. The same feeling applies to a man (assumed to be hetereosexual) who spots a sexy woman, although he is unlikely to use this expression, which is used only by women or effeminate gay men.

Resuscitate the Heart
pám hŭaa jai (v.) ปั๊มหัวใจ

When a defibrillator is used to start a stopped heart the appropriate phrase is *pám hŭaa jai*. It is the act of pressing the machine against the chest, or the act of using one's hands to restart a heart that is no longer beating. This is one of those *Heart Talk* expressions that you don't want to hear being said about you.

See Another's Final Breath
than hěn jai (v.) ทันเห็นใจ

In Thai culture, there is a wish to see your loved one take his or her last breath. There is a desire to be present before an injured person or patient dies. Close friends or family are often present before death occurs. Someone's mother may be terminally ill and in hospital in another province. The daughter takes the overnight bus to see her mother, arriving an hour before the mother dies. She is able to see her mother and hold her hand while she has these last moments of life. The daughter's act of seeing her mother's final breath is *than hěn jai*.

Heart Disease
rôok hŭaa jai (n.) โรคหัวใจ

This is a medical term to describe a physical condition of a heart which suffers from disease. In other words, this is not a metaphor but the physical organ beating in the chest of each person. If you hear your doctor using this phrase, it is time to make certain that your will and health insurance policies are in good order.

Shriveled Heart
hŭaa jai lîip (n.) หัวใจลีบ
hŭaa jai fÒO (n.) หัวใจฝ่อ

One meaning of the heart phrase "shriveled heart" (*hŭaa jai lîip*) is to describe that broken heart caused by a lover's sudden departure. The second meaning applies to the medical opinion from a doctor breaking the unfortunate news that a person has heart disease. *Hŭaa jai fÒO* is used in the same context.

Fainting

Fainting Heart
jai wǐw (v.) ใจหวิว

"Fainting heart" is a physical sensation of feeling dizzy or about to faint. When you stare down from the top of a forty-story building without safety railings, you may feel dizzy, as if you might faint. At this point a friend may ask if you are *jai wǐw*. This physical feeling can result from the sense of terror that something terrible is about to happen. The mother of a child attending a school where a mad person has stabbed students will feel *jai wǐw* upon hearing news of the attack.

You might have spent too much time sunbathing on the beach under a hot tropical sun or have checked the bar bill after entertaining a half-dozen friends at an expensive club; afterwards you may feel shocked or *jai wǐw*. That sense of being light-headed, dizzy, giddy, is the precursor to losing consciousness. Remember that monster of a roller-coaster ride at the amusement park? The one that caused sheer terror as time appeared to stop. That is another way to have experienced *jai wǐw*. The *jai* phrase can also be used to express the overwhelming attraction a man or woman feels toward another.

Kicking

Kicked Below the Belt Heart

klÒOng duaang jai (n.) กล่องดวงใจ

This phrase, literally "box of heart," has its origin in the Thai classical literature *Ramakian* (*Ramayana*). In a a clever attempt to protect his life, the ten-armed arch villain, Tossakan, removes his heart and puts it in a box and hides it in a safe place. But ultimately—as the fate of most villains can be expected—Tossakan is killed by the hero, Phra Ram (Rama), who shoots an arrow through his chest, and the Monkey King, Hanuman, who simultaneously squeezes the box that contains his heart. Only through this coordinated effort the villain is slain and his "box of heart" destroyed. From this origin, *klÒOng duaang jai* became a metaphor for something that is the most precious for a person.

The usage has evolved and its modern usage is slang for male genitalia. It is a polite way of saying something that is more hard-edged in

Thai. It may be used in a Thai kick-boxing match. One boxer kicks the other below the belt. But this *jai* phrase doesn't apply only to professional boxing. A woman who is angry with a man may also have a fast and well-aimed foot or fist hitting the man below the belt. The man's *klÒOng duaang jai* has been hit.

Shake, Rattle & Roll

Fast Beating Heart
jai tên (v.) ใจเต้น
hŭaa jai tên rEEng (v., adj.)
หัวใจเต้นแรง

This feeling occurs in circumstances where you are surprised or thrilled. Vinai is busily brushing his teeth alone in the bathroom. His girlfriend sneaks in behind him and he catches sight of her in the mirror. This unexpected event may cause him to feel *jai tên*—his heart dancing in his chest from the shock of seeing the unexpected. A young person who is crazy about a superstar, meets the superstar and, while waiting for his or her autograph, the youngster will feel *jai tên*. Another formulation is *hŭaa jai tên rEEng*. If you are jogging you feel your heart beating faster and that is *hŭaa jai tên rEEng*.

Absent-minded Heart

jai mâi yùu kàp tuaa (adj.) ใจไม่อยู่กับตัว

jai mâi yùu kàp núeaa kàp tuaa (adj.) ใจไม่อยู่กับเนื้อกับตัว

9
perception

In Thai, certain perceptions, such as astonishment and surprise, impression and satisfaction, issue directly from the heart. Most mental and intellectual processes, such as awareness, concentration, imagination, intuition, knowledge and understanding, also involve the heart. The *jai* phrases in this chapter provide examples of how the Thai emotional and intellectual spheres overlap and how the Thai heart and mind often work as one. Take the process of understanding for example. In English, we would rarely associate our understanding of what has been said, or what another person has said to us, with our heart—unless the conversation contained an emotional component.

Understanding in the Thai context is not limited to understanding in the sense of romantic or other feelings in relationship but is inclusive of understanding of people, things and subject matters that require the working of the intellect. The translation of many heart phrases in this chapter suggests the limitation of the English language to provide accurate translation of these *jai* expressions.

As indicated in the introduction, mind and heart have been for centuries divided in a fashion that is not true for the Thai language. In English, the mind would "understand" the rational, logical and analytical information, process that information and use it. While the heart might also "understand," it would be implicit in English that this understanding is qualitatively different in nature. In Thai, the heart is involved in all matters of understanding and perception. It is the heart that is surprised, amazed, satisfied, impressed, and responsible for imagination and intuition. It is also the heart—not the mind—that concentrates and contains knowledge and awareness of the environment. The heart is involved in thinking, understanding people and subject matters, and realizes the truth.

Awareness & Realization

Touch One to the Quick Heart
sà kìt jai (v.) สะกิดใจ

A person with a "touch one to the quick heart" is reminded in a flash about something important involving people, events or situations. She may be driving and remember that she forgot to turn off the rice cooker. It is that flash of insight that results from a reminder. This momentary feeling of remembering is the essence of *sà kìt jai*. The key element is being reminded of something. It may be a gesture, a facial expression, an article of clothing, a certain tone, intention, or a movie that reminds you of a feeling, a person, or an important moment of your life. A private investigator should be prone to *sà kìt jai* like Sherlock Holmes, who could deduce the murderer from the fact that the dog didn't bark at the time of the crime.

Sudden Realization Heart
chùk jai (v.) ฉุกใจ
sà dùt jai (v.) สะดุดใจ

You have the abrupt realization that you have forgotten something. The memory of the forgotten thing returns in a flash. Another use is the sudden realization of something not understood before, for example, when hearing for the first time the difference in tone between the Thai words for tiger and shirt, dog and horse. Having left the house to go shopping, you remember an hour later that you have forgotten your credit card and cash. Someone misplaces their passport and suddenly wakes up in the middle of night and remembers where it has been misfiled.

Sudden Realization Heart

núek è jai (v.) นึกเอะใจ
chà lĭiaw jai (v.) เฉลียวใจ
è jai (v.) เอะใจ

When you feel a sudden doubt or uncertainty, then you have a case of *núek è jai*. A friend tells you that he will show up at the restaurant at seven for dinner. By eight, you are waiting, glancing at your watch; your friend still hasn't arrived. You have a flash of doubt—*è jai* or *núek è jai*—that you may be at the wrong restaurant.

Chà lĭiaw jai has three meanings: (i) suspecting a deception has occurred (also see *rà wEEng jai*); (ii) doubt or uncertainty in the same sense as *núek è jai*; and (iii) something reminds you about something else, such as when someone at the table says "Chiang Mai" and you realize that you are late to pick up a friend who is arriving from Chiang Mai.

Unaware Heart

mâi chà lĭiaw jai (v.) ไม่เฉลียวใจ
mâi núek è jai (v.) ไม่นึกเอะใจ

The *jai* phrase *chà lĭiaw jai* is used on its own to convey suspicion or that you are wary of another person or situation. The person who feels *chà lĭiaw jai* is fearing that something adverse is happening to him. Adding the word *mâi* means that a person is unaware of what ought to be causing him fear or suspicion. Ben, a handsome but poor office worker, loves his girlfriend Mimi who is a beautiful model with many admirers. She tells him that she loves only him and will never want to be with another man. He's not aware of any reason why she would leave him; he believes her. It never occurs to Ben that Mimi would be tempted by one of her many admirers. Ben is said to be *mâi chà lĭiaw jai* or *mâi núek è jai*.

Concentration

There are times when you want to concentrate all of your efforts and energy to accomplish a task or reach a specific goal. Or you may concentrate your heart on another person, and by so doing, show a genuine interest in that person. The failure to focus or concentrate is another context in which heart phrases appear.

Concentrated Heart
jai jòt jai jÒO (adj.) ใจจดใจจ่อ

This heart phrase means one has developed the ability to fully focus on a project and to complete it without being sidelined by the usual distractions of life. A professional painter, writer, film director, athlete are examples of workers who require a "concentrated heart" in order to survive in fierce competition. At the same time, a "concentrated heart" may be the quality of being available to meet the emotional needs of someone. For instance, another person may be telling a long, emotional story and the listener pays full attention and gives understanding words and gestures as the story unfolds. The person telling the story will feel that such a listener is *jai jòt jai jÒO*.

Single-minded Heart
jai nÊEw (adj.) ใจแน่ว

This is the opposite of *jai wÔk wÊk*, "distracted heart." It belongs to the same family of *jai* phrases as *jai jòt jai jòt jai jÒO*. This is a stronger expression for someone who is totally focused or in the groove. Their concentration is firm, intense and unwavering. A golfer, snooker or chess player who is *jai nÊEw* has an advantage. A person who is *jai nÊEw* also makes a good employee or student. For example, you wish to study nineteenth-century poetry. Everyone in your family and all of your friends think this isn't a good idea because you can't earn money. But you are determined to take this course of study; your mind is fully concentrated on this subject and you are willing to forgo money and luxury to pursue your dream.

Paying Attention Heart
tâng jai fang (v.) ตั้งใจฟัง

A large part of concentration is paying attention to what someone else has to say. This heart phrase applies to certain formal relationships where paying attention is expected. You listen with your heart (*tâng jai fang*). For example, you listen and have a "paying attention heart" to the words of a doctor, a professor or a respected monk. Part of the paying attention is respect for their position, and part is for the benefit of the wisdom or advice such a person is giving. It can also be used in an informal setting among friends or colleague.

Distraction

Floating Heart
jai lOOy (adj.) ใจลอย

This heart phrase is used to describe absent-minded conduct or a person who is absent-minded. An example is the person who has a chronic inability to concentrate. This is a personality trait and such a person has no attention span beyond a few minutes.The story in the *jai lOOy* person's mind shifts randomly, and he or she does not connect one event with another. This is not someone you hire to operate heavy machinery. Nor is it someone you want behind the wheel of your taxis from Don Muang Airport. *Jai lOOy* is the expression used by an observer of such an unfocused person.

Someone who suffers from attention deficit is *jai lOOy*. It would be rare for a person with this type of personality to describe herself or himself as *jai lOOy*. A second meaning is the temporary lapse of concentration that most of us experience. It is important to distinguish between someone who sometimes has a "floating heart" and someone whose heart appears to be forever floating. The sense of focus and concentration inherent in this phrase is connected to the Buddhist concepts of awareness of what is what, and of being aware of what one is doing as one acts.

Absent-minded Heart
jai mâi yùu kàp tuaa (adj.)
ใจไม่อยู่กับตัว
jai mâi yùu kàp núeaa kàp tuaa (adj.) ใจไม่อยู่กับเนื้อกับตัว

These heart phrases describe the absence of concentration. They describe someone who is doing one thing but thinking about something else. You are thinking about the stock market and sticking a pen (rather than a key) into the lock on the front door. Attending a football match you are thinking about an MTV video. Noi leaves her ATM card in an ATM machine because she is thinking about how she is going to spend the money rather than concentrating on the business at hand. She loses her card as a result. The above are all examples of someone with an "absent-minded heart."

Fear may cause one to be scatterbrained in the sense of this term. When you're going through immigration at the airport, the official may ask the purpose of your stay. You say that your purpose is tourism but the official fears you are coming on business and he takes you aside for further interrogation. You may feel *jai mâi yùu kàp núeaa kàp tuaa* during the questioning as you are fearful of the authorities.

Distracted Heart
jai wÔk wÊk (adj.) ใจวอกแวก

Something or someone has disturbed your concentration. In this distracted condition, you are unable to concentrate on the task at hand or to focus your mind to perform your duties. Your mind is somewhere else. When a beautiful young woman walks into the party and the conversations stop as everyone's attention is diverted, the guests feel *jai wÔk wÊk*. When you are working, head down over your paperwork, and your office mate strolls in and wishes to gossip about her boyfriend or the latest Channel 7 soap opera, your heart is distracted. When a student is sitting an important examination and outside the window a truck backfires, his concentration on writing the answer is destroyed in that moment. He feels *jai wÔk wÊk.*

Stirred-up Heart
kuaan jai (v.) กวนใจ

This heart phrase means that another person or thing is distracting or disturbing you from a task that you wish to perform. Usually, the cause of the disturbance is nearby. Such disturbance or distraction reduces if not eliminates your ability to concentrate and may cause you to experience a bad mood. You may wish to concentrate on reading the newspaper, watching your favorite TV program, but someone in the household—your spouse or child—wants attention and pulls down your newspaper or changes the TV channel. Or your new Jack Russell dog jumps onto your lap when you are checking your email. The spouse, child or dog *kuaan jai* you.

Aimless Heart
plÒOy jai (v.) ปล่อยใจ

"Aimless heart" is appropriate to describe someone lost in a state of reverie, or someone whose mind meanders aimlessly. These mental states involve momentary feelings which arise in two circumstances: (i) when you think there is nothing worth doing, and (ii) when doing something but it is boring or appears useless. In both instances, you feel a lack of direction or purpose. This feeling is lifted when you find a renewed sense of purpose or the boredom drifts away. Lek works in a factory where her job is to stuff baby corn into cans for ten hours a day, six days a week. She feels bored with this work. Her mind drifts from the baby-corn stuffing to a daydream about going out to see a film with her friends. Her act of daydreaming is *plÒOy jai*. Often you can spot this emotional state in someone's eyes. They appear to be very far off, lost in their personal thoughts, and you may ask what they are daydreaming about by reference to this heart phrase.

Forgetting

Erase from the Heart
lóp man pai jàak jai (v.)
ลบมันไปจากใจ

This heart phrase is the equivalent of the English expression: "Forget it." Usually the memory to be forgotten is associated with a painful or unpleasant experience. For instance, Lek believes that her boyfriend Vinai has a regular job and is well regarded by the community. She discovers that in fact he is a car thief and is on the run from the police. After she breaks up with him, when her foreign friend asks about Vinai, Lek replies in a combination of Thai and English: "I have already *lóp* Vinai *pai jàak jai*." I have already forgotten Vinai. As this example indicates, a person's name, an event or an object can be used in place of the Thai word *man* to express the notion that he, she or it has been erased, deleted from the heart.

Wash One's Heart
láang jai (v.) ล้างใจ

A person has some ill feelings, a bit of heartache, and is suffering. Somchai is suffering from the abandonment of his lover, and goes into the monkshood. The idea is to undertake actions to forget the suffering of the past. Any task that assists the person in forgetting the bad experience may *láang jai* or wash the heart of the heartache inside. Giving someone a good book to read may take their off their suffering. A trip to London or Paris may have the same effect. Changing jobs, hair styles, meeting new friends are all well-tested techniques of getting over and putting the past behind one.

Imagination

Imagination Heart
wâat phâap nai jai (v.) วาดภาพในใจ

Noi has been nominated for Best Actress of the Year at the annual Thai Oscars ceremony. On the day of the event, she is in her apartment dreaming of her moment of glory when her name is pulled out of the envelope and she is declared the winner. She imagines herself going on stage to receive the Oscar from M.C. Chatri, Thailand's renowned film director, and thinks of her acceptance speech. The essence of this heart phrase is imagining a future or past event. Imagination is not always glamorous and pleasant. As they drive, someone might imagine having a car crash. Another person might imagine what it would be like to have been born in another country and within another family. Imagination is this mental ability to wonder "what if" about the present, future and past.

Reflection in the Heart
phâap khûen nai jìt jai (a sentence)
ภาพขึ้นในจิตใจ

This sentence is normally confined to the written (as opposed to spoken) form. Someone describes their trip to Vancouver, British Columbia in such vivid terms that the listener is able to mentally picture Stanley Park and English Bay. The essence of "reflection in the heart" is the internal visualization of an experience, event, or place.

Impression

Pleasing to the Eye, Pleasing to the Heart
tÔOng jai (v.) ต้องใจ
tÔOng taa tÔOng jai (v.) ต้องตาต้องใจ

Red roses and chocolate cake may be two items that *tÔOng jai* or *tÔOng taa tÔOng jai*; they please your eye and please your heart. This expression can also be translated as "fondness heart." What causes the heart to feel fondness for an object arises as the eye catches a pleasing object of desire. The initial excitement of finding this beautiful object is the essence of the phrase. One may be shopping and come across the perfectly pleasing dress, shirt or necktie.

Tempted Heart
wăm jai (adj.) หว่ำใจ

This is an ancient *jai* phrase. It is no longer commonly used. A middle-aged man who sees a young woman in a short skirt and skimpy tank-top, might use this expression as his disapproval of the woman's sexually provocative dress. On the other hand, it can also mean that the man who sees the provocative dress on the young woman responds with a feeling of thrill or sexual interest. This example of linguistic ambiguity leaves open the true intention of the person using this phrase. Is he offended? Or is he aroused? You would have to know something about the personality and attitude of the person to know the intention behind the use of this *jai* phrase.

Buried in the Heart
făng jai (v.) ฝังใจ
făng yùu nai jai (v.) ฝังอยู่ในใจ

When you were a child you may have heard many stories and witnessed many incidents in the company of your family. You store them away as memories, good or bad. The stories or incidents become buried in your heart and later in your life something or someone causes you to remember what was laid down when you were a child. Or the memory might be associated with your romance at school. Later in life, memories of the incidents which occurred during your early relationship experiences may be triggered by things said and done by your current spouse or lover. Your first kiss, your first date, or the first time you traveled abroad. The memory of the past is *făng jai* or *făng yùu nai jai*—"buried in the heart."

Staying in the Heart
trueng jai (v.) ตรึงใจ
tìt trueng jai (v.) ติดตรึงใจ
trueng taa trueng jai (v.) ตรึงตาตรึงใจ
tìt taa trueng jai (v.) ติดตาตรึงใจ

These heart phrases are confined mainly to the written word, although you may hear *trueng jai* and *tit taa trueng jai* used in normal conversation. These four phrases have a similar meaning to *făng jai*. The main difference is that these phrases only describe a memory that is pleasant and happy. You go on a holiday to Phuket and experience the good beaches, seafood, and comfortable hotel accommodation. Later you would recall these experiences with a sense of wellness or happiness. Special vacations like a honeymoon would be the best candidate of happiness that will stay in the heart.

Imprint in the Heart
rOOy phim jai (n.) รอยพิมพ์ใจ

ROOy phim jai, literally "printed in the heart," is another example of something or someone who has caused a person to keep a good memory of an event, thing or person. A person may impress with her wisdom, intellect or talent. A beautiful painting may impress with its aesthetic quality. The lingering memory of a wonderful cool evening on Koh Samet with a loved one is *rOOy phim jai* as well. The impression may be for bad or good. Usually, however, *rOOy phim jai* is used in connection with a good impression. The emotional imprint of the impression stays locked in the heart.

Intuition

Clairvoyant Heart
taa jai (n.) ตาใจ

A person who can read the past or see into the future is said to have *taa jai*, a "clairvoyant heart," The usual candidate is a fortune-teller or a monk. When going to a fortune-teller, one may ask friends whether the person reading the fortune has *taa jai*. That is, does the fortune-teller have true insight into that person's life?

Intuitive Heart
lá wái nai thăan thîi khâw jai (v.)
ละไว้ในฐานที่เข้าใจ

If you feel that another person understands you or what you are saying without having to express yourself in full, then you can leave the matter as understood. There is no need to discuss or explain the matter any further. This act of leaving it as understood is called *lá wái nai thăan thîi khâw jai* in Thai. The essence of this heart phrase is the reliance upon intuition as a firm and reliable guide to understanding another and acting upon that understanding. Being around someone with an "intuitive heart" ensures that non-verbal methods of communication will succeed in getting across the essential information concerning moods, wishes, dreams, and desires. It often applies in the context where it isn't necessary to fully explain what you mean, on the basis that you assume that the other person understands by way of implication. This works best between people who are friends, family or colleagues and for whom filling in the blanks is much easier. For others outside of the loop, short of mind-reading, it can be frustrating to guess at unstated meanings.

Premonition Heart
săng hŎOn jai (v.) สังหรณ์ใจ

When someone has a sixth sense or an intuitive feeling about someone or something then they *săng hŎOn jai* and the subject matter is usually dark or bad. You go into a business meeting with a premonition that the deal will fall through, or you are driving home and have a feeling your spouse is in a bad mood or your soi has flooded with the afternoon rains. It matters less whether these things happened or not, it is the feeling about what will or will not happen in the future that makes you *săng hŎOn jai*. This is a good quality in a private eye or other investigator but not in ordinary people, as the preoccupation is on the negative, bad, evil side of life.

Knowledge

Full Knowledge Heart

rúu yùu tem jai (v.) รู้อยู่เต็มใจ

The essence of this heart phrase is to have full knowledge of something but to act contrary to such knowledge, usually to the detriment of oneself or another's. The person knows that a small child cannot swim but allows the child to go along to the swimming pool without a lifeguard present. The child nearly drowns. The knowledge at the point of making the decision to permit the child to swim alone is *rúu yùu tem jai*. The company executive knows that Thursday is a national holiday in Thailand and that a foreign client is coming to Bangkok with the expressed desire to meet and discuss financing with a banker, but the executive says nothing to warn the client of the bank closing for the holiday. When the client arrives and finds that no business can be transacted, he becomes angry. The company executive is *rúu yùu tem jai* about the holiday, the closure of the bank and the client's expectations in Bangkok, but failed to inform the client accordingly.

Know in One's Own Heart

rúu yùu kÈE jai (v.) รู้อยู่แก่ใจ

rúu kÈE jai (v.) รู้แก่ใจ

Closely related to *rúu yùu tem jai* are these two *jai* phrases. When someone has done a good deed, they know in their heart that they have added some goodness to the world. They comprehend the consequences of their words and actions on others. Thus, if they do something bad or wrong, despite having knowledge that their action would cause another to suffer harm, then they *rúu yùu kÈE jai*. This is their conscience talking through their heart, monitoring the quality and kind of behavior they do or don't exhibit.

Well-etched in the Heart

khûen jai (v., adv.) ขึ้นใจ

When you learn a certain kind of information about the world by heart, then the recollection becomes etched into your heart or is *khûen jai*. For instance, a person who has learned a poem, a Thai phrase, or another's face, has the poem, the phrase or the image of the face etched in his or her heart. Acquiring new information and the retention of this knowledge makes the person *khûen jai*. This phrase can be used as a verb or as an adverb. You may ask someone to help you to pay your rent. Even though you've seen this person help others, he refuses to help you. You will remember his refusal to help very well (*khûen jai*) and will not ask for his help again.

Satisfaction

As you enter that state of feeling satisfied, you have a number of heart phrases to express your sense of satisfaction. Each phrase is a variation on the theme that one has accomplished or is presented with something that is the cause of the satisfaction. There are shades and nuances in this category, from simple satisfaction and pleasure to feelings of gratification and satiation. In Thailand there is such a thing as too much satisfaction.

Satisfied Heart

phOO jai (v., adj.) พอใจ
yin jai (v., adj.) ยินใจ
phueng jai (adj.) พึงใจ
phueng phOO jai (adj.) พึงพอใจ

Perhaps the best known and most commonly used heart phrase for satisfaction is "satisfied heart" (*phOO jai*). When you are satisfied with your latest haircut, new cell phone, an important meeting, or in your job or relationship, you will have a "satisfied heart." If your spouse says he or she is *phOO jai*, that's a very good thing. It means that he or she is satisfied. But if your spouse claims to be *mâi phOO jai*, then he or she is dissatisfied with an act, the failure to act, or with life itself. *Yin jai* is an ancient Thai expression that corresponds to *phOO jai*. If you use this with a native Thai, they will think you are a time traveler from the deep past.

Like many heart phrases, there are degrees of intensity and preferred usage. Some examples of *phueng jai* are in circumstances when a person witnesses or experiences an object of beauty such as a work of art, the sea at sunset, smelling flowers, or listening to music; and *phueng phOO jai* applies when these feelings of satisfaction are the result of close proximity to the object of beauty. It is also used to express a feeling of fondness or affection for another. Lastly, when a person completes a project with excellence, the boss will feel *phueng phOO jai*.

Gratified Heart

thǔeng jai (adj.) ถึงใจ

thǔeng òk thǔeng jai (adj.) ถึงอกถึงใจ

These two heart phrases are appropriate for expressing your feeling that someone or something has satisfied you fully. You well up with a sense of glee. It may be that a personal goal has been wonderfully achieved and that, having crossed the finish line, you feel gratified. It may come from watching a football match in which your home team has performed exceptionally well. These heart phrases are also considered to be slang. You go up in a helicopter for your first skydiving experience, then jump out of it. The parachute opens and you land safely on the ground. As you pick yourself up, you feel *thǔeng òk thǔeng jai*. The expression comes from the quality of experience that makes you feel extremely satisfied with the outcome. In action films, when the bad guy is defeated by the hero after a long battle, the audience feels *thǔeng jai*.

Satiated Heart

sǎa jai (adj.) สาใจ

sǎa kÈE jai (adj.) สาแก่ใจ

What is pleasing to one person may not necessarily be a good result for another. For example, someone who exacts revenge by taking another life may feel *săa jai* or *săa kÈE jai*. In this case, the person feeling *săa jai*, or having a "satiated heart," has been the active agent in bringing about this feeling of satisfaction. On a more joyful note, members of an audience at a concert may experience a communal joyfulness while listening to the music. Between the two expressions, you are more likely to hear the second phrase *săa kÈE jai* in conversation as *săa jai* is a rather old expression and has fallen out of use. *Săa kÈE jai* is often used to express the feeling when knowing or witnessing someone getting their just deserts. *Săa jai* is not the same as *sà jai*, "satisfy wild side heart," which has another meaning connected with justice.

Fully Satiated Heart

jù jai (adj.) จุใจ
chàm jai (adj.) ฉ่ำใจ
năm jai (adj.) หนำใจ

You have taken as much emotionally as you can. In other words, you have reached the emotional upper limit, whether it is with an activity or interpersonal relationship, for example, going to a concert of your favorite singer, playing your favorite video game, going out to a favorite bar with friends. You have had an excessive quantity of something that you like. It can also be used in a judgmental way—in the context of a scolding. You got in a quarrel with with your boss. He unleashed a verbal assault against you (unreasonably, of course). You let him shout at you until he ran out of his verbal ammunitions and after lunch you quit your job. You let him scold you to his heart's content; in other words, you let him *dàa jon jù jai* (scold until the heart is full). Another example is when Lek hasn't eaten for many days to lose weight for a beauty contest; after the contest is over and she lost, she rushes off to the buffet and loads up on cakes and ice cream and everything she has been craving for. Lek is said to be *kin jon jù jai* (eat until the heart is full). You can play or do other activities until your heart is full or fully satiated. The other two phrases are used in the same way.

Surprised, Amazed & Alarmed

As a general rule, surprising another is not welcomed in Thai culture. In public, where the mask and costume are worn, and the interactions carefully scripted for the social situation, a surprise can cause confusion and discontent. By its very nature, a surprise is outside of the script, beyond what is expected. Amongst friends a surprise is one thing, but in a formal setting of strangers, any act that surprises another should be avoided.

Astonished Heart

prà làat jai (adj.) ประหลาดใจ

You feel *prà làat jai* when someone acts out of character, or when you confront an unexpected situation. It corresponds to feelings associated with suspicion or doubt in the context that what you expected is not what you received. It is a versatile heart phrase that can be employed in many situations. Gop is putting on weight and her friends ask whether she is pregnant. Later a doctor confirms that she is really pregnant. This being totally unexpected news because she is on the pill, Lek feels *prà làat jai*. The *jai* phrase can also be used to express feelings of astonishment evoked by everything from the weather to the environment. The weather forcast said it was going to be sunny today, but the rain started pouring down around mid-day. You feel *prà làat jai*. Looking at Thai children swimming in a dirty, polluted khlong a tourist has the feeling of *prà làat jai*.

Surprised Heart

plÈEk jai (adj.) แปลกใจ

The meaning is similar to *prà làat jai*. *PlÈEk jai* is slightly less formal; and though used in both spoken and written Thai, it is most often an oral expression. There is a sense of strangeness or weirdness in an event or a person's action that brings on the condition of the "surprised heart." The key component is the element of the unexpected or the unfamiliar. You see your best friend from fourth grade, someone you haven't seen in thirty years, walking down Sukhumvit Road with your ex-spouse. The sight of the two together would make you feel *plÈEk jai* (among other things).

Amazed Heart

àt sà jan jai (adj.) อัศจรรย์ใจ

There is an element of surprise leading to this state of amazement, which is akin to excitement. When people go to a freak show and see a two-headed snake or an eight-foot woman with a beard, they are amazed and feel *àt sà jan jai*. The essence of this phrase is appropriate for highly unusual situations, events or persons. When a bomb goes off in a subway, people feel *àt sà jan jai*. When a four-year-old child sits down to the piano and plays Mozart perfectly, this causes a sense of wonderment. The discovery of a new planet might also cause this feeling for some. The phenomenon that causes the "amazed heart" is usually other-worldly, weird, outside of the normal realm of experience and expectation.

Alarmed Heart

(tùuen) trà nòk tòk jai (v.) (ตื่น) ตระหนกตกใจ

As the world collapses around you, the emotional spasm is one of alarm. In this heart wake-up call, you are submerged in difficult times and feel panic. There is an upheaval which leaves you feeling helpless and not knowing which way to turn. You pick up the newspaper and read that the stock market has fallen 25 per cent overnight, and you are *tùuen trà nòk tòk jai*. You go to the office and discover that your building has burned down, or you go to your tailor and learn he has increased his prices by 100 per cent. In each case, the person who is *tùuen trà nòk tòk jai* is responding with alarm to a situation.

Startled Heart

tòk jai (v.) ตกใจ
tòk kà jai (v.) ตกกะใจ
tòk òk tòk jai (v.) ตกอกตกใจ
tòk núeaa tòk jai (v.) ตกเนื้อตกใจ

There is a range of emotions that can be described as "startled heart." The first two expressions are appropriate for the mild surprises of daily living, and the last two expressions apply when the fright is more severe and immediate. A heart might be said to fall (*tòk*) when you quietly sneak into the shower and frighten your lover—his or her heart falls (*tòk jai*). This is a feeling of your pulse beating in your throat, the terrifying sense of being in sudden danger. Surprise and shock combined. The act of making someone scared out of their wits is *tham hâi tòk jai*.

Tòk kà jai is slang—a rather feminine expression. It is mainly used by women and children. When Lek goes up the staircase late at night, her boyfriend with a bad sense of humor makes ghostlike sounds and Lek is startled and shouts out, *"Tòk kà jai mòt looey,"* I am totally frightened. In this context it is an expression of fright. A car may backfire and the surprising noise startles you. Someone at the next table drops a plate and it smashes on the floor; this would cause some to feel *tòk jai* or *tòk òk tòk jai*. *Tòk núeaa tòk jai* is an old-fashioned expression.

Exclamation Mark Heart

khrûeaang măay tòk jai (n.)
เครื่องหมายตกใจ

Khrûeaang măay tòk jai means the exclamation point used in writing. It is used to signify an exclamatory sentence—a kind of written sign posted to announce the writer intended an effect such as surprise.

Lost and Overturned Heart

jai hăay jai khwâm (v.) ใจหายใจคว่ำ

This is another example of a nasty surprise or turn of events lurking out there. Suddenly, you turn a corner and find yourself in a burning hotel with the fire doors locked, in the middle of a street riot, or in a major road accident. The feeling is one of being stunned. *Jai hăay jai khwâm* is akin to a significant jolt—an emotional shock rolls over the person experiencing it. The literal translation is "heart lost, heart overturned." This sense of loss and overturning of the heart arises from a near-miss with disaster, violence, or the trauma resulting from a brush-with-death experience. In the Phuket area, each time there is a warning of an earthquake, the residents feel *jai hăay jai khwâm* upon hearing this news as they fear a tsunami may cause massive flooding and loss of life.

Panic Heart
jai túm túm tÒOm tÒOm (v.)
ใจตุ๊มๆต่อมๆ

This heart phrase anticipates an emotional state arising out of a sense of danger or uncertainty. You have run a red light and a policeman pulls you over. As the policeman approaches your car to issue a ticket, you may feel a sense of panic—your heart races, beating uncontrollably (*jai túm túm tÒOm tÒOm*). Or you are alone in your house reading and hear the sound of glass breaking in an empty bedroom. It's likely your heart will be racing in your chest, and you experience the physical sensation associated with terror or fear. When it is dark and stormy, and you must walk alone down an unlit village path, you fear the presence of ghosts, and this sense of fear of encountering a ghost causes you to feel *jai túm túm tÒOm tÒOm*. The unrest in the southern part of Thailand also creates this feeling in teachers, policemen and civil servants who are uncertain as to their fate in coming and going to work.

Total Panic Heart
jìt jai mâi yùu kàp núeaa kàp tuaa (adj.) จิตใจไม่อยู่กับเนื้อกับตัว

When you have an "alarmed heart" you can control your feeling after the surprise happens. But with "total panic heart" you lose control over your emotions. Your fears or emotional background often don't prepare you for certain unexpected happenings. When Lek tells you that last night she was visited by a ghost, her face is still white with fear, and she's trembling. At the time of "seeing" this ghost she goes into a state of complete panic: she might scream, cry, shout or faint—all done without any ability to control her reaction to the "sighting." John has lived in a mountain sanctuary for five years practicing mediation. When he comes down the mountain, walks along Sukhumvit Road and sees a number of very beautiful women, John breaks into a sweat, can't speak and starts to tremble. Fortunately, he starts after a few minutes to remember a good mantra and finally controls himself so that he's *sà ngòp jai* (his heart is pacified) and regains his self-composure.

Thinking

Think Inside One's Heart
núek yùu nai jai (v.) นึกอยู่ในใจ

When you think to yourself (without voicing these thoughts to others) or have an expectation of an act or course of conduct, then you *núek yùu nai jai*. Some people have ongoing internal dialogs with themselves. *Should I take the train to Chiang Mai on Saturday? I would like a salary increase; now, if only I could find a way to ask— That is a beautiful, attractive person sitting at the next table, should I go over and start a conversation?* These are examples of what goes on when you "think inside your heart" or *núek yùu nai jai*. Your lover may feel *núek yùu nai jai* that you will have brought him or her a gift when you return from abroad

Think in the Heart
khít nai jai (v.) คิดในใจ

This is a more generic phrase to describe your internal thought process. We all experience thinking about what to buy on the way to the supermarket or shopping mall.

As you ride the BTS and *khít nai jai* about the peanut butter, pasta sauce and milk, your mind is actively engaged in adding to the shopping list. As you prepare for an important business meeting, you think over the options you have and the goals you wish to accomplish and this, too, is *khít nai jai*.

High Math Skill Heart
lÊEk khà nít khít nai jai (n.)
เลขคณิตคิดในใจ

This *jai* phrase describes a type of math skill. The person who has this skill needs no calculator or computer; all of the calculations take place in the mind. If you see a game show and the contestant is asked a complicated math question and can work out the answer in his or her head, then the person has a skill for *lÊEk khà nít khít nai jai*. This skill or talent of math ability is a good quality in a bank teller, accountant, stockbroker and poker player. The student who can answer the math quiz with a perfect score has demonstrated *lÊEk khà nít khít nai jai*. Albert Einstein's work showed that he possessed this kind of heart.

Truth

Truth in the Heart
khwaam jing jai (n.) ความจริงใจ

If you desire others to believe that you are sincere, you are asking them to believe that you possess *khwaam jing jai*. One's lover, spouse, friends and colleagues wish to believe that one is sincere in one's words and actions. This is a common heart phrase, which indicates the importance that Thais place on sincerity. As with *waang jai*, politicians frequently use this phrase in order to gain the support of voters for their views and policies. It is often an excuse to not answer questions about the precise details of those policies; instead of explaining their actions or policies, they may say, "There is no need for details. Please trust the truth in my heart."

Understanding

When you wish to communicate ideas about learning, comprehension, or failure to comprehend, these heart phrases are useful.

Understand in the Heart

khâw jai (v.) เข้าใจ
khâw jăi (v.) เข้าใจ๋

A frequently heard phrase, *khâw jai*, translates as to understand what someone else has said or meant by what they have said. This literally means that what the other person has said has "entered" your heart and that you have the understanding in the heart. This is not limited to understanding the expression of emotions but any source of information that has been communicated, from understanding a technical manual on operating a computer to whether a person has properly filled out a bank form. This is a state of understanding what has been said, demonstrated or written. If you want to ask someone if they understand what you have said, you can ask, "*Khâw jai mái kráp?*" (for a male speaker) or "*Khâw jai mái khá?*" (for a female speaker).

The second phrase *khâw jăi* is slang. There is important tonal difference here. When pronounced with a middle tone (*khâw jai*), the verb is innocuous and is used in both statements and questions. When pronounced with a rising tone, it is slang and is always a question. For example, two young gangsters have a discussion: "I told my mother that I am going to the wat, but don't tell her that we are going to rob a gold shop. You have to tell my mother that we are going to the wat, *khâw jăi*?"

Understand with Sympathetic Heart

khâw òk khâw jai (v.) เข้าอกเข้าใจ

The phrase means to understand the emotional state of another person. One of the two gangsters in the above example was scolded by his mother after she found out that he went to rob a gold shop rather than going to the temple; he calls his friend and tells him that he's been scolded, and his friend replies that he understands: *khâw òk khâw jai*. Using this phrase allows you to show your understanding and feelings of sympathy in the face of another person's suffering or unhappiness.

The Heart of the Matter
jai khwaam (n.) ใจความ
khÔO yài jai khwaam (n.)
ข้อใหญ่ใจความ

These phrases can be used to explore the meaning, substance or gist of the matter at hand, for instance, a heart phrase. The gist of *săng hŎOn jai*, "premonition heart," is the intuitive feeling that someone has about an event or person or thing. When in doubt about the meaning of a heart phrase, you ask a native Thai speaker for the *jai khwaam* of the phrase in question: what is the gist, the essence of the phrase? *KhÔO yài jai khwaam* means the crux of the matter. The village chief explains a new law to the villagers. There are many complicated details and the villagers are confused. So one of the villagers asks the chief to just give them the *khÔO yài jai khwaam* of the new law.

Clear in the Heart
jÊEng jai (adv., adj.) แจ้งใจ

This phrase describes a person's ability to see a situation with clarity and explain a solution to a problem. A computer expert has the expertise to clearly see the problem causing the computer to hang. Thais also like this quality in those who read palms or their tarot cards in order to predict their future. The *mŎO duu* (fortune-teller) spreads out the cards on the floor and studies them, puts on a performance that suggests that he or she is *JÊEng jai* about the customer's future and gives a prediction based on this quality of seeing. Of course it is a guess or speculation but the illusion is one of comprehension. To understand something clearly within its context is the essence of the phrase. There may be a difficult math problem or a legal document that leaves you feeling that you don't understand the principles involved. A good math teacher, in the case of the math problem, or a good lawyer, in the case of the legal document, who can explain simply and accurately what is involved, makes you feel *JÊEng jai*.

Rehearse Understanding of Each Other's Heart
sák sÓOm khwaam khâw jai (v.)
ซักซ้อมความเข้าใจ

This heart expression is employed in a process to double-check that two or more people share the same understanding of something. It might be a report, an event, an accident, an appointment, or an order given by a superior. The purpose of the process is to make certain that each person clearly understands the situation. The literal translation of the phrase is to "rehearse" with one another that everyone has the same understanding: *sák sÓOm khwaam khâw jai.* For example, when a big customer comes to visit the company, the employer briefs the employees on how they should answer questions from the customer so that everyone working for the company is able to effectively communicate the same policies and message.

Misunderstand the Heart
khâw jai phìt (v.) เข้าใจผิด

If you have misunderstood what has been communicated, and acted upon that misunderstanding, then once the mistake comes to light and you are asked why you acted or behaved in that fashion, it is appropriate to say you have *khâw jai phìt*. The literal translation would be that the information has gone into the heart the wrong way. Either you cannot make sense of it, or you acted on the misunderstanding. For example, if you make an appointment for a meeting with your friend at ten in the morning and your friend believes the appointment was intended for ten at night, your friend would have misunderstood the time of the meeting, arriving twelve hours late. After the error has been discovered about the meeting time, an appropriate response to the mix-up from your friend would be *khâw jai phìt*.

Remember by Heart
jam khûen jai (v.) จำขึ้นใจ

Jam khûen jai means to learn by heart a person, thing or event. You remember by heart a friend's birthday, lunch appointments, telephone number, or street address. This is the essence of *jam khûen jai*. A witness at a crime scene may remember the face of the criminal. Later, at the police line-up, the witness can say that he or she can *jam khûen jai* one of the suspects. If a dog bites a person, that person will likely remember that dog and avoid it thereafter. You also remember when someone lent you a helping hand at a moment of crisis, and those who turned away when you needed help. You may also remember by heart, *jam khûen jai*, a math formula, the names of all the capital cities in Europe or a poem by Rudyard Kipling.

Silent Reading Heart
àan nai jai (v.) อ่านในใจ

This heart phrase describes the act of reading silently to yourself. You are reading a book or report, concentrating on its contents and wishing to take the substance of the printed word directly into your heart. "Silent reading heart" is often used in the context of study and examination. The phrase is mostly employed by students attending schools and universities, or lip readers as they mouth every word, for example, when poring over a restaurant menu.

Glutton Heart

taam jai pàak lam bàak tÓOng (v.)

ตามใจปากลำบากท้อง

10
self-control

Although this chapter on self-control is relatively short, feelings of restraint are expressed in some of the most important heart phrases in the Thai language. In Thai culture considerable value is attached to a person's ability to exercise restraint or control over his or her feelings of rage, anger or upset.

The ideal, in the Thai tradition, is not to be drawn into an emotional reaction when provoked. There is an attempt to avoid confrontations and heated exchanges. Of course this is an ideal, and anyone pushed hard and long enough will react with anger. The fighting words and words of rejection and criticism are examples of the kind of provocation one seeks to overcome with heart phrases contained in this chapter. There is a competition for the heart. In one orbit around the heart are the heart warfare phrases on the attack; and in another orbit are the deep-seated cultural values of using restraint to deflect the attack. This contradiction is not always easy to resolve. Indeed, it might be thought that the need for resolution is a Western rather than a Thai notion. The heart expressions are the front line of emotional defense against such attacks, insults or provocation.

At the same time, self-control as embodied in these heart phrases is a broader concept than simply an attempt to avoid anger. Also valued are ideals of calmness and concentration. Thai culture values a person with a heart capable not only of suppressing rash action based on random impulses, but also of overcoming constant distractions of the thousand daily things that compete for one's attention.

Calm & Composure

Cool Heart

jai yen (adj.) ใจเย็น

If you want to truly understand what Thais value in a person, *jai yen* is a good place to start. The culture places considerable importance on a person who is cool-headed and avoids confrontation. Even in the face of provocation, the man or woman who can maintain a smile has the respect and admiration of all. A second usage of *jai yen* is to remind someone who has lost their cool (it may be yourself) to calm down and to restore a sense of inner peace and harmony.

In one respect *jai yen* is the Thai equivalent of a stiff upper lip in the face of adversity or provocation. You may have suffered an emotional setback or disruption but you are able to feel (or give the appearance of feeling) emotionally collected and cool in the face of the problem. John is stuck in a traffic jam for hours or has a flat tire on the expressway while driving at 100 kilometers per hour. The key is the ability to remain in control. John does not panic when the car tire blows out. Being stuck at Asoke and Sukhumvit intersection for forty minutes does not cause him to explode. If John does not show anger or swear, or express any other outward emotion, but deals with these incidents of distress with patience and composure, then it can be said that he is *jai yen*.

If you frequently hear others asking you to be *jai yen* it is a signal that your actions are impatient or hot-blooded or you have trouble controlling your temper. None of these personal attributes will serve you well in personal or business relationships in Thailand.

Calm One's Heart

sà ngòp jai (v.) สงบใจ
sà ngòp òk sà ngòp jai (v.) สงบอกสงบใจ

When you feel an unpleasant emotional upset, then you will try to *sà ngòp jai* or calm yourself. The concept behind "calm one's heart" is to reach a state in which you can try to control how you feel in the midst of an emotional thunderstorm. A friend may advise another, who is experiencing emotional turmoil, to *sà ngòp jai*. It is the ability to control the hurtful or negative emotions like anger and replace them with a sense of calmness. Assuming that you have succeeded in calming yourself at the moment of crisis you will feel *sà ngòp jai*. *Sà ngòp òk sà ngòp jai* also applies to a situation where the unpleasant emotion causes considerable upset. Both phrases can be appropriately used in the circumstances of the death of a friend, parent or spouse. Or the loss of a job, after many years, because the business is leaving Thailand. In such situations friends and family would recommend the person suffering the upset to *sà ngòp òk sà ngòp jai*.

Pacify One's Heart
rá ngáp jai (v.) ระงับใจ

This heart phrase is a variation of *sà ngòp jai*. When you blow your top and the anger flows like lava, someone else may tell you to *rá ngáp jai*. That is, calm down, take a deep breath, and don't let the anger carry you away into doing some act you may later regret. You feel angry with your child who won't stop crying in the department store and you are about to strike the child, then you tell yourself to *rá ngáp jai*. You have overcome your impulse driven by anger and can calmly talk to your child in a rational, non-threatening manner.

Concentrate One's Heart
săm ruaam jai (v.) สำรวมใจ

The idea of "concentrate one's heart" comes from the Buddhist notion of meditation. In a Buddhist country like Thailand, the idea of meditation translates in this heart phrase as concentration, focus and calmness. You are centered, not distracted or off balance. You are in the groove of the moment as your heart concentrates. During the time you are focused and concentrated you are in the act of *săm ruaam jai*.

Concentrate One's Body, Speech and Heart
săm ruaam kaay waa jaa jai (v.)
สำรวมกาย วาจา ใจ

This heart phrase emphasizes the concentration on the good deed or on speaking the appropriate or kind word. To *săm ruaam kaay waa jaa jai* is to be in the state of awareness that what is being done, said or thought is right and appropriate for the circumstances. For example, in Thai society, women are expected to dress, act and speak appropriately (this means in a highly conservative, modest fashion). Children are taught to show deference to elders. The essence of instilling these values in Thai women is in part associated with the *jai* phrase *săm ruaam kaay waa jaa jai*; mothers and teachers and monks teach this as an important value for Thai women and especially for children. Thais value and admire as their role models public figures who use appropriate speech and behavior without resorting to excessive emotions or overly dramatic gestures to color their words.

Patience

Brief Moment of the Heart
ùet jai (n.) อึดใจ

The control of the heart is required for a brief time in the case of *ùet jai*. One is requested, or requests another, to hold or wait for a short period of time. The reason may be that someone is not available. Or it may be that waiting is desirable. Normally, the phrase is used among family and friends and not between strangers. The sister may be using the telephone and the brother needs to make a phone call. The sister, upon hearing the request, asks her brother to wait a brief moment (*ùet jai*). In another situation, the phrase may be used to tell someone to muster up the courage to endure a moment of pain. A child who is frightened when given an injection may be gently assured by his mother and the attending nurse that the pain will last only a moment. It can also be used in the context of physical labor when a person stops for an instant before pushing forward with a concentrated effort. Such a person may be a weightlifter who must bench press an amount beyond what she has lifted before.

Another Brief Moment of the Heart

ìik ùet jai (n.) อีกอึดใจ

A woman is in labor at hospital and the doctor uses the phrase *ìik ùet jai*, to reassure her that the child is on the way. Or the brother who wants to use the phone is told by his sister who is occupying it to wait another brief moment (*ìik ùet jai*).

Reassure Another's Heart

chûaa ùet jai (adj.) ชั่วอึดใจ
bàt dĭiaw jai (adj.) บัดเดี๋ยวใจ

The literal translation of *chûaa ùet jai* is the amount of time a person can hold his or her breath in anticipation of something happening. It is closely related to both waiting and the amount of time passing before an event takes place. "Reassure another's heart" is used in circumstances where a person is anxious about reaching a destination or the outcome of an event. After many hours on the road, Lek is driving to Chiang Mai, and her father calls and asks where she is. Lek says she is in Lampang, *chûaa ùet jai* (soon) she will arrive in Chiang Mai. Daeng is stuck in Bangkok traffic and her boss, Somchai, calls her and asks if she is going to be on time for an important meeting. Daeng says to him, "*Chûaa ùet jai* Khun Somchai, I will be on time." *Bàt dĭiaw jai* is rarely used outside of a period drama.

Peace

Calm Heart

jìt jai sà ngòp (adj.) จิตใจสงบ

This is a quality of calmness and tranquility resulting in peace of mind. In this state you aren't disturbed by the activities of others, nor distracted by negative thoughts. Meditation is often used to achieve this state of mind. When you know someone well enough under circumstances of stress or disturbance, you are able to judge whether they wilt emotionally and are overwhelmed by the pressure or stress. Alternatively, you have achieved an inner peace that allows you to rise above this disturbance and, with a clear, unafraid mind, to take a course of action based on reason. When your life is one of performing good deeds, when you are not caught up in the cycle of material acquisition and success, you are more likely to have a peaceful, calm heart: *jìt jai sà ngòp*.

The Light of the Heart in the Dark World
jai sà wàang klaang lôok mûuet
(adj.) ใจสว่างกลางโลกมืด

This heart phrase has several different meanings. The first is for the blind. Those who are born or later become blind live in the world with a disadvantage. But when others give them friendship, love and compassion, the blind will have feelings of light entering the world of their heart and eliminating the darkness. The actions of others may bring a warm light into their otherwise dark world. The second meaning is connected with Buddhism and concentration practice. If you meditate on a regular basis, then you may experience feelings beyond emotion, a state of non-being, which releases you from the darkness, pressures and demands of the world. The third meaning is connected with those who have entered a dark phase of their life, and finds a person or a book that allows them to feel a ray of hope or light; as a result the darkness inside their mind leaves their life even though the environment in which they live remains unchanged.

Restraint

Control One's Heart
khòm jai (v.) ข่มใจ
bang kháp jai (v.) บังคับใจ

Control becomes a powerful metaphor when linked with the heart. In the face of adversity you attempt to *khòm jai* and control the impulse to become angry or sorry or react in a negative, hostile fashion toward the person who has rejected, criticized or hurt you. When you are under emotional attack as a result of an insult or provocation, to try to *khòm jai* means you restrain yourself from saying something hurtful or mean-spirited.

Bang kháp jai is used in the sense of exercising restraint or self-control. When you see the latest computer screen in Pantip Plaza, you can't help but stop and have a look. If you can *bang kháp* (control) your own heart, you keep on walking, suppressing the impulse to buy the new super-cool flat screen. Or if you are about to fall in love with a married woman and you know this path will lead only to heartache, you try to *bang kháp jai* yourself and to forget about her. When you are at a party and have to drive home and the host offers to refill your wine glass, you must *bang kháp jai* yourself and pass on the refill, knowing that driving while drunk can cause an accident.

Forbid One's Heart

hâam jai (v.) ห้ามใจ

sà kòt jai (v.) สะกดใจ

sà kòt òk sà kòt jai (v.) สะกดอกสะกดใจ

These three heart phrases share the same core quality of controlling one's feelings. *Hâam jai* is similar to *bang kháp jai* as it is also used in the context of controlling your impulse to do something that would allow desire to trump over other interests. You may also "forbid" *(hâam jai)* your heart to buy a new super-cool flat screen or to fall in love with a married woman. Another example: Lek would very much love a new dress and sees that her mother has left her handbag unattended. For a moment she considers the possibility of helping herself to her mother's cash. But she controls this impulse.

The latter two phrases are used in the same sense as *khòm jai.* In heavy Bangkok motor traffic, a motorist who is stalled for fifteen minutes at an intersection because the light appears to stay red forever may initially shout and curse, but before fully losing his temper, the motorist brings the feelings of rage under control. This act of control is *sà kòt jai*. In other words, *sà kòt jai* is the anger cut-off valve in the Thai language. Just as the anger reaches boiling point, the heat is turned off, the temper cools down and calmness (or at least resignation) is restored. If you don't phone your girlfriend for many days and each day she looks at her cell phone, restraining herself from phoning you, she can be said to *sà kòt jai* by not placing the call. When you *sà kòt jai* you suppress your feelings or bring your temper under control. Your neighbor makes a careless, hurtful remark and rather than enter into an argument you may *sà kòt jai* and let it go.

Cut with One's Heart
tàt jai (v.) ตัดใจ
tàt òk tàt jai (v.) ตัดอกตัดใจ

When you *tàt jai*, you cut the impulse or the desire out of your heart. There is an object of desire that may be compelling you to go forward without thinking, as if you are on automatic pilot. When you "cut" your heart, you attempt to eliminate such non-reflective, reflex actions, and regain control and exercise self-restraint.

In the context of a great loss or emotional upheaval a person may tune out the pain and suffering of this loss or upheaval: *tàt jai*. It is a way of coping with emotional trauma. When overwhelmed by a death or loss, the person deals with the emotion by way of resignation. When two women have a heart-to-heart talk, and one is crying that her husband has a minor wife, the friend tells her to *tàt òk tàt jai*, to put it out of her mind, let him be.

Pause and Weigh One's Heart
yáp yáng châng jai (v.) ยับยั้งชั่งใจ

This is another way of controlling your impulse. You pause and weigh your words or action when you *yáp yáng châng jai*. Without *tàt jai* or *yáp yáng châng jai* your raw impulses and desires may take control over your life. By stopping to consider your words before saying them or your action before taking it, you give reason a chance to stop yourself from doing something that you may later regret.

Restrain One's Heart
hàk jai (v.) หักใจ
hàk òk hàk jai (v.) หักอกหักใจ
hàk hâam jai (v.) หักห้ามใจ

Thais often use these three *jai* phrases in the context of a love affair or a relationship. When one's lover dies in a car crash or in war, then one must *hàk òk hàk jai* to avoid the painful sense of loss, which naturally arises. In less dramatic circumstances, one may *hàk jai* to avoid the feeling that comes with the end of a relationship or with the knowledge that it must end. When a wife discovers that her husband has a minor wife, she must (under traditional social custom) restrain her heart. In modern-day Thailand the tradition of *hàk jai* is not always tolerated by the unwilling major wives.

Other examples would include when a man who has a taste for risks daydreams about buying the multimillion-baht penthouse and toys with the idea of betting his life savings on a horse race in order to come up with the purchase price. But at the end of the day, the person controls his impulse and avoids the racetrack. The act of controlling his desire is *hàk jai* or *hàk òk hàk jai*. Such a person is placing restrictions on himself. By "restraining" one's heart, one is able to set limits on the things one's wishes to do or acquire.

Forgo One's Heart
òt jai (v.) อดใจ

"Forgo one's heart" is yet another expression of restraint. The emphasis is on the ability to restrain your immediate emotional response in an attempt to act more rationally. The English translation of the expression suggests the heart is propelling us toward an emotional response which we ought to suppress. The essence is the delay of gratification. Lek's friend wants to buy a beautiful dress and Lek asks her to wait, as in one week the shop will have a "50 per cent off" sale and she can buy the dress at a much better price. Lek would advise her friend to *òt jai.* Another example is when you go to a buffet and you hear a mother say to her child to *òt jai* as he comes back with the third plate filled with cakes.

Temptation

Attracted Eye, Attracted Heart
tìt jai (v.) ติดใจ
tìt taa tìt jai (v.) ติดตาติดใจ
tìt òk tìt jai (v.) ติดอกติดใจ

These phrases apply when any of the senses are attracted to an experience, a person or an object. It could be to a grandmother's somtam (Thai papaya salad). Here the sense occupies the boundary between attraction and addiction. Vinai is a keen collector of the art of Khun Thawan Datchanee (one of Thailand's most famous painters) because he feels *tìt jai* the dramatic effects of Khun Thawan's paintings. His wife teases him that he is suffering from his attraction/addiction (*tìt jai*) to Khun Tawan's art.

There is often the desire to repeat an activity or an experience, especially one that has a strong element of excitement attached. For instance, someone may become addicted to certain sports, such as golf, swimming, roller-blading, or skiing. The sports enthusiasts achieve a thrill from one of these activities and, in the extreme case, give up all other activities in order to pursue the one that gives them the adrenalin rush they demand. *Tìt òk tìt jai* might apply to a man addicted to a beautiful woman, or a woman addicted to a handsome man. The addiction may be solely based on the appearance of the person, his or her love-making skills or personality. A friend might describe the addicted person as *tìt òk tìt jai.*

Satisfied Heart

phueng phOO jai (v.) พึงพอใจ

Many years ago this *jai* phrase was used in the context of courtship and arranged marriages. Parents would ask their sons or daughters if they felt *phueng phOO jai* to the person they had chosen for them to marry. *Phueng phOO jai* means feeling satisfied or attracted to a person or thing. When one likes something, one usually tries to acquire it.

Tempting to the Eye, Tempting to the Heart

lÔO taa lÔO jai (adj.) ล่อตาล่อใจ

The eye sees what the heart desires and you are genuinely tempted to indulge the desire. Those who love lobster, but have an allergic reaction if they eat it, will be tempted to eat a particularly delicious-looking lobster, but will stop themselve from doing so. A person passes through a shopping mall and sees the latest computer game and wants to buy it. Unfortunately, he or she does not have the money and must carry on walking, empty-handed. The lobster and the computers are *lÔO taa lÔO jai.*

Over-consumption Heart

taam jai pàak mâak nîi (proverb) ตามใจปากมากหนี้

In today's materialistic world temptations to acquire abound. This proverb serves as a warning about giving in to the temptation to consume. The greediness over food, clothes, cars, electronics and computer games, for example, is the target of the lesson found in this proverb. *Taam jai pàak mâak nîi*, "over-consumption heart," translates as: if you give in to the demands of your mouth then you will have much debt. If you are constantly thinking and dreaming about the next material acquisition, you will always be in debt and the debt will hang heavily over your life. The anti-materialistic message in the proverb may have less impact with policies that encourage everyone to get rich and buy more and more things.

Glutton Heart
taam jai pàak lam bàak tÓOng
(proverb) ตามใจปากลำบากท้อง

This is another proverb for self-restraint, which focuses on over-consumption of food. *Taam jai pàak lam bàak tÓOng*, "glutton heart," translates as: if you give in to the demands of your hungry mouth then your stomach will suffer. It is a way of telling you to moderate or control your hunger and desire for food. For example, the greedy person who eats three plates of spicy salad may have a stomachache. This applies to people who lack self-control and indulge themselves to excess; as a result of this self-indulgence they suffer from a number of unpleasant consequences. However, it is unlikely that you will see this written on a sign hanging inside a restaurant serving buffets.

Exhilarated Heart

lá laan taa lá laan jai (v.) ละลานตา ละลานใจ

lá laan jai (v.) ละลานใจ

11
choice

Each day in a hundred different contexts one is confronted with a number of choices to make. Indeed the average day is about choosing among options. A person makes judgments and decisions about what to wear, where to eat dinner, who to telephone and where to plan a holiday. It is not uncommon for someone to be unable to make up their mind. They are uncertain what to do, where to go, what to choose. In the Thai language the heart plays a large role in the expressions concerning the ability to make judgments and decisions.

In this chapter, heart phrases illustrate a range of statements about the process of making or changing a decision or plan. One has the chance to explore certain patterns involved in the following, changing, weighing, and wavering of the heart. In each heart phrase, a nuance is revealed about the way a person has made, changed, or failed to make a decision or judgment.

There is also issue of free will. It is an important value in Thai culture that everyone is "free" to make their own choices, and there are a number of heart phrases which reflect this deep-seated cultural value. However, there are times when decisions and judgements collide, and when this happens there is a vocabulary for the battle of will as well.

DISCISION-MAKING

Choices

Exhilarated Heart
lá laan taa lá laan jai (v.)
ละลานตา ละลานใจ
lá laan jai (v.) ละลานใจ

A woman who has never been in a jewelry shop is taken into an exclusive jeweler's and the shelves are filled with diamonds. The sight of all of these diamonds overwhelms her with a flood of happy emotions. The key factor when using this *jai* phrase is the "quantity" of the thing that causes an overwhelming feeling of awe and happiness. The implication is that there is lot of something over which to become excited, and you may have trouble deciding which thing to choose.

Another aspect of *lá laan taa lá laan jai* is that because of the large quantity, one cannot easily make up one's mind which item to choose. On going to a sale at Central department store where there are hundreds of beautiful watches, after looking at so many watches, one finds it difficult to select one. A man walks into a room where there are fifty beautiful women and he doesn't know which one to strike up a conversation with; of course, it is also possible for a woman to walk into a room where there are fifty handsome men and have the same experience of indecision. If you love chocolate and someone hands you a box of chocolates and invites you to take one, then you will experience an "exhilarated heart."

Look Inside One's Heart Before Deciding
thǎam jai duu kÒOn (v.) ถามใจดูก่อน

This *jai* phrase is used for the big decisions of life. It is a way of asking another or oneself to reflect seriously before deciding on a course of action that has broad implications. A mother may ask her daughter if she is sure she wants to marry her boyfriend. She asks her daughter to look into her heart before making a decision. A wife tells her husband that she wants a divorce, and the husband asks her to *thăam jai duu kÒOn* and if she really wants to divorce then he will comply with her decision. A young man receives acceptances to a good university in Thailand and a good university in Canada, and he asks his father whether he should go to university in Thailand or in Canada. His father tells him to ask his own heart (*thăam jai duu kÒOn*) before making a decision on which university he should attend.

Weigh One's Heart
châng jai (v.) ชั่งใจ

In order to reach a decision, you carefully weigh the pros and cons, considering all the possibilities of whether to go or stay at home, to walk or drive to the office, to sit or stand at a reception. Each decision requires a person to assess the relative benefits of alternative courses of action. The "weigh one's heart" process is a way of reaching an ultimate decision among competing possibilities. A woman is thinking of resigning her position at a company to become a housewife but her married friend tells her to *châng jai*, "weigh her heart," before making the final decision. When choosing lotion, cream, shampoo, shoes—the list is nearly endless—factors of brand recognition, quality and price must all be weighed before making a decision to buy. Deciding which path has more merit, more benefit or more reward is *châng jai*.

Certainty

Sure Heart
nÊE jai (v.) แน่ใจ

You may wish to make an absolute judgment or decision, or you may wish another person to make such a judgment or decision. For example, Lek discusses taking a possible trip to Chiang Mai with her friend, Somporn. Lek may want to ask Somporn if she is *nÊE jai* about traveling on the proposed dates. Used in this context, *nÊE jai* becomes a way of expressing a feeling of certainty about a judgment. The boyfriend has offered to buy his girlfriend a gold chain, and she asks him if he is certain. To say you are *nÊE jai* is to give reassurance that you are sure in your heart about your desire to follow through on your judgment or decision.

Convinced Heart
pàk jai chûeaa (v.) ปักใจเชื่อ

This is a stronger variation of *nÊE jai*. A person with a "convinced heart" will not change his or her mind since the mind is made up. Lek lost her money but doesn't know who took it. She remembers that her friend came in and she's *pàk jai chûeaa* that this friend stole the money because a day later this friend bought a new watch, and another mutual friend told Lek that this person had also stolen from her. Whether or not the friend really took the money, Lek is now *pàk jai chûeaa* that she did. In the situation when a decision is made with a "convinced heart," there is usually indirect evidence and/or prejudice involved.

Decision-Making

Decide with One's Heart
tàt sǐn jai (v.) ตัดสินใจ

Tàt sǐn jai is the verb form for deciding on a course of action. It does not necessarily imply that the decision was carefully considered. It may have been spontaneous in nature. Thus you may decide to accept a new job or ask your lover to marry you. In doing so you may have decided on the spot. Another example of *tàt sǐn jai* is when, after long hours of negotiating a contract, the manufacturer decides not to accept the agreement from his supplier. The decision can be either positive or negative. When one company decides to work with another company that, too, is *tàt sǐn jai*. The decision in this case can be made on the spur of the moment or after a careful consideration.

Agree with One's Heart

tòk long jai (v.) ตกลงใจ

kaan tòk long jai (n.) การตกลงใจ

Tòk long jai normally involves careful consideration before finally reaching a decision or entering into an agreement. The defining feature of *tòk long jai* is that before deciding you ponder the conditions and terms and then agree to what is offered. After reading a review you may decide that you are convinced to see a new film, or dine at a new restaurant, or have your hair styled in a new fashion. This verb is a common and applicable in many situations. When the time comes to make a decision, and one decides what to do, what one wants or what one values, and then agrees with one's heart and make the decision. The noun form is *kaan tòk long jai*. Two companies wish to enter into a joint venture agreement and when they finally come to a decision and sign the agreement the principals involved have *kaan tòk long jai*.

Agree to Commit Heart

plong jai (v.) ปลงใจ

tòk long plong jai (v.) ตกลงปลงใจ

Plong jai or *tòk long plong jai* means that you commit yourself to a course of action. The expression describes the feeling of resolve when one has decided, consented or agreed to perform (or not to perform) a task or favor, or undertake an obligation. The stress is on the finality of the decision-making and willingness to stick to the decision. It doesn't necessarily follow that the person making the decision has no reservations but, despite such reservations, he or she chooses to make a binding decision. A woman's acceptance of a proposal to marry will have this quality of heart. When you decide to trust another absolutely or make a total commitment to that person, you commit with your heart. In these circumstances, you retain no reservations about your decision concerning the trustworthiness of the other. In your heart, you have no doubts and are committed to your choice. The phrase can also be used outside a relationship. When you decide to buy a car, you look a various models and brands and finally commit (*tòk long plong jai*) to buying the Honda.

Fast Heart
jai rew (adj.) ใจเร็ว

The verbal spin of "fast heart" translates as someone who acts with undue haste. A person makes a quick decision in response to another person or an event, and afterwards he or she comes to the realization that the decision was flawed or wrong. Such decisions may be due to time pressures arising at that moment or the impatient or impetuous nature of the decision-maker.

Intention

Intent Heart
jong jai (v.) จงใจ
tâng jai (v.) ตั้งใจ

If you intend, while at work during the morning, to phone your friend, spouse, colleague or lover later that evening, then you feel *jong jai*. You have formed an intention to do some specific act. The person with "intent heart" may intend to go out during the lunch hour and buy a gift for a friend's birthday. The act of forming one's intention is *jong jai*. It is not the actual carrying out of the intention but the emotion that arises from having made a decision to do something later. *Tâng jai* is a synonym of *jong jai.* At the present time, be warned; both phrases are often used in a negative way, especially as an excuse for careless behavior. The person who knocks over the expensive vase that smashes on the floor says he didn't intend to break the vase (*mâi dâay tâng jai*) and that it was an accident. The reckless driver who injures several people may also resort to saying he *mâi dâay jong jai* (didn't intend) to cause the accident.

Mark with One's Heart

măay jai (v.) หมายใจ

This *jai* phrase is applied to the state of mind when one expects or aspires for something. For example, when the publisher of *Harry Potter* announce the date the latest book will be available, many Thai children *măay jai*, "mark with their heart," and remember this date to go to the bookstore. Another example is when a man sees a beautiful girl waiting at the bus stop and he wishes to have a conversation with her. He experiences a feeling of attraction and establishes a conscious intention to act upon his attention; to establish contact. There are two aspects to keep in mind. First is the act of expecting or aspiring. Second is the follow-up and acting upon the expectation or aspiration by doing something to make it come true. The emphasis is on the first. It is one thing to "mark" something with one's heart but another to act upon the intention. One may *măay jai* to establish contact with someone one is attracted to or to buy that beautiful watch but may never follow up on the intention.

Resolve

Endure Heart

khĔng jai (v.) แข็งใจ

tham jai khĔng (v.) ทำใจแข็ง

These two phrases describe strong, stoic behavior in the face of adversity. A woman falls down on the street and injures her ankle, and after picking herself up she limps that last mile home. Along the way she has to *khĔng jai* or *tham jai khĔng*. The notion of "endure heart" is that one is forcing oneself forward despite the pain being suffered. When someone has a task that they would rather not perform but are compelled through circumstances or position to carry it out, then they too must *khĔng jai*.

Prepare One's Heart

treaam jai (v.) เตรียมใจ

The essence is preparing one's heart before confronting a situation that suggests dread, fear or uncertainty. A patient on the eve of a serious operation will prepare her heart for the operation and this may bring on feelings of fear. A worker who repeatedly makes careless mistakes in his work and is told he has an appointment to meet his boss to discuss his sloppy work is likely to be fearful in preparing himself for the meeting. If you are fearful of flying, you will prepare yourself for the flight or, in other words, *treaam jai* before boarding the plane. Three hours before her wedding a woman may also prepare herself for marriage, to make her mind strong, and this preparation is *treaam jai*. A doctor may break the news to a patient's family that the patient's chance of recovery is small and they should prepare themselves for his death. The doctor would advise them to *treaam jai*.

Ready One's Heart

tham jai (v.) ทำใจ

The essence is preparation to confront reality. There are many circumstances in life when one is called upon to confront an unpleasant task or duty, for instance, visiting a terminally ill person in hospital who is hooked up to a life-support system. In such a situation, you must *tham jai*, "ready your heart," before entering the patient's room. The student who has failed his examination must *tham jai* before handing over the report card to his father. The parents may also feel *tham jai* as they accept that their child who has worked as hard as he can, simply isn't very clever. As a result they can't feel anger, only regret. The employee who has lost a customer for the company due to a careless mistake, and must explain this mistake to the boss, must *tham jai* before such a meeting.

FREE WILL

The idea of free will relies upon several important metaphors such as to follow and master one's heart to express subjection to the control of others and the exercise of personal freedom. These Thai phrases recognize the balance between independence and interdependence, between the individual and the family, and the constant play between getting one's way and giving way to the wishes of another. Associated with free will is the notion of will power, for which there are also several heart expressions.

As One's Heart Wishes

dàng jai (adv.) ดั่งใจ

yàang jai (adj.) อย่างใจ

You have the freedom of choice to do something or the ability to do what you wish. The essence of these heart phrases is the free will to act independently and freely. There is an absence of external pressure or intervention, which forces a certain decision. The decision-maker comes to the decision without coercion or influence. This is an ideal state for making a decision that one rarely finds in reality. No one is telling you what you must or have to do. This is the perfect state, whether in a job, relationship, or in life, that you have the good fortune to act according to your personal desires. As long as your wishes determine what you will or will not do, then you will continue to exist in this emotional state. *Tham mâi dâay yàang jai* means one does not have free will or free choice to do what one wishes.

Follow One's Heart

taam jai (v.) ตามใจ

This is an important heart phrase. You can *taam jai* yourself, your child, spouse, friend, employee, maid, etc. In one way, it means spoiling the other; in other variations, it means giving the other person control to decide whether to do something. It can be used as an escape valve that prevents someone else from losing face. It can provide the other person an "out." Whether the decision is about what TV show to watch or which restaurant to go to, it is common for a Thai speaker to defer to another person's choice or decision, especially when that person is considered above them in the social ladder, older than they are, or their mother or father.

Battle of Will

Force One's Own Heart
fŭuen jai (v.) ฝืนใจ

When someone asks you to do something against your will or inclination but you are in no position to refuse, you force (*fŭuen jai*) yourself to do what you are asked. The "force" comes from the inside as a result of outside pressure in this case. For instance, Lek dislikes a particular customer of the company but her boss requests that she takes this client to dinner. This is important for the company. Lek *fŭuen jai* to comply with her boss's request. Another example is someone who has lost their job in the financial sector and is forced (*fŭuen jai*) by economic circumstances to accept employment in the night-time entertainment industry. In loving relationships, you sometimes have to force yourself to comply with the wishes of your loved ones. The children force themselves to eat vegetables and the husband grudgingly tags along shopping with his wife; the children and the husband *fŭuen jai* to please the woman they love.

Force Another's Heart
khŭuen jai (v.) ขืนใจ
khòm khŭuen jai (v.) ข่มขืนใจ

The nature and emotional anguish of the force is significantly more profound in the context of *khŭuen jai*. *Khŭuen jai* is used to denote someone compelling or forcing another to act against his or her will. For example, Lek has been seeing Vinai for eighteen months and they have a serious relationship. Only Vinai is a noodle vendor and Lek's parents disapprove of her relationship with him. The parents "force" or *khŭuen jai* Lek to marry a man with a higher status. She does not love this man. Lek feels *fŭuen jai* in carrying out the obligation she feels is owed to her parents by marrying a man of their choice and abandoning the man she loves. In the extreme case, the phrase describes the act of the person who rapes or violates a woman. Such a crime leaves a deep scar on the woman's heart. *Khòm khǔuen jai* has the same meaning but is a legal term. You are more likely to hear this expression used by lawyers in courts or find it in legal documents.

Lose to One's Own Heart
phÉE jai tuaa eeng (v.) แพ้ใจตัวเอง

To "lose one's own heart" is to feel a sense of defeat that follows once one's will to continue is exhausted. For instance, a smoker feels such a lost heart, having kicked the habit only to pick it up again six months later. The heart phrase means someone has been defeated by the strength of their own desires, which they have not succeeded in overcoming. A person who is on a strict diet succumbs to the temptation; the lost weight has been regained and the cycle of diet restarts. This person has "lost" to his or her own heart (*phÉE jai tuaa eeng*). Such a person knows that a certain course of conduct must be put to an end but can't find the will power to do so. Another example: A politician works hard on a project to help fight AIDS but his project is turned down, and this causes him to "lose to his own heart" and to become passive and uninterested in his work.

Master of the Heart
pen jâw hǔaa jai (v.) เป็นเจ้าหัวใจ

This heart phrase means there is the absence of free will or choice. Someone is using control and authority to impose their wants, demands, desires onto another. Someone described as "master of the heart" (*pen jâw hǔaa jai*) takes away another's freedom of choice. The "master of the heart" person is often a bully, and has a tendency to dictate others how to live their lives—what to eat, when to sleep, what to wear, what to say. Their actions smack of thought control. If you find yourself constantly resorting to this heart phrase it is possible that you have found yourself on the wrong side of a control freak. On the other hand, there are those who willingly give up control to another. Some people are more comfortable having a master of their heart who relieves them from the responsibilities of making decisions.

Unwilling Heart

jam jai (v.) จำใจ

The feeling of "unwilling heart" comes from carrying out your responsibility even though you might wish that you were doing something else or were someplace else. The "unwillingness" comes from either inside the person or outside pressure. The obligation is fulfilled, but grudgingly. You would rather be at a party with your friends than staying late in your office finishing your mid-term report or taking your mother shopping. One day Narong's mother wakes him at 6.00 a.m. He'd rather sleep in but forces himself to get out of bed and take his mother to the morning market. The neighbor's ten barking and hungry dogs wake Daeng early on Saturday morning. In order to restore peace and quiet she takes food next door and feeds the dogs. They stop barking, she goes back to sleep. By forcing herself out of bed and feeding the dogs she has acted unwillingly in the circumstances. You can feel *jam jai* by performing obligations and tasks (which you would otherwise wish to avoid) required by your family, friends or employer. You do your duty to please the inner circle of people important in your life. It avoids one of the worse sins in Thai culture: confrontation. It is very difficult for Thai people to say they are unwilling to do something. Or, as in the last example of the barking dogs, you can *jam jai* yourself for your own personal reasons, independently of others.

Uncertainty

There are several heart phrases to illustrate that deciding upon a course of action is difficult. By taking one path, another path is abandoned. By buying one dinner, another dinner is excluded. Sometimes there are too many choices; other times there are individuals whose type of personality means they find it difficult to make up their minds.

Carried-away Heart

phlŏoe jai (v.) เผลอใจ

The essence is when you mistakenly or temporarily lose your heart to someone or something—an object of desire. You might not be conscious that it is happening at the time. Before you know it you've lost your heart, which may or may not return. A couple of examples, however, illustrate that this phrase has its own sphere of meaning. For instance, two people have been dating for two years. The boyfriend returns to England for a couple of months. His girlfriend, shortly after his departure, meets another man who is attractive and interesting, and within a week she realizes that she is attracted to this man. She starts going out with him; she *phlŏoe jai* with him. This may be a temporary change and she will ultimately return to her old boyfriend or she may decide to dump her old boyfriend.

Lek is much taller than Vinai. Because there is a cultural expectation that men should be taller than their lover or spouse, Lek dismisses the idea of a relationship with Vinai. Vinai, as it turns out, is a very nice guy with a good heart and after a while Lek no longer thinks that the height difference is that important. Lek *phlŏoe jai* as a consequence of his other good qualities. *Phlŏoe jai* might equally apply to changes in perception about weight, race, age and social status. All of these factors may initially cause one person to exclude or discount another as a possible friend, colleague, lover or spouse.

Change One's Heart

plèaan jai (v.) เปลี่ยนใจ

Plèaan jai, "change one's heart," is a common heart phrase. A person changes his or her mind about ordering rice and orders French fries, or changes his or her mind two or three times in one morning about what colors to wear. In other words, there is a wide range of possible changes involved, from trivial matters in daily life to life-altering decisions about a job, relationship, or housing. The verb *plèaan jai* is the proper heart phrase for when you change your mind. In Thai you don't change your mind; you change your heart.

Troubled Heart

yûng yâak jai (v.) ยุ่งยากใจ

In some cases, the choice between alternatives causes confusion. The person facing the choice falls into a state of emotional chaos caused by worry and anxiety. There is also a sense of nuisance from the trouble. The feeling can arise from either large or small things: your son is adjusting to a new school, your spouse has a gambling or drinking problem, or your neighbor cranks up the music full blast at midnight. The "troubled heart" may also be a pretext for a failure to act when a person wishes to retain the best of all worlds. For example, the man with three minor wives is faced with a delegation demanding that he select one as the "major" wife. After considering this demand, the husband is much troubled over which of the minor wives he ought to choose. Your daughter wants a new car and you tell her that you don't have enough money to buy one for her. Her expression of sadness makes you feel *yûng yâak jai.*

Two Minds, Two Hearts

sǑOng jìt sǑOng jai (adj.) สองจิตสองใจ

The state of "two minds, two hearts" is Hamlet-like. You can't make up your mind whether you want to holiday at the beach or in the mountains, choose Lover No. 1 or Lover No. 2, a house or an apartment, a sports car or a sedan. This phrase has its English equivalent, "two minds," but in Thai the hesitation involves not only the mind but also the heart. This is not necessarily a personality trait but reflects the indecisiveness of the moment when faced with several options or alternatives. The chronically indecisive person who simply can never choose one thing over another is definitely a candidate for inclusion in the *sǑOng jìt sǑOng jai* hall of fame.

Wavering Heart

lang lee jai (v.) ลังเลใจ

If someone spends a long time deciding what course of action to take, or which alternative to follow, the act of being uncertain, indecisive or wavering is *lang lee jai.* This is another of several heart phrases to cover the Hamlets of the world who are forever asking "to be or not to be" in many circumstances of life.

Will Power

Fighting Heart
jai sûu (adj.) ใจสู้

You are driven by pride and perfection. Your drive and energy is focused on accomplishing a goal or task. Some might call this perseverance. A Thai kick-boxer who is matched against a superior fighter is determined to use all of his efforts to win. In the home or office, you feel that you want to do something over again until it is perfect. You play a bad round of golf and want to return to the course after lunch for another round to practice your game. This sense that somehow you failed and wish to return for another chance to do something better or to do it right is *jai sûu.* A *jai sûu* person has a fighting spirit and is driven by a strong motivation to succeed. Those who have seen the film *Groundhog Day* with Bill Murray will have experienced an entire film dedicated to characters in a state of perpetual *jai sûu.*

Keen heart
jai rák (adj.) ใจรัก

When someone is thoroughly one with what they are doing—the Zen state of perfect completion and satisfaction—then they are *jai rák.* They are devoted to the task at hand or love the activity. This is a good feeling of being in the groove of life in a particular activity such as painting, collecting antiques or taking Thai language lessons. Although *jai rák* might be translated as "love heart," this would cause a misleading impression that the phrase is linked to romance and relationships when in fact it is used as an expression of keen interest in an activity.

Keenly Interested Heart
fài jai (v.) ไฝ่ใจ

While *sŏn jai*, "interested heart," is an expression of interest in someone or something, *fài jai* combines intention with the element of action. You are not only interested in golf but also play the game. At work the project assigned to you is something that you are interested in and are actively involved in, realizing the potential of the project. Others will see that you are *fài jai* when your intentions and actions coincide, whether it is a sport, hobby, education or work. If your actions are *fài jai* you demonstrate a high level of emotional involvement. No one needs to motivate you as you are self-motivated.

Single-minded Heart
jai jòt jai jÒO (adj.) ใจจดใจจ่อ
tâng jai (v.) ตั้งใจ
tâng òk tâng jai (v.) ตั้งอกตั้งใจ

You have devoted yourself to a project such as learning Thai. You take your course of study seriously and spend considerable time and effort, leaving other things in your life in the background. At this point you would be said to have *jai jòt jai jÒO*. This may be translated into a kind of self-responsibility.

When a group of Liverpool fans gather to watch a match on TV (and in particular if they have placed bets on the outcome) they will forgo all other distractions including women, drink and food until the match is finished. Their absolute devotion to the game is an example of *jai jòt jai jÒO* conduct.

Tâng jai and *tâng òk tâng jai* are verbs also applying to single-minded, concentrated efforts. When one *tâng jai* or *tâng òk tâng jai* at work or studies, one is likely to reap the rewards of one's efforts and single-minded dedication.

Heaven in the Chest, Hell in the Heart

sà wăn nai òk ná rók nai jai (proverb) สวรรค์ในอกนรกในใจ

sà wăn yùu nai òk ná rók yùu nai jai (proverb) สวรรค์อยู่ในอกนรกอยู่ในใจ

12
romance

This chapter contains *Heart Talk* phrases which most lovers who are fluent in the Thai language wish to hear from the object of their affection. Every language has its "pillow talk," and the Thai language is no exception. "Pillow talk" is found in the metaphors linked to the heart. When you use one of these heart phrases, remember that the listener is expecting you to reveal the true condition of your feelings. In most cases, the Thai listener has an experienced ear, judging each heart phrase with a view to determining if it is sincere.

The Thais are world-class experts on knowing whether one's expression of heart and the actual status of the heart match; whether the speaker is being genuine or is merely trying to please with a pleasant phrase. The quickest way to lose credibility is to use a heart phrase for an ulterior motive, that is, in an effort to gain something from the listener rather than communicate a true emotional state of being.

A number of the heart phrases appearing in this chapter have appeared in earlier chapters. For the die-hard romantic a review of such heart phrases from the point of view of romance is a useful exercise.

A good place to start is with heart phrases about commitment and then to examine the heart phrases one might find inside a full cycle of romance: boy wishes to meet girl and suffers until he finds her, then boyfriend and girlfriend have an argument and the relationship ends with the girl walking out, and the boy is left to nurse his emotional wounds. Of course the cycle is the same when girl wishes to meet boy. At each point in the cycle there is a heart phrase. Terms of endearment and other emotional states related to romance such as infatuation, intimacy and loyalty are included, so are trust and unfaithfulness.

Commitment

There are romantic relationships that last a day and others that last a lifetime. The degree of personal commitment to the relationship is conveyed in a number of heart phrases. The common link with each phrase is the importance a special person occupies in the life of another. Given this chapter is about romance—one kind of relationship—the object of communication is assumed to be a spouse or lover.

Body and Heart
tháng kaay lÉ jai (adv.)
ทั้งกายและใจ

The heart of romance is when two people achieve that state of being when they feel a communion of body and soul. "Body and heart" means that you feel an absolute, unconditional commitment to the other person in the loving relationship. The "separateness" from another has evaporated in a shared feeling of oneness. *Tháng kaay lÉ jai* is one step beyond *plong jai rak*, "irrevocable heart." When your spouse or lover whispers that they love you *tháng kaay lÉ jai* it is the ultimate Zen state of commitment. In the best relationship, you and your partner both feel this level of commitment. But soap operas on Thai TV often feature a couple where only one person in the relationship has such an unconditional commitment while the other person keeps his or her options open. In an ideal romantic scene she has held nothing back and neither has he; they exist together as body and soul. You should be deep in the heartland of romance and commitment before using the phrase *tháng kaay lÉ jai*.

Confident Heart
mân jai (v.) มั่นใจ

To have a "confident heart" means to be confident of one's feeling about one's spouse or lover. In the context of romance, the confidence is specially about the relationship. To say that you feel *mân jai* is regarded as an expression of commitment between two people in a relationship. When you ask your lover about his or her feelings concerning the relationship, and if *mân jai* is the reply, it means your lover trusts you and is committed to being with you.

Contract of the Heart
sǎn yaa jai (n.) สัญญาใจ

"Contract of the heart" is another weighty emotional heart phrase that can be used in a serious, long-term committed relationship. One has committed one's heart to a permanent relationship or marriage. This commitment is *sǎn yaa jai*—it is the contract that you make with your heart. And the terms are clear: you are in the relationship for keeps. This phrase is not appropriate for an idle conversation or for the first date. The language of contract means one has sealed a lover's bargain for staying the course over the long-haul. Break this contract and the damages are considerable for all those involved.

Gold Chain Around the Heart
sôo thOOng khlÓOng jai (n.) โซ่ทองคล้องใจ

The commitment between two people deepens when they have *sôo thOOng khlÓOng jai*, meaning children. For most Thai couples, a child is the prize, the pride and joy, and the seal of their love. The child is the "gold chain" around the parents' hearts, which further strengthens their love and commitment to one another. This is a metaphor often used by Thai parents to express their feeling about the importance of their children in their relationship. Like the heart phrase below, this one is the real "inside stuff" on what Thai speakers say to express that special relationship. It would be unusual for a non-native speaker to know and use this phrase. By so doing, you are likely to draw an amazed smile. The spin is this, "An emotional gravity holds us in a tight orbit, and nothin', but nothin' ain't gonna pull us apart."

Irrevocable Heart
plong jai rák (v.) ปลงใจรัก

When you have made that final, ultimate commitment to another—in the sense that there is no pulling back, no second thoughts or changing your mind—then this act of commitment is *plong jai rák*. The notion of irrevocability is weighty and meaningful in any language. If you wish to use *plong jai rák* it should be understood that "irrevocable heart" is an expression of a lifelong commitment. To revoke the irrevocable is probably an exempted risk on Thai life insurance policy; one should check it before carelessly using this heart phrase. These are the words every Thai (indeed everyone) wishes to hear—but not as *phûut aw jai* or flattering talk. The words are powerful in the degree of intensity because they convey the "forever" quality of the feeling. Thus an "irrevocable heart" is one that is committed for the long term.

This Heart of Mine
jai duaang níi (n.) ใจดวงนี้

This romantic heart phrase is an expression you can use with that special person in your life. If you desire to articulate to that special person your love and commitment, you can proclaim, "I love you and *jai duaang níi* is for you only."

Cycle of Romance

Lonesome Heart
nǎaw jai (adj.) หนาวใจ

"Lonesome heart" is the opening scene of romance. A man or woman who claims to feel *nǎaw jai* is giving a signal that he or she wishes to have a relationship with another and is suffering from the lack of such a relationship. The heart phrase is the stuff of poetry, films and novels. The emotional state is like an arctic cold front blowing through your heart and leaving you with the feeling of aloneness; in this snowbound world of the heart, your life is cold, and you experience *nǎaw jai*. When this inner sense of loneliness occurs then the desire arises to seek refuge in a relationship. On the other hand, a man or a woman who is constantly complaining of this emotional state might be said to be *khîi nǎaw jai*—an emotional characteristic that may be pathological and potentially problematic in a long-term relationship.

Beautiful to the Heart
sà khraan jai (v.) สะคราญใจ

This *jai* phrase is used to describe a beautiful woman. But if you want to chat up a beautiful young woman, this is not exactly a phrase to use; she might be wondering if you are a time traveling poet from the early twentieth century. This is Thai poetry at its best. It is laced with the promise of romance.

Stolen Heart
thùuk khà mooy jai pai (v.) ถูกขโมยใจไป

The heart is "stolen" when the love or attraction is secret; the object of the affection is unaware of being the object of someone's affection. In this situation, the one who is in love feels painfully alone. "Stolen heart" is the Thai version of unrequited love. The person who experiences this one-sided love may confide his or her condition to a friend. Seeking advice about unrequited love is a way of dealing with it. The phrase is also used to flirt with another, by saying to the person that she or he has stolen your heart.

Capture Another's Heart
khà yûm hŭaa jai (v.) ขยุ้มหัวใจ

This slang heart phrase is similar to "stolen heart," but offers a more dramatic expression of the attraction. It describes the feeling that comes when another person has so powerfully captured your heart. It is as if an eagle has swooped down and grabbed your heart and won't let go.

Have a Heart for One Another
mii jai hâi kan (v.) มีใจให้กัน

This is one way of saying that two people have mutual attraction and fondness for each other. This phrase can be used to ask a question about whether or not another person loves you: "*Khun mii jai hâi phŏm rŭue plàaw?*," Do you have a heart for me? A couple has been friends for a long time and this grows into love, then one day one of them acknowledges this transition from friendship into love. They now "have a heart for one another": *mii jai hâi kan*.

Tie Another's Heart
mát jai (v.) มัดใจ
phùuk jai (v.) ผูกใจ

Tie, as in tying the lace of a shoe. In this case, the heart phrase signifies the tying together of two hearts. So how do you persuade another to tie their heart to your own? A simple answer is that through your actions you cause another person to love you. What actions achieve this tie to another's heart? By being loyal, faithful, witty, patient and compassionate you can usually succeed in tying another's heart to your own. Alternatively, if one does not possess such lofty qualities of character, one might try making gifts of a Rolex, a BMW and a penthouse condo. Cash or gold can also create a tie. The correct *jai* phrase in these circumstances is *mát jai*. *Phùuk jai* is less frequently used. Whether the heart tied with gold is as well "tied" as one tied with the qualities mentioned above is beyond the scope of this book.

Possess Another's Heart

khrOOng jai (v.) ครองใจ

The underlying message is that when possessing another's heart there is an obligation to look after and take care of the emotional well-being of that person. Lovers can employ this heart phrase when talking about their feelings. Often it is used among friends to describe how they feel about their loved ones. Sometimes the heart phrase pops up in commercial advertising as well. For instance, it has been used to sell house paint. The paint, which is claimed to be of very good quality, possesses the heart of the people who love their house.

Heaven in the Chest, Hell in the Heart

sà wăn nai òk ná rók nai jai (proverb) สวรรค์ในอกนรกในใจ

sà wăn yùu nai òk ná rók yùu nai jai (proverb) สวรรค์อยู่ในอกนรกอยู่ในใจ

The literal translation is that one feels heaven in one's chest and hell inside one's heart. The essence of these *jai* expressions is that whether others judge your actions as good or bad, in your heart you know whether you have done right or wrong. The sayings are a way to focus your conscience on your actions. You remind yourself that heaven or hell is not in the afterlife but present in the here and now. If your actions are good you will enjoy the rewards bestowed upon those who perform good deeds, and you will have happiness in your heart. But if your actions are bad you suffer hell inside your heart because you know that what you did was wrong. In the context of romance, acts of betrayal and secret affairs, even when they stay secret, are often the on-going dramas that call for these heart phrases.

Broken Heart
ráaw raan jai (v.) ร้าวรานใจ
hŭaa jai ráaw raan (v.) หัวใจร้าวราน

"Broken heart" occurs along with "heaven in the chest, hell in the heart" in the love-affair cycle. After finding a lover to rid you of the feeling of *năaw jai*, "lonesome heart," your lover splits from the scene. The pain of the separation causes heartbreak. Now you find yourself in another state of heart, a "broken heart." This feeling of hurt should not be confused with *jèp jai*, "resentful heart," which is a broken heart for which the broken-hearted person may seek revenge. When dealing with broken hearts, it is important to distinguish between emotional conditions. *Ráaw raan jai* or *hŭaa jai ráaw raan* is when the hurt is turned inward and is the language of poetry, songs, films and novels where a love affair has ended.

Heartache
rá thom jai (v.) ระทมใจ
chám jai (v.) ช้ำใจ
pùaat jai (v.) ปวดใจ
pen khâi jai (v.) เป็นไข้ใจ

These are all expressions of heartache, the feelings that follow the end of the love affair or arise when the romance is surely heading toward its final destruction. These expressions are used when you have endured a period of long-suffering heartache from disappointment and pain in the relationship. Your heart is battered and you feel depressed.

Melted Heart
jai lá laay (v.) ใจละลาย

"Melted heart" is another heart phrase for disappointment in love. The emotional state is one of heavy, hurt feelings over the loss of a loved one. The phrase can be heard when a man spots a sexy woman across the room, approaches her and uses it as a chatting-up line (though it is likely a modern, educated Thai woman would find such a line tacky). Another example is when the lover is filled with anger and the husband returns home with flowers and a gold chain and the wife's anger melts away (at least in theory).

Shattered Heart
jai sà lǎay (v.) ใจสลาย
hǔaa jai sà lǎay (v.) หัวใจสลาย

This is heartache in a league of its own. These phrases are used only in the major cases of broken heart, extreme sadness and disappointment. The state of "shattered heart" usually follows the most unfortunate events in the relationship, such as a severe case of betrayal or a sudden death of the love of one's life.

Endearments

The use of terms of endearment has a different cultural basis in Thai than in English. English speakers in a relationship often employ "darling" and "sweetheart" to refer to a special loved one. However, such endearments are rarely used among Thai couples. Using most of endearments described below would be done for effect, as a kind of joke, but almost never as a direct expression of affection.

Many Thais would consider such endearments to be in the class of cartoon language if used between lovers. These terms are not thought of as signs of affection in that context. One may wish to come across as Humphrey Bogart using a "sweetheart" line, but what is being heard is a Jay Leno or David Letterman line. They can be and are used, however, in other relationships, say between a mother and child.

Dearest of the Heart
yÔOt duaang jai (adj.) ยอดดวงใจ

YÔOt means the best or the highest level or the top of something. This *jai* phrase is used to express that your lover is number one in your life. It is best to leave out who is number two, three, etc. This is a term of endearment that can be used by either a man or a woman. If you propose marriage to a Thai woman, this might be a good opening line before you ask for her hand. A man may say to his lover, "*Khun pen yÔOt duaang jai khŎOng phŏm.*"

Healer of the Heart
yaa jai (adj.) ยาใจ

In earlier times *yaa* was used as a verb meaning to patch a boat, and the same word in the noun form also means medicine. This is another term of endearment, like sweetheart or darling, which a Thai mother might bestow as a name for her child. But if you try to use it romantically, as saying the other is medicine for your heart, then you will be greeted with laughter. This is a good line if one wishes to create a Thai laugh track but otherwise to be avoided. Context is everything when using *yaa jai*. For example, when a woman experiences a great feeling of disappointment in life, and a man comes into her life and his words and presence remove the heavy feeling of disappointment, it is appropriate for her to say that he is *yaa jai* for her.

Iris of the Heart
kÊEw taa duaang jai (n.)
แก้วตาดวงใจ

The person who is the "iris of the heart" is the most important or vital person residing in the center of one's heart. You want to be programmed into this place in your lover's heart. It is common for Thais to say the most important thing in a mother's heart is her child. And a daughter will invariably say her mother is the most important thing in her heart. It is less common for a lover to use this phrase; but when used in the romantic context what follows is often an emotional meltdown.

Most Beloved of the Heart
sùt jai (adj.) สุดใจ
sùt sà wàat khàat jai (adj.) สุดสวาทขาดใจ

The two phrases translate as the "most beloved of the heart." It is possible to find Thai women with the name *sùt jai*. *Sùt jai* is, however, another heart phrase that is not normally used in conversation. It more likely to be found in passages from classical Thai literature. *Sùt sà wàat khàat jai* is more commonly used but often in a non-romantic context to refer sarcastically to another person. If you used it seriously it would sound like a blast from the past, excessive and overly dramatic.

Sweet Heart
wǎan jai (n.) หวานใจ

This is "sweetheart" in Thai. But should one employ the endearment, one's spouse or lover may say that one is *pàak wǎan* or sweet-mouthed. The chances are very high it would be met with a laugh and treated as a joke. It is used to tease a friend: "Where's your *wǎan jai*? Why isn't he with you today?" Unless you are aware of this cultural difference the joke may be on you. The concept of *wǎan* is associated with a gentle, soft-natured and innocent person. But this heart phrase is thought excessive and insincere.

Infatuation

Love's second cousin is infatuation. An emotion sometimes confused with love itself.

Addicted Heart
tìt jai (v.) ติดใจ
tìt òk tìt jai (v.) ติดอกติดใจ
tìt núeaa tÔOng jai (v.) ติดเนื้อต้องใจ

When one feels an attraction to someone, one can be said to *tìt jai* the person. *Tìt òk tìt jai* is a stronger expression for this attraction. It often has a sexual connotation. One can be said to *tìt òk tìt jai* the taste of food in one's favorite restaurant. In the same way, one can be said to *tìt òk tìt jai* one's lover—what is implied as the cause of the addiction is the "sexual taste" or skills of the lover. *Tìt núeaa tÔOng jai* has the same meaning as *tìt òk tìt jai* but is an old-fashioned expression. On a negative note, the romantic or sexual addiction can lead to obsessive conduct, such as repeated phone calls and protestations of undying love. In the case of a break-up, the "addicted heart" may follow the script from the classic movie *Fatal Attraction*.

Compatible Heart

thùuk jai (v.) ถูกใจ
thùuk òk thùuk jai (v.) ถูกอกถูกใจ
mŭeaan jai (adv.) เหมือนใจ

These are more phrases for attraction, but without the "fatal attraction" connotation. When two people are pleased with each other, they feel *thùuk jai* with one another; they enjoy the same movies, books, wine and friends. They are compatible in their worldview, their outlook and taste. They feel a sense of common ground when their lover gives them exactly the right gift at the right time; they sense that the lover knows and understands their taste, desires and wants.

Heartthrob

khwăn jai (n.) ขวัญใจ

Khwăn jai is the appropriate expression for heartthrob. The heartthrob may be a movie star, singer, sports hero or celebrity figure. The "heartthrob" is not limited to the teen years and extends to the office, the classroom, a members' club. The object of the infatuation can be a boyfriend, girlfriend, spouse, office colleague or boss; each can be *khwăn jai*. A husband can affectionately refer to his wife as his *khwăn jai*. Some public figures also elicit this feeling among the general population in Thailand.

Thrilled Heart

sà yĭw jai (v.) สยิวใจ

If you hear someone say this about you, it means that they find you sexy and desirable. It is highly unlikely that you would hear this phrase from a *rêaap rÓOy* (well-behaved) Thai woman, who would be too embarrassed to use such language with a foreigner. But don't fear, even if she would use this phrase, unless you look like Brad Pitt or Arnold you are unlikely to hear this phrase said about you in Thailand. *Sà yǐw jai* applies to the circumstances where a woman finds a man attractive. It also applies when a man sees an attractive woman and exclaims that he feels *sà yǐw jai*.

Intimacy

Romance is marked by intimacy. The closeness, joy and happiness that spring from an intimate relationship are the subjects of a number of heart phrases. This section provides a few examples of how to extend the heart vocabulary to express one's intimate feelings toward another.

Captivating to One's Heart

jàp jai (adj.) จับใจ

This phrase can be used in two circumstances. The first is when one shares one's feelings and shows a vulnerability, and the experience of revealing oneself to another leads to a feeling of intimacy. The person who is open and revealing himself or herself can capture another person's heart. The second circumstance is when one is highly touched by another in the sense of *tìt jai* and may use *jàp jai* to express one's feeling that one's heart has been captured.

Darling of the Heart

klOOy jai (adj.) กลอยใจ

To get your spouse's or lover's attention, you can use the "darling of the heart" phrase to convey to him or her that he or she is your *klOOy jai*. The heart phrase conveys the sense that two people are emotionally and spiritually merged into a single person. Most often, this expression is used in the context of a mother and child relationship. In a romantic relationship, however, it can be used with someone special.

Intimate Heart
chûuen jai (adj.) ชื่นใจ

The phrase appears in other chapters as "fragrant heart" and "joyful heart." Outside of romance it is used to express pleasure and joy. In the romantic context, it is used to express the feeling of intimacy and closeness. When one person in the relationship gives the other a special gift, she or he will likely feel *chûuen jai*. The definition of intimacy is understanding what brings joy to the heart of another and acting upon that knowledge. What does it take to make someone joyful? This is a list for all lovers to work on together. It is often the small gesture, such as touching her hand, brushing away a strand of hair, or a light kiss on the cheek.

Open One's Heart
pòoet jai (v.) เปิดใจ

When two people are close enough to disclose their most secret, hidden feelings to each other, then they an "open heart" with one another: *pòet jai*. The heart phrase may also apply outside an intimate relationship, to an entertainer such as a singer, who has created a bond with his or her audience.

Soft Heart
jai ÒOn (adj.) ใจอ่อน

It is said that intimacy softens the heart, takes away the rough, harsh, judgmental edges. Someone who has a soft heart (*jai ÒOn*) does many things for their friends, family and children. They place personal relationship higher than self-interest.

The person who is *jai ÒOn* is giving, respectful, and thoughtful in his or her relations.

Touch One to the Quick Heart

jîi hŭaa jai (v.) จี้หัวใจ

This heart phrase means to be touched emotionally by something or someone. The literal translation is that the heart is touched or tickled: *jîi hŭaa jai*. In the context of a romantic relationship, the small gesture of love, such as a phone call, a card, a gift, may touch the heart of the person receiving it.

Pair of Hearts

khûu jai (n.) คู่ใจ

A precondition to experiencing a "pair of hearts" is to understand and trust another person—this mainly applies to a spouse or lover—then that person is your *khûu jai*. One feels joined together with another person in a couple. Their union is cemented with trust. The two people involved feel a match has been made between them. This heart phrase appears frequently in the context of a husband and wife. The word *khûu hŭu* or "pair of ears" is used in non-romantic situations between friends.

Love

Love is implicit in many of the heart phrases contained under the headings of commitment and loyalty. There are degrees of love. Some hearts burn with a hot fire and passion. There are a number of heart phrases included below which deal specifically with the wide range of feelings associated with love.

Same Heart

jai diiaw kan (adj.) ใจเดียวกัน
jai trong kan (adj.) ใจตรงกัน

There are two aspects to the expression of "same heart." First is the initial mutual attraction between two people: *jai trong kan*. Second is the state of being that ideally one should share with one's spouse or lover—harmony and compatibility. When two people first meet, it's love at first sight. These two people can say to one another or relate to their friends later that they and their love interest feel *jai trong kan*. In the second sense, there is an absence of conflict in the love relationship. You are in complete union with the other. You like the same movies, food, friends and holidays. You both drink fresh-squeezed orange juice and put strawberry jam on your wholewheat toast while listening to contemporary jazz. You both have the same favorite color, and prefer a hard mattress to a soft one.

Brimming-over Heart

lón jai (adj.) ล้นใจ
rák jon lón jai (v.) รักจนล้นใจ

This heart phrase is used to provide emphasis to your feelings of love. Thus a person who wishes to declare that his or her feelings of affection or love rise significantly above the ordinary may resort to this heart phrase. For example, you may say to your lover, "*Rák khun jon lón jai*," I love you so much my heart brims over with love. In this case, *lón jai* acts as an exclamation point added to an expression of love. In Thai culture, a Thai woman might experience the feeling of *lón jai* but she would be highly unlikely to use the phrase. It is more common for a Thai man to use this phrase with his girlfriend or wife.

Love Sickness

khâi jai (n.) ไข้ใจ
pen khâi jai (v.) เป็นไข้ใจ

"Love sickness" befalls the true romantic who sees someone across a crowded room and falls in love. At the office a man is secretly in love with a colleague and he finds out that the woman of his interest is already happily married. What is at work in this "love sickness" is the tendency to love someone at a distance with the disappointment that she can never be his. The landscape of this love ballet is deep inside your own imagination and dreams. The love is locked inside your head. When two people split up, one of them may feel such "love sickness" at the absence of the other that she or he can't sleep and doesn't want to eat. In this case, their friends would say they have *khâi jai* or *pen khâi jai*. Another context for using *khâi jai* is when two people have the kind of relationship where they are so wrapped up in love that even a short separation causes them to experience *khâi jai*.

Love with All of One's Heart
rák jon mòt jai (v.) รักจนหมดใจ

Another expression of love is the concept of loving with all of one's heart. The heart has feelings (and room) for only one person other than oneself. You give your entire heart to one person and have none left to give to another. As a romantic heart phrase, it conveys loyalty, devotion and faithfulness to another.

Pour Out One's Heart
thee jai (v.) เทใจ

This is the right romantic *Heart Talk* phrase when one person has poured out his or her feelings of love for the other. This is informal slang mostly used by teenagers to express their feelings of love. *Thee jai* is descriptive of the act of expressing one's love for another. What pours out of your heart is the attraction you feel for another: her laughter, the way she smiles, her eyes, her slim figure. If you are pouring out your heart to someone who is indifferent to you or lukewarm, then it's time to move on.

Most Beloved of the Heart
sùt sà wàat khàat jai (adj.)
สุดสวาทขาดใจ

This romantic heart phrase is used to emphasize the depth of someone's emotional feelings for another. The phrase is descriptive of love and devotion. Often it is used when two people are discussing a third person. Two women talking about a mutual friend might use the phrase to describe that friend's devotion to her husband. It can be used in an ironic sense as well, for example, when your child spills his milk again and your wife tells you to look at your *sùt sà wàat khàat jai* child now. If you use this phrase with a Thai as an expression of love, though, he or she would probably laugh. It is the kind of phrase found in sappy Thai country music.

To the End of the Heart

sùt khûaa hŭaa jai (adj.)
สุดขั้วหัวใจ

This romantic phrase is used when lovers wish to express the feeling that their heart is filled to the maximum with love for the other person in their life. "To the end of the heart" is a useful phrase to reassure another about one's feelings of devotion and love for one's lover. If one's lover is feeling insecure in the relationship, then hearing the phrase *sùt khûaa hŭaa jai* may allow him or her to overcome the feelings of insecurity. To many Thai ears, though the phrase sounds as if it has been taken from the script of a TV soap opera.

Loyalty

Missing-Another Heart

jai hùaang thŭeng (v.) ใจห่วงถึง

This phrase is used in the context of someone who is worrying about the well-being of another. A wife worries about her husband who stays out late. His absence and silence make her suffer from worry. When he finally comes through the door, she may say (if she's the literary type) that she has *jai hùaang thŭeng* him. Then she punches him. She's suffered, so why shouldn't he suffer too? This is rarely used in daily conversation and is more likely to be found in Thai literature. A more commonly used (non-heart) phrase for this situation would be *pen hùaang*.

One Love, One Heart
rák diiaw jai diiaw (adj.)
รักเดียวใจเดียว

These two *jai* phrases are expressions of one's deep love, exclusive commitment and loyalty to another. *Jai diiaw*, "one heart," is deep commitment and loyalty but *rák diiaw jai diiaw* expands that commitment to another level. The *rák diiaw jai diiaw* person has the love that is exclusive to just one person; the person is not interested in having minor wives or girlfriends, or secret affairs of any kind. When the girlfriend spots her boyfriend talking with another woman she storms away and sulks in the corner. The boyfriend follows, puts his arm around her and whispers sweetly that he feels *rák diiaw jai diiaw* only toward her. This means she shouldn't worry about any other woman in his heart.

Save One's Heart
kèp jai (v.) เก็บใจ

Someone is saving their heart for another. Someone other than their lover or spouse does not occupy this "saved" heart. Jeab's boyfriend has gone abroad to study. During the period that he is away in New York, Jeab has many guys floating around her, wanting to date her. But she pays them no attention and remains faithful to her boyfriend. She saves her heart (*kèp jai*) for her boyfriend. In another circumstance, a woman who has had a bad experience with love decides to not give her heart again. Thus it can be an emotional defense after having been hurt to *kèp jai*.

Studying & Testing the Heart

Study Another's Heart
duu jai (v.) ดูใจ

There are a number of expressions for courtship in Thai and one of the central ones is *duu jai*. During the courtship process you study the heart of the other person to determine how sincere he or she is about the relationship. At the same time your lover is studying your heart to determine your sincerity. In this respect, all lovers are students of the heart. The subject of this study includes, in addition to evidence of another person's sincerity, qualities such as loyalty, honesty, kindness, compassion, and gentleness. While the act of studying is an ongoing activity, the term is rarely used between lovers. This heart expression is more commonly used by a friend who confesses that he or she is studying the heart of his or her lover. *Duu jai* is used as a verb. There is also a second meaning: when you see for the last time the face of a dying friend or relative.

Test Another's Heart

yàng jai (v.) หยั่งใจ

In matters of the heart, you will often put the other to the test in order to determine his or her true feelings and intentions. There may be some doubts as to the nature of the relationship and one person wishes to put this to the test. For instance, Lek and Vinai have been friends for six months. Vinai asks Lek to be his girlfriend; however, she is not really certain about the degree of his commitment and Vinai remains silent on this issue. To put the matter to the test, Lek accepts a date with Worachai. Soon after discovering Worachai's interest in Lek, Vinai proposes that they become engaged.

Truth & Trust

It is natural to wish to convey how important truth and trust are in a relationship. Issues such as truth-telling, certainty of feeling, loyalty, sincerity and compatibility are at the heart of any relationship. In this section, the required vocabulary to provide these necessary emotional assurances are set forth.

Straight to the Heart

trong hŭaa jai (adj.) ตรงหัวใจ

One lover expresses feelings to the object of his or her love. If the expression is one of love and affection, the listener will feel happy. On the other hand, if a husband says to his wife that she looks ugly, this will most likely cause her to feel unhappy. One feels happy or sad in one's heart. Words that are "straight to the heart" (*trong hŭaa jai*) may make one feel happy or sad, depending on what is being said and how the listener feels about the words that come out of the mouth of his or her beloved. Like any other kinds of relationships, a successful love relationship requires truth to be told, but there is also a consideration of another's feelings. A skilled lover knows how to tell the truth while also protecting the heart of his or her love from feeling hurt.

One Heart

jai diiaw (adj.) ใจเดียว

Someone who is and remains faithful to their partner is *jai diiaw*. Every lover's dream is to find the partner who has eyes only for him or her. This is the Thai way of expressing that desire of "one woman, one man." The importance of this heart phrase cannot be overemphasized. Thais, like everyone else on the planet, dislike being set up with phony expectations. If you promise to be *jai diiaw*, your lover will likely question you, test you, do everything in her power to see if you are serious. The indiscriminate use of "one hear" can create a balloon of expectation that—when it goes—may go with a bang and not a whimper.

Sure Heart

nÊE jai (v.) แน่ใจ

In a relationship, when you are certain of your feelings toward the other you are *nÊE jai* about the person. This is the feeling of being sure. In other contexts it may be used to signal certainty. Before a woman and man decide to marry, they must be certain of the qualities of the other. The quest for certainty is a very human one, and in the decision to marry the couple must assure themselves that they experience no doubts about the other.

True Heart
jing jai (adj.) จริงใจ

A person who expresses his or her feelings of love, caring or consideration to another is *jing jai*. The essence is sincerity of feeling. There is no mask or deceit in the words or behavior of a person who is *jing jai*. The heart phrase often comes in the form of a question from a Thai speaker. He or she is looking for reassurance. Who isn't? After one has heard a hundred pitches, a thousand lies, it is wonderful to think one still has enough resilience to even ask, "*Khun jing jai rúue plàaw*?," Are you of true heart or not? It is a question a lover asks and then reads your eyes for the answer.

Trust with One's Heart
wái jai (v.) ไว้ใจ

The feeling of trusting another comes from the heart in Thai. *Wái jai* is the act of trusting. When someone trusts another person, they say they *wái jai* that person. In this heart phrase one is saying, "In my heart I trust you." Trust, in this case, is based on telling the truth, and not deceiving or betraying another who relies on one's words and actions. There isn't a lover alive who doesn't want to trust his or her partner. This is always a question of timing. If the statement comes too soon, it sounds like an obvious lie. If it comes late, it may come too late and your lover may have fled the scene for a more trusting person.

Unfaithfulness

Unfaithfulness is a category of betrayal. While betrayal is a general term covering many kinds of relationships, the concept of unfaithfulness is mostly restricted to husband and wife or those in a committed relationship. In this context, the following *jai* phrases provide a rich vocabulary to describe adultery, promiscuous behavior and cheating on spouses.

Adulterer in the Heart

chúu taang jai (n.) ชู้ทางใจ

This *jai* phrase is used only in the context of a romantic relationship. On the surface the couple are in love and happy, but the husband (in this example, but it could well be the wife) has a secret desire for another woman. He is said to have a *chúu taang jai*; he is an adulterer but only in the heart. He may or many not have a platonic relationship with his object of secret desire, but he will not act upon his desire. If he crossed the line and acted upon his longing that would be another story with a list of *jai* phrases below. The essence is that your heart maintains a secret love affair with another but the longing is emotional and is not acted upon.

Cheating Heart

nÔOk jai (v.) นอกใจ

When this phrase is used, the unfaithfulness is no longer just "in the heart" but usually acted upon. When either the husband or the wife maintains a relationship with another person outside of the marriage or committed relationship then his or her action is *nÔOk jai*. The man with a minor wife, mistress or girlfriend exhibits classic *nÔOk jai* behavior. Like *sŎOng jai*, "two hearts," and *lăay jai*, "promiscuous heart," this heart phrase is used as a condemnation.

Divide One's Heart

pan jai (v.) ปันใจ

When a man has a major wife and continues to love and support her, and at the same time has a minor wife whom he also loves and supports, it is said his heart is "divided" between the two women. The heart phrase can also apply to a woman who has two husbands, or one husband and a lover. This slang expression is taken from a Thai song. The phrase also applies to other contexts. For example, Vinai officially works for one company but also has another job on the side. Increasingly he spends more time at the sideline job and even uses inside information from his official workplace in his other job. Vinai has a divided loyalty. He divides his heart between two jobs: *pan jai*.

Heart with Many Rooms
jai mii lăay hÔOng (v.) ใจมีหลายห้อง

This heart phrase is another description for someone who attempts to juggle several lovers or partners at the same time. The person who has several simultaneous relationships has a "heart with many rooms." Sometimes the *jai* phrase is used to rationalize a man's decision to maintain several ongoing relationships. The phrase is associated with an incorrigible polygamous man (or woman). The context of usage varies from a serious condemnation of a man to light repartee between friends. In most cases the phrase covers the same conduct as *lăay jai*.

Promiscuous Heart
lăay jai (adj.) หลายใจ

In the context of romance, "promiscuous heart" refers to the character of a person who cares for many lovers. A person who is *lăay jai* cannot be faithful to one person. While the phrase implies a less serious condemnation implicit in related heart phrases such as "cheating heart" and "two hearts," to be called *lăay jai* is a clear message that someone has been written off as faithless and unreliable. No thinking person wishes to get deeply involved with a *lăay jai* person. You can sometimes hear Thais use the English word "butterfly" to describe someone with a promiscuous heart.

Two Hearts
sŎOng jai (adj.) สองใจ
jai sŎOng (adj.) ใจสอง

A person who loves two or more partners at the same time is *sŎOng jai*.

The idea of loving more than one partner is translated into a person who possesses two hearts. This overcomes the obvious difficulty of cutting up a single heart for use with two lovers. Such a two-hearted person is frequently the subject of Thai TV soap operas, films and books. In many such stories the battle is between a husband and his relationships (and divided loyalties) with a major and a minor wife. The origin of the *jai* phrases, however, was to condemn a woman who had divided loyalties between two men, as in the classic story of *Khun Chang Khun Phaen*.

Benevolent Heart

plùuk rueaan taam jai phûu yùu phùuk ùu taam jai phùu nOOn

ปลูกเรือนตามใจผู้อยู่ ผูกอู่ตามใจผู้นอน

13
heart proverbs

Proverbs are found in every culture. In many ways they are historical defining moments of culture handed down from generation to generation. The Thai proverbs often provide moral lessons. Some say parables are distinguished from proverbs on the basis that the former are moral lessons. In the case of Thai proverbs this line is not so clear, as proverbs in this chapter illustrate.

Often they are taught in school or by monks, appear in ancient literature and folklore, and pop up in mass cultural TV programs, newspapers, magazines and books. Most proverbs teach moral lessons of empathy, trust, freedom and the dangers of deceit, greed and betrayal.

Every society has a moral code and proverbs are one way this code is taught to children. Proverbs survive because they are timeless. Each new generation learns messages such as "Wealth is hard to come by, but poverty is always at hand." As this example of a Western proverb illustrates, along with Thai proverbs, it matters little whether you lived in a remote village two hundred years ago or live in modern Bangkok today.

Chinese literature is also rich in proverbs. "To negotiate with a tiger for its skin" comes from the Song Dynasty (AD 938). This translates into the moral that it is useless to negotiate with a tyrant to act against his self-interest. A Qing Dynasty (seventeenth century) proverb, "The night is long and the dreams are legion," teaches that even when success is near you shouldn't take it for granted until it actually happens.

It is hoped that couples wishing to teach their children some of the ancient moral lessons in Thai culture will find these proverbs useful, entertaining and thought-provoking tools.

Benevolence

Benevolent Heart
plùuk rueaan taam jai phûu yùu phùuk ùu taam jai phùu nOOn
ปลูกเรือนตามใจผู้อยู่ ผูกอู่ตามใจผู้นอน

Young students learn this proverb in school. In traditional Thai literature there are two well-known stories: (i) *Khun Chang Khun Paen* and (ii) *Srithanonchai*. In the first story, when Khun Paen was a baby he cried a great deal, and one day a monk visited the house and advised his mother that if she retied the cradle the baby would stop crying. The monk told Khun Paen's mother this proverb. In *Srithanonchai*, the mother asked her child, Srithanonchai, to take care of his young brother by washing him completely and then placing him in a cradle. But Srithanonchai, being a cunning person, takes the instructions a little too seriously and opens his brother's stomach to clean the intestines, and then puts him in the cradle. This is an example of how the literal application of a proverb can allow a clever, tricky person to cause harm or damage.

This "benevolent heart" proverb translates as: Build the house according to the dictates of the heart of the owner and tie up the sling (cradle) according to the wishes of the one who will sleep in it. In the old days, the mother would tie a sling between two trees or poles so as to have a place to rock her baby to sleep. She must tie the sling in the proper place or the baby could fall and be harmed. The proverb now means we must act to ensure that others will be happy and in comfort. A person who is a modern example of this proverb shows a willingness to take care and be considerate to others.

Concentration

See with the Heart, Listen with the Ear
aw jai duu hŭu sài เอาใจดูหูใส่

In early junior high school, students learn this idiomatic phrase in a course on ethics and morality. The teacher uses the idiom to teach what qualities (such as paying attention) make for success in life. This Thai idiom means to concentrate the eye and the ear. The heart is used to focus both. This is compatible to the Buddhist teaching of awareness. Be aware of one's mind and actions: pay attention to the task at hand. Don't have one's mind somewhere else. When doing homework don't at the same time watch TV and listen to the radio. When playing sports don't be occupied about playing the next video game. This phrase provides a guide to practice concentration and to develop a sense of responsibility.

Daydreams

Big Dream Heart
mâng mii nai jai lÊEn bai bon bòk
มั่งมีในใจ แล่นใบบนบก

Many students first learn about this proverb in school, during courses about culture and society, and the Thai language. Monks also use this proverb upcountry in farming communities. Traditional Thai society rests on self-sufficiency and on being grateful for what one has in life and not wanting more. In recent years the political message has been that everyone has the chance to work to become wealthy. It is unclear, as the economy develops, whether the message in this proverb will continue to find a receptive audience.

This proverb, literally translated as "wealthy in the heart, sailing on the land," describes the desire to achieve impossible goals or acquire unattainable things. Someone in a small village dreams one day to become a famous movie star, neglecting the fact that they have no

acting skills. The person who earns $5 a day dreams of buying a 7 Series BMW. The high school student dreams of having a date and marrying a famous actor from Hollywood. The janitor who cleans the floors at night dreams of becoming the CEO of the company. These are all examples of people with dreams and expectations larger than the reality of their life. It doesn't mean that one can't dream of winning the lotto, but the chances of that happening are like those of being struck by lightning. This is an uncommon *jai* phrase and Thais may be perplexed to hear it used by a foreigner because they have likely not come across it themselves.

Differences

Distinctive Heart
máay lam diiaw yang tàang plÔOng phîi nÓOng yang tàang jai
ไม้ลำเดียวยังต่างปล้อง พี่น้องยังต่างใจ
tôn máay tàang plÔOng phîi nÓOng tàang jai
ต้นไม้ต่างปล้อง พี่น้องต่างใจ

In junior high school students would learn this proverb in the context of understanding and appreciating the differences between brothers and sisters in the same family. Grandparents would use this proverb to teach their children who have children of their own. It is a lesson passed down from generation to generation about how to value individual members of the family.

The literal translation of the two variations of this proverb is: As in a length of bamboo each section is distinctive, likewise brothers and sisters though of the same piece of bamboo have different or distinctive hearts and points of view. The proverb is used to explain that as each piece of bamboo is distinctive, each older and younger sibling is different too. "Distinctive heart" recognizes that it is natural for there to be a divergence of taste, likes, dislikes, talents, personality and temperament among members of the same family. It is important to appreciate and respect these differences.

Empathy

Empathetic Heart
aw jai khăw maa sài jai raw
เอาใจเขามาใส่ใจเรา

This Thai idiom translates literally as taking another person's heart into your heart. The English equivalent is to ask someone to put themselves in the other person's shoes. The message is to be considerate and thoughtful to others. It is a common expression that every Thai knows.

This expression is taught to children at an early age, in school and Thai households, in an attempt to instill the importance of showing compassion and sympathy to others. There is a project to promote good habits in a primary school, and the teacher uses this proverb as a lesson about working together on assignments. The students must take into account the feelings of other students when allocating the work among the group. And they must share the burden of the work and help each other. It teaches a collective attitude toward a common project.

Sit in Another's Heart
nâng nai hŭaa jai
นั่งในหัวใจ

This is another idiom that is learned early. A teacher explains that the good deeds you do sit in your heart. Monks also teach it to young novices. The literal translation is: To sit in another's heart is to have knowledge of their mind and soul. Thus it is putting oneself in the place of another in order to know how they think and feel. With such understanding it becomes easier to anticipate the other person's wants, desires and moods. It is useful in instructing children to be sensitive in their relationship with others. For example, when two children have a fight, you can ask both of them to reflect on their own actions and then try to understand each other's point of view by "sitting" in the other person's heart: to understand how the other thinks and feels and to have empathy for the other.

False Promise

False Promise Heart
khÓ kà laa hâi măa dii jai
เคาะกะลาให้หมาดีใจ

In junior high school students are taught to write essays or stories and they are encouraged to use a proverb, such as this one, as their subject. The literal translation is that by tapping the top half of a coconut shell you will make the dog happy. Someone makes a promise to do or give something to another but when the time arrives for performance, the promise-maker does not deliver. The promise was false. There will not be a positive outcome or a reward.

In the illustration, the brother promised his younger sister that if she gave him her money, he would buy icecream for her, their baby brother and the family dog. However, after she gave him the money, the brother pretended to forget what he said. He bought icecream only for himself and pocketed his sister's money. The brother *khÓ kà laa hâi măa dii jai*: he has a "false promise heart." This is an act of dishonesty that children would best learn to avoid.

Freedom

Small Place is Livable, But a Tight Heart is Not
kháp thîi yùu dâay kháp jai yùu yâak คับที่อยู่ได้ คับใจอยู่ยาก

This proverb teaches a sense of personal freedom and dignity. It refers to an uncomfortable emotional space; the proverb literally says, "A small place is livable, but a tight heart is not." The "smallness" or "tightness" (*kháp*) is not physical but an internal state of being. For example, many people can stay together in what is physically a small place and remain content—this is physical "tightness" (*kháp thîi*) that is livable and does not cause emotional discomfort (*yùu dâay*). But in the state of emotional "tightness" (*kháp jai*) where you have people who get under your skin and drive you to despair it doesn't matter how big the space is, you will feel a great sense of discomfort (*yùu yâak*).

Usually, the emotional discomfort in the sense of *kháp jai* comes from the feeling that you lack personal freedom or are being mistreated by those close to you. The people who cause emotional discomfort in others tend to be bullies—at school, at work or in the family.

Guilt

Fear of Retribution Heart
wuaa sǎn lǎng khàat hěn kaa bin phàat kÔO tòk jai
วัวสันหลังขาด เห็นกาบินผาดก็ตกใจ

This is a university-level proverb. Monks teach it as well as university lecturers. This isn't a proverb that small children would be able to grasp easily. The literal translation is: The cow with a torn out spine is frightened when seeing a crow fly past quickly. The essence is dread of retribution. Attention is focused on the guilty person. The person who has done something wrong (the cow) dreads that his wrongful act will be discovered, so the person becomes easily rattled by any small hint of that possibility (such as the crow flying past).

A child knocks over her mother's favorite vase and it smashes into a hundred pieces on the floor. He sweeps up the broken pieces and hides them from his mother. When the mother enters the room and seeing the vase missing enquires what has become of her vase, the

child replies, "I didn't do anything." In this case the son who has the wound is the "cow" of the proverb, and the mother is the "crow" who will keep up her enquires until she discovers exactly what has happened.

Immature Acts

Spoilt Heart

jai tÈEk (adj.) ใจแตก

Jai tÈEk can be translated literally as "a heart that has broken." However, this is not the same as broken heart. In this case, the word *tÈEk* indicates the quality of the heart that has gone bad or out of control. The phrase carries a strong tone of moral judgment. Thai teenagers who are led down the wrong path by their friends might be described by those in those in the older generations as *jai tÈEk*. This is the equivalent of teenage rebellion—the James Dean syndrome. *Jai tÈEk* teenagers don't trust their parents.

The essence of the phrase is misdirection in life. The fact that the heart is described as "broken" or "spoilt" suggests that it used to be

in a good condition. The teenage girl who has always been a straight-A student started going out on a date and became pregnant is said to be *jai tÈEk*. Similarly, the teenage boy who was a good student and a well-behaved young man but got involved with a wrong group of friends and became a drug addict can also be described as *jai tÈEk*.

The main meaning of this heart phrase is hence a loss of innocence, and is applied in the context of sexual or immoral behavior. Unfortunately, these actions are not confined to those in their teens. The phrase also applies to anyone who has lost their good judgment and starts doing something stupid or self-destructive.

Indulgence

Glutton Heart
taam jai pàak lam bàak tÓOng
ตามใจปากลำบากท้อง

Children and adults who cannot control their hunger or appetite and eat whatever they want have a "glutton heart." This Thai proverb translates literally as: If you give in to the demands of your hungry mouth then your stomach will suffer. To give in to the demands of your hungry mouth is to *taam jai pàak*. Thai parents often say to their children, "*Yàa taam jai pàak*," Do not indulge your appetite, or you will be sorry later (*lam bàak tÓOng*).

The proverb is taught to senior high school students as part of their studies about culture, religion and society. It is a way of telling them to moderate or control their hunger and desire for food. If you are greedy for food (especially if it is hot and spicy Thai food), your appetite will cause you stomach troubles. A child who has troubles controlling himself when it comes to food would benefit from this proverb.

Over-consumption Heart

taam jai pàak mâak nîi
ตามใจปากมากหนี้

Literally translated as: If you give in to the demands of your mouth then you will have much debt, this proverb comes from stories told about previous lives of the Buddha. Monks also use this proverb in lectures about a very rich man who was careless about his money and, as a result of his greed for things, lost his wealth and became poor.

This is a good proverb to use when warning young people about paying too much attention to consuming things. Expensive consumer products like fancy cell phones, computer games, designer clothes and bags are beyond the means of most people, not to mention school children and teenagers who do not yet have their own income. Teachers use this proverb to teach the value of saving money. It is also a lesson about the accumulation of debt. Students learn about the relationship of law and debt as a warning about borrowing too much.

Marriage

Child Disturbs the Body, Husband Disturbs the Heart
mii lûuk kuaan tuaa mii phŭaa kuaan jai มีลูกกวนตัว มีผัวกวนใจ

This *jai* proverb expresses the concern of many women (both married and unmarried) who have to combine the demands of child-rearing with looking after their husband's or boyfriend's needs and desires. Many modern Thai women feel that the domestic pressures leave them very little personal time and freedom. This proverb has become more relevant as more women enter the workplace and have the same time constraints placed on them as their male counterparts, while the traditional view of what is expected of women has not changed as rapidly.

This is a *jai* proverb that a Thai woman would use with her husband, lover or child when she's in a complaining mood. She's expressing a feeling that has a germ of truth but is not intended seriously; it is more an expression of being tired, and it allows her to vent her sense of feeling disturbed. It can also be used as a warning from married women when a friend says she wants to get married. Single women never have to use this Thai proverb and this may explain why so many Thai women choose to remain single.

This proverb, though not directly applicable to children, may help them understand their mothers better and have more sympathy for the mothers' double burden of work and housework. The proverb can be used to encourage them to help around the house to ease the burden of their mothers.

Mistakes

The Stumble that Breaks the Heart

thà lăm lông chák ngâay thà lăm jai chák yâak

ถลำล่องชักง่าย ถลำใจชักยาก

This is a Thai proverb which translates as: If we take a misstep, it is possible to recover without much difficulty, but if we misstep with our heart, then it is much more difficult to step back without falling down. When the parents discover their daughter loves a man who is already married, they will likely use this proverb as a warning that if the daughter continues this illicit relationship she will break her heart. The lesson taught is the gravity of emotional commitment and the adverse consequences that result from making an important decision too quickly. The subtext is: "Have you thought through carefully if this is what you really want to do?"

It is used in health education classes, and the message conveyed in the context of sexual relations is one of restraint and self-control. Middle-class children would also have this proverb reinforced by their parents. In senior high school it would be used to teach restraint. The example might be the receipt of a gift-wrapped package and the instruction is not to open it for three days. Children would naturally wish to open the gift immediately.

Obedience

Obey the Host's Heart
long rueaa taam jai pÉ
ลงเรือตามใจแป๊ะ
long rueaa pÉ taam jai pÉ
ลงเรือแป๊ะตามใจแป๊ะ

The basic principle is that once you get on another person's boat you follow the orders of its owner. This heart phrase is appropriate for use in connection with a person's office, house, car, boat, motorcycle (not to mention airplane, water buffalo or other forms of transportation). It teaches the notion of *kreeng jai*, "awe heart," to the host, to whom one owes consideration and respect. It is important to "obey" the host's wishes. Whatever the host wants to do, one has to comply, as one is not in the position to demand otherwise.

For instance, Noo Lek, who is from upcountry, goes to school in Bangkok and lives in a house owned by a friend of her mother. The mother's friend enforces a curfew rule that Noo Lek must return each day no later than 9.00 p.m. Although Noo Lek does not like these rules, she must comply by returning to the house before 9.00 p.m. In so doing Noo Lek is following the "boat owner's" rule: *long rueaa taam jai pÉ*.

Self-Reliance

Beware of Others Heart
yàa wái jai taang yàa waang jai khon jà jon jai eeng
อย่าไว้ใจทางอย่าวางใจคนจะจนใจเอง

The proverb translates as: Don't trust other people because to do so will invite trouble. In primary school children would be taught this proverb through literature. A teacher may use stories such as *Little Red Riding Hood* or *Snow White* as examples of the lesson of the proverb. Children in all classes and regions in Thailand would learn and understand its message. The proverb is also taught in the family.

Sometimes you will see the proverb posted on a tree in the grounds of a temple. The idea behind it is to create a sense of danger about relying not only on strangers, but also on people close to oneself including mothers, fathers, uncles, teachers, sons, daughters, lovers, or spiritual leaders. The essence is that relying on others is dangerous. It teaches self-reliance and using one's own judgment rather than going along with the wishes or views of others, as this leads to a road of many dangers.

Borrow Another's Nose to Breathe Heart
yuuem jà mùuk khon ùuen hăay jai
ยืมจมูกคนอื่นหายใจ
phûeng jà mùuk khon ùuen hăay jai
พึ่งจมูกคนอื่นหายใจ

The crux of this metaphor is in self-reliance. To borrow another person's nose to breathe refers to reliance on others to do things for you. It can be inconvenient and the result may not be what you expect. Therefore, if you like to have things done to your liking, it is better to do them yourself. That is, do not *yuuem jà mùuk khon ùuen hăay jai*. In other words, use your own nose to breathe.

Phûeng jà mùuk khon ùuen hăay jai has the exact same meaning, although it literally translates as "to depend on another's nose to breathe." This phrase has been replaced in common usage by *yuuem jà mùuk khon ùuen hăay jai*. You might come across this in an old book but it is less likely that you'd hear it in contemporary conversations, on TV, or in a modern book.

Sincerity

Sweet Words But Want to Slit the Throat Heart
pàak praa săi jai chûeaat khOO
ปากปราศรัยใจเชือดคอ
pàak praa săi náam jai chûeaat khOO ปากปราศรัยน้ำใจเชือดคอ

Most Thai children would learn this proverb in school between the ages of ten and twelve. In Thai literature *Phra Aphaimanee*, Phra Aphaimanee's son was searching for his lost father. The son wishes to find his father and, after a long journey and many false attempts, he finds a magic black horse. Later he finds an old man who wants the horse. He tells the son that he will help find the father but the boy must first give him the horse. The son gives the horse but the old man fails in his promise to help.

The son goes to see his teacher and tells him this story about the magic black horse and the old man, and the teacher teaches him that

he shouldn't easily believe in sweet words because the heart is complicated and can't always be believed.

This Thai proverb is another lesson about sincerity and hypocrisy. It gives warning to children (and adults) not to trust others so easily. Someone may have a credible exterior mask and speak soothing and friendly words (*pàak praa săi*), but have evil intentions in the heart (*náam jai chûeaat khOO*).

Skill

Appropriate Heart
jai dii kÊE dâay jai ráay kÊE măi
ใจดีแก้ด้าย ใจร้ายแก้ไหม

This *jai* proverb isn't common at the present time and a lot of Thais have not heard it. The literal translation is: Good heart unties thread, cruel heart unties silk. The proverb used to describe group or community activity. The rural texture of the phrase should not be thought of as a limitation on more general usage. In essence, it means that work is best given to people who have the capability of performing the task or assignment, and withheld from those who cannot efficiently do the work. Thus the person who is able to untie the thread may be unable to untie the silk. Conversely, the person who is good at untying silk may be inept at untying thread.

Children, like people in general, have different skills. Some are good at things that others are not. This proverb can help children understand their own strengths and weaknesses and apply them appropriately.

Spirituality

Heaven in the Chest, Hell in the Heart
sà wăn nai òk ná rók nai jai
สวรรค์ในอก นรกในใจ

This proverb is a Buddhist concept of personal suffering. Monks would preach this proverb. Mothers also teach it to their children. A mother may warn her child not to tell a lie, because by telling a lie the child will have *ná rók nai jai*, "hell in the heart." Friends can also use this proverb with each other.

The literal translation is that one feels heaven in one's chest and hell inside one's heart. The essence of this proverb is that whether or not others are aware of the good or bad deeds you have done, you always know in your heart whether you have done right or wrong. If you have performed good deeds, you will feel happy in your heart, in other words, you have heaven in your chest (*sà wăn nai òk*). But if you have done what you know are bad deeds, you will suffer hell in your heart (*ná rók nai jai*). Whether others judge your actions as good or bad, your conscience will tell you whether you have done right or wrong.

This proverb is a way to focus one's conscience on one's actions. It is also a reminder that heaven or hell is not in the afterlife but present in the here and now. For children, this Thai proverb illustrates the principle that our actions can cause us to experience a sense of personal suffering. The degree of suffering can be great or small in

nature, depending on your actions. If you steal money from your mother, your conscience will cause you to feel guilty. And living with guilt from bad actions makes one experience a kind of personal hell.

Treachery

Face of Deer, Heart of Tiger
nâa núeaa jai sǔeaa
หน้าเนื้อใจเสือ

In a course on the Thai language, students of around ten years old learn this proverb. The story comes from traditional folklore *Pla Bu Tong*. An evil stepmother killed her husband's first wife, and the dead wife is reborn as a fish. The stepmother knows the fish is the first wife. She catches the fish, kills and fries it, and takes it to a daughter of the first wife. She pretends to be nice to the girl and gives the fish for her to eat but the daughter refuses to eat the fish. When the stepmother cajoles the stepdaughter to eat the fish, she has the face of a deer but the heart of a tiger: *nâa núeaa jai sǔeaa*.

In the story, the stepmother ends up eating the fish. The stepdaughter later finds out the fish was her reborn mother and buries the fish bones. She secretly blames the stepmother but keeps this secret to herself. This is an ancient Thai proverb and is similar to the saying: A wolf in sheep's clothing. In Thai culture the disguise comes in the form of a deer that in fact has the heart of a tiger.

In today's world, there are many dangers lurking around every corner, especially for children who are vulnerable. In Thailand school children are known to have been abducted from school. The abductors would put on the "face of a deer" and persuade unsuspecting children with sweets or kind words to get them in a van or an abduction vehicle. This proverb serves as a good teaching tool for children not to trust strangers.

Trust

Keep Secrets to Yourself Heart
cháang săan nguu hàw khâa kàw meaa rák mâi khuaan wái waang jai
ช้างสารงูเห่า ข้าเก่าเมียรักไม่ควรไว้วางใจ

This proverb forms part of the traditional story of *Khun Chang Khun Phaen,* which is a story of love, intrigue and betrayal known by every Thai. It translates literally to mean a man can't trust the elephant, cobra, old servant or beloved wife.

The proverb teaches that one can't trust an elephant even though it has been well fed and housed since it was a baby; it might turn on the owner and step on him when he's not looking. While, in theory, a cobra and elephant can be trained, we can't really trust that their true nature won't one day suddenly appear; on that day they will revert to their dangerous nature and strike without warning. The old servant and the wife are in the same boat as the cobra and elephant. Their loyalty is not certain.

One can be certain that Thai wives in modern Thailand would find the proverb offensive. It lingers from an ancient time when the role of wives and servants diverged in meaning from their role today. In the old days the proverb taught that the old servant who has been looked after may gossip to the neighbors, so one shouldn't tell him secrets. And at the same time, a husband shouldn't tell his wife secrets because she might disclose them to her friends at local village well.

Many middle-class, educated Thais would question the appropriateness of teaching this Thai proverb without explaining its ancient usage and that it should not be accepted literally in modern Thailand. A more modern interpretation of the proverb is simply: We cannot always trust those closest to us as one day they may betray that trust. The best way to keep a secret is not to share it with anyone.

Sweet Heart
wăan jai (n.) หวานใจ

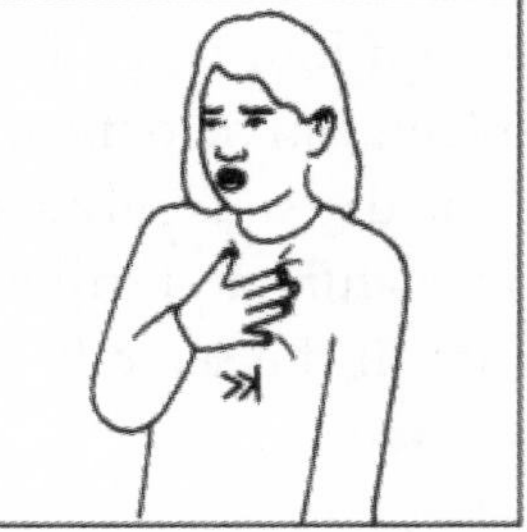

Sympathetic Heart
hĕn jai (v.) เห็นใจ

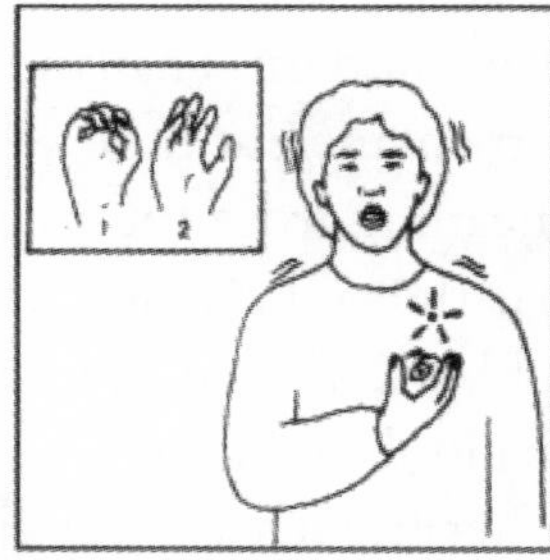

Jerkily Dancing Heart
jai tên (v., adj.) ใจเต้น

14
hand talk

Heart Talk is not limited to spoken language. The deaf in Thailand have their own distinct sign language and culture. And in Thailand the deaf are a visible and important part of the community. Many of the street vendors found on Silom and Sukhumvit Roads are deaf. This, however, in no way prevents them from expressing heart phrases with the same skill and precision as Thai speakers using the spoken word.

The following selection of *Heart Talk* sign language will assist you in communicating with this group of Thais who have a highly evolved vocabulary of the heart. In many cases, the influence of spoken and written Thai is apparent and has crossed over into Thai sign language. But there are examples where the sign language and spoken language diverge.

For example, the Thai phrase *khâw jai*—or understanding—illustrates the absence of separation between the heart and the mind. In spoken and written Thai, *jai* refers to both heart and mind. In the case of sign language, the hand is raised to the head, suggesting that this is the place of understanding. In Thai sign language the gesture for "love" is a movement toward the heart, but in spoken and written Thai *rák*, or love, is not a *jai* word, although there are a large number of *jai* phrases related to love and romance.

It is outside the scope of this book to explore the intriguing possibility that spoken and written Thai and sign language Thai may, at least in part, have been shaped by different concepts, ideas and influences.

Anxiety & Worry

Hot Heart, Hot Chest

rÓOn jai (v.) ร้อนใจ

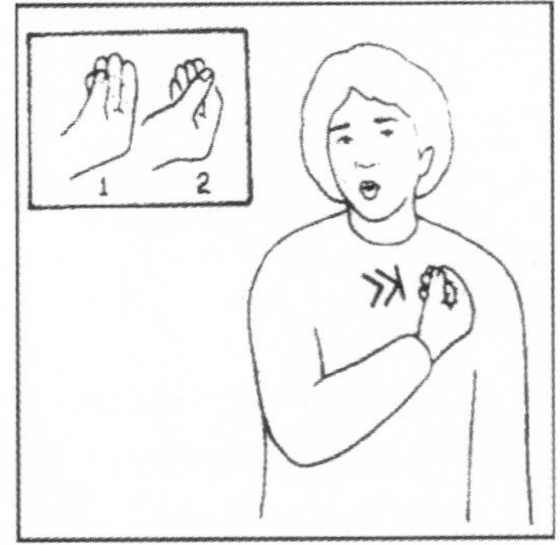

worried, anxious

The sign has a repeated tapping on the body indicated by the symbol in the drawing. At the same time there is a rubbing of the thumb over the fingers, referring to a last heartbeat. There is one rub for each tap.

Class & Hierarchy

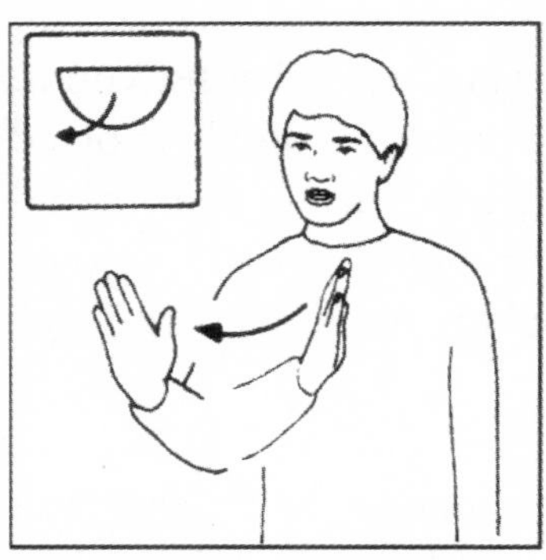

Thank You Heart

khÒOp jai (v.) ขอบใจ

thank you

Awe Heart

kreeng jai (v.) เกรงใจ

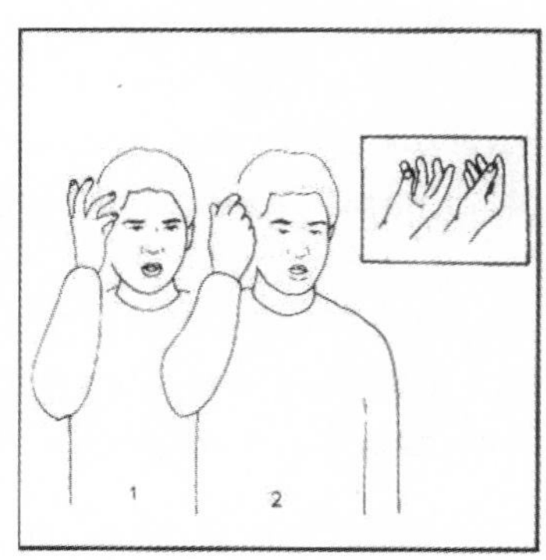

reticent, reluctant to impose, consideration for (others, situation)

The facial expression indicates awe. The movement usually occurs once.

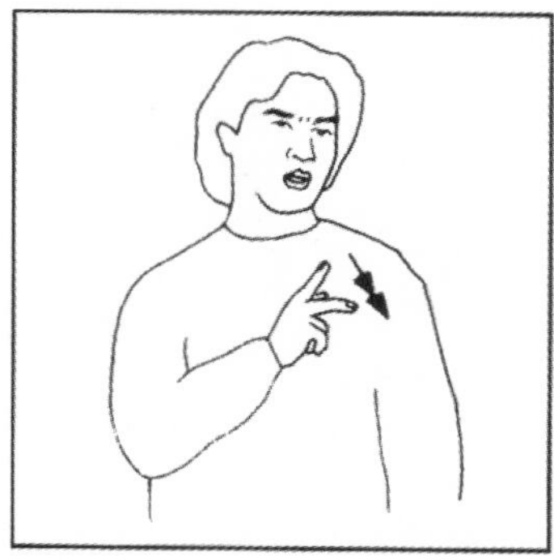

Awe Heart

kreeng jai (v.) เกรงใจ

reticent, reluctant to impose, consideration for (others, situation)

Compassion

Sympathetic Heart

hĕn jai (v.) เห็นใจ

Console Another's Heart

plÒOp jai (v.) ปลอบใจ

to concern, to care for

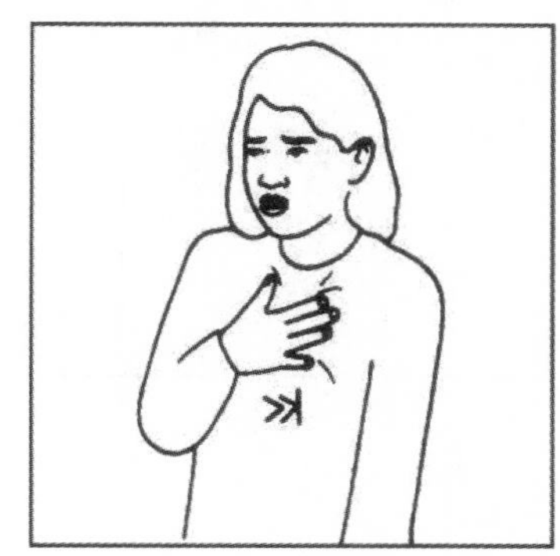

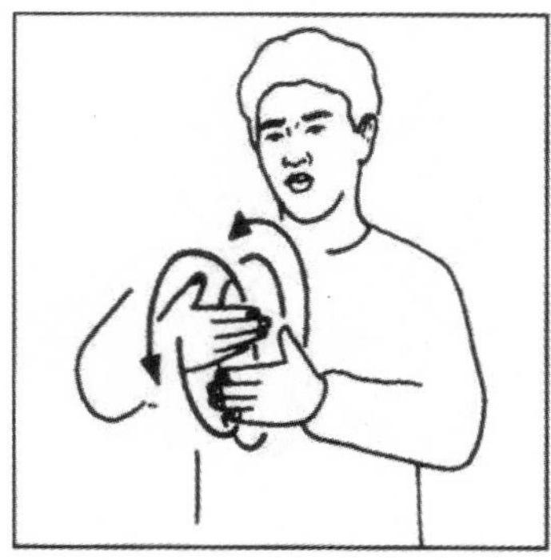

Sympathetic Heart

hĕn jai (v.) เห็นใจ

pity, sympathy

These two signs illustrate the dropping of a base hand in two-handed alternation forms, a pattern common in sign languages. These signs are related to signs referring to consoling a person.

Confidence

Unconfident Heart
mâi mân jai (v.) ไม่มั่นใจ

don't want to, no confidence in (from fear or misgivings), no desire to

This sign combines several meanings: lack of confidence, trepidation, lack of desire, and no interest in (going, doing, etc.)

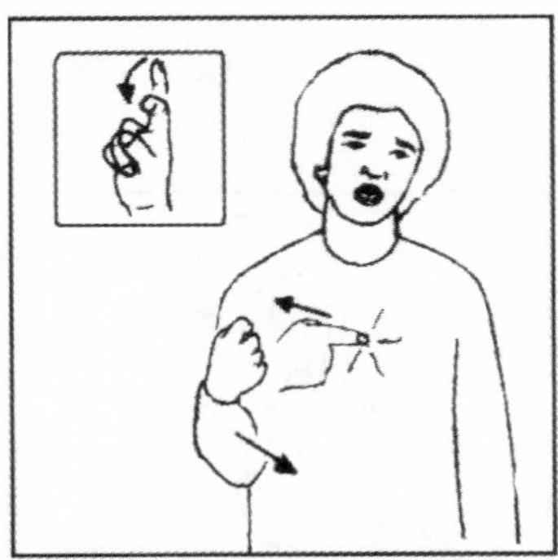

Insecure in One's Heart
mâi chûeaa jai tuaa eeng (v.)
ไม่เชื่อใจตัวเอง
mâi mân jai (v.) ไม่มั่นใจ

diffidence, overwhelmed (apprehensive of situation), overawed (intimidated by task or situation)

"It'd be the end of me!" (Used as an exclamation in a situation the speaker feels is overwhelming)

Decision-Making

Agree with One's Heart
tòk long jai (v.) ตกลงใจ

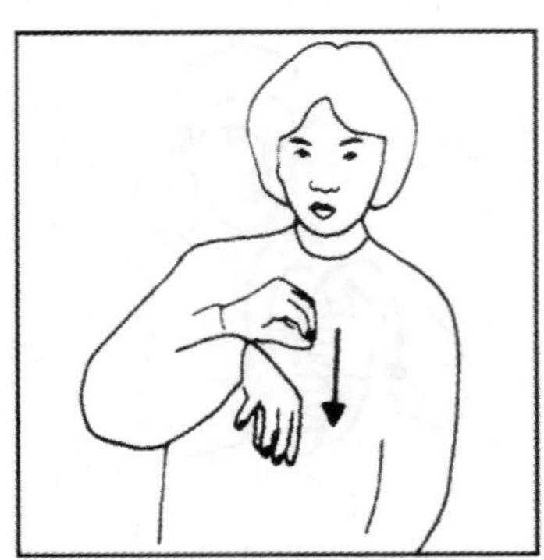

to accept, to agree, okay

Unable to Decide with One's Heart

tàt sǐn jai mâi dâay (v.) ตัดสินใจไม่ได้

indecision (from too many conflicting choices), to vacillate (can't pick one option over another), to waiver (between choices or options)

Dying

Have a Heart Attack

hǔaa jai waay (v., n.) หัวใจวาย

Breathe One's Last Breath

khàat jai (v.) ขาดใจ

This sign is done quickly to show the sudden nature of a heart attack.

Encouragement

Give Power of the Heart

hâi kam lang jai (v.) ให้กำลังใจ

to support, to encourage

Endearments

Sweet Heart

wăan jai (n.) หวานใจ

affection, fondness

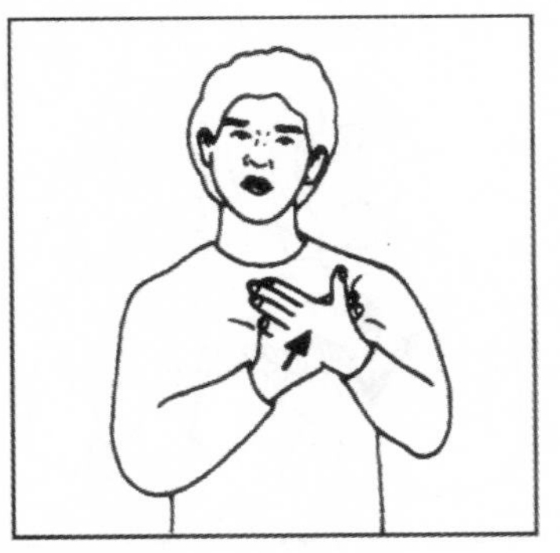

Love

rák (n.) รัก

love

Excitement

Fast Beating Heart

hŭaa jai tên rEEng (v., adj.)
หัวใจเต้นแรง

pounding heart, heart beats strongly

This sign has a repeated opening of the fingertips from under the thumb.

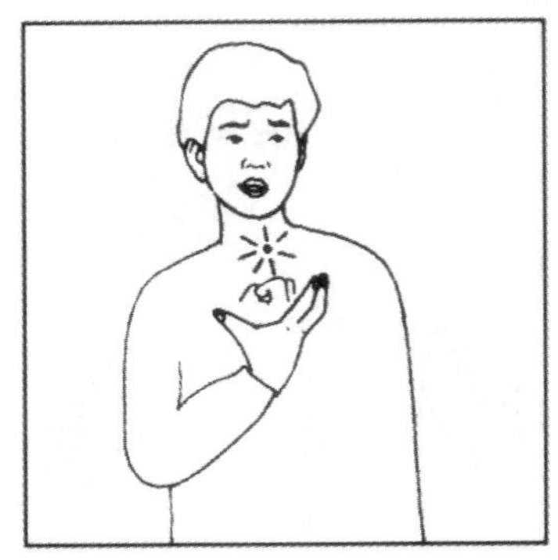

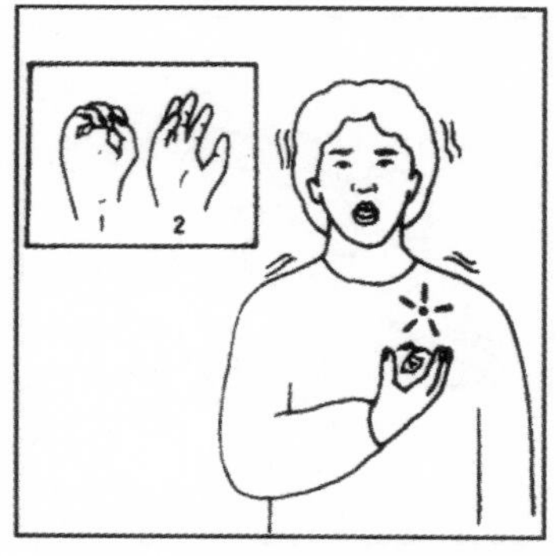

Jerkily Dancing Heart

jai tên (v., adj.) ใจเต้น

palpitation of the heart, heart beats rapidly

This sign has a repeated opening of the fingertips from under the thumb. The openings are smaller and more than in the sign above.

Free Will

Follow Another's Heart

taam jai (v.) ตามใจ

whatever, whichever, anything will do, either is acceptable

The signs use alternating movements. Notice also that in English and other spoken languages one "weighs" alternatives. TSL uses the same metaphor.

Grudge & Resentment

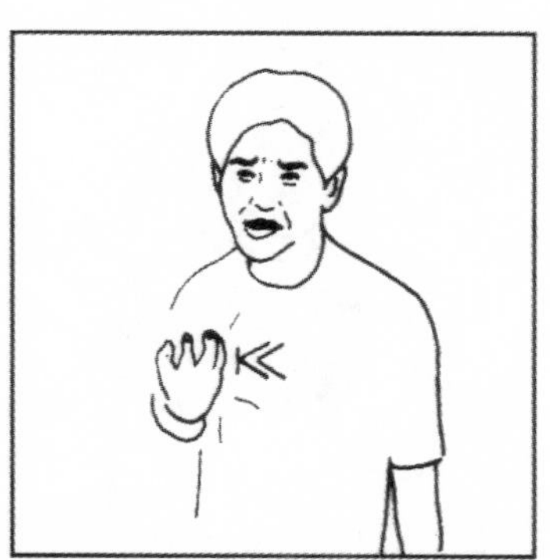

Resentful Heart

jèp jai (v.) เจ็บใจ

to hold a grudge, rancor, angry heart

Resentful Heart
jèp jai (v.) เจ็บใจ

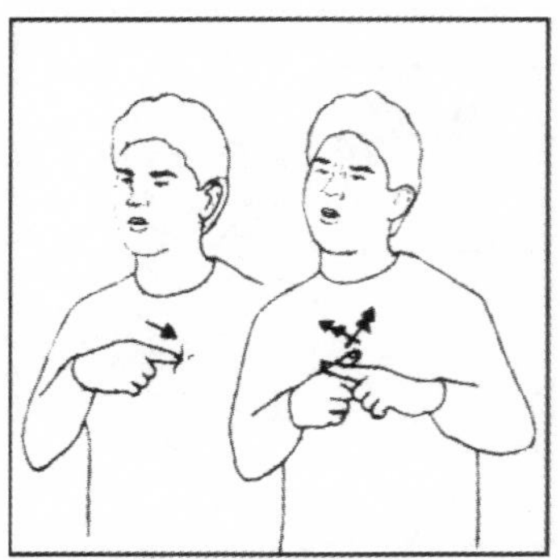

heartache

This sigh refers to an emotional hurt, not a physical ones.

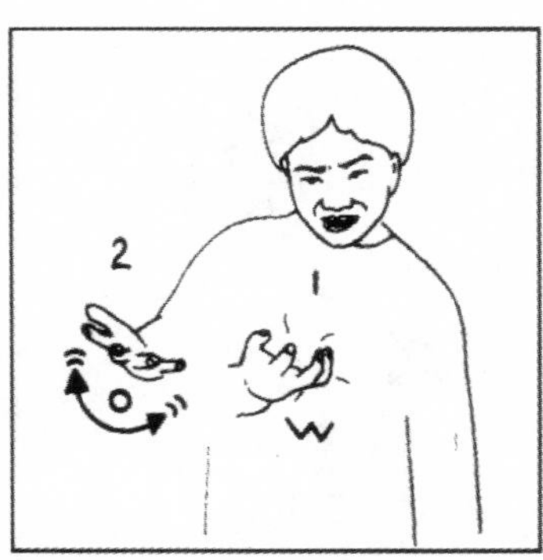

Holding No Grudges Heart
mâi jèp jai (v.) ไม่เจ็บใจ
mâi khÉEn jai (v.) ไม่แค้นใจ

no rancor, not angry, to hold no grudges

A negation formed by a compound with the sign "don't have."

Insults

Brutal Heart
jai ráay (adj.) ใจร้าย
Despicable Heart
jai leew (adj.) ใจเลว
Perverted Heart
jai saam (adj.) ใจทราม

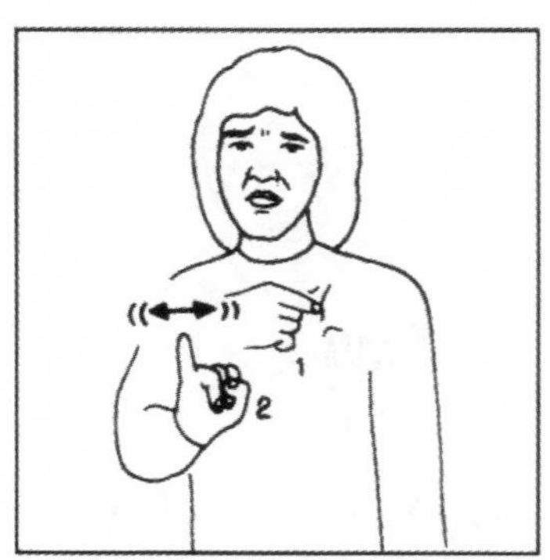

bad-hearted, wicked

Memory

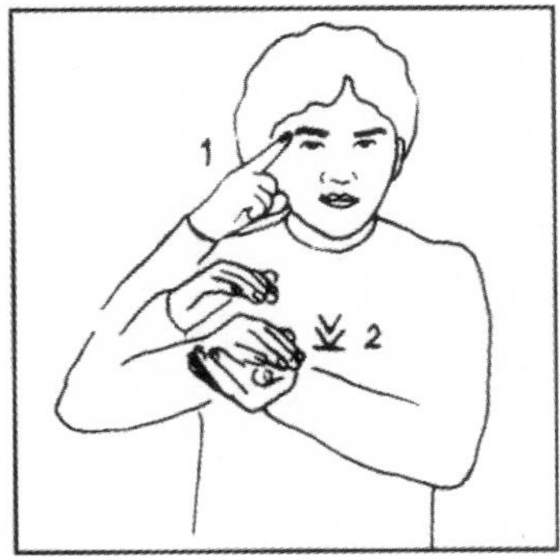

Retained in One's Heart

tìt yùu nai hŭaa jai (v.) ติดอยู่ในหัวใจ

to remember carefully, to retain in one's memory, to fix in one's mind

Nobility

Noble Heart

jai sŭung (adj.) ใจสูง

high-minded, well-educated, high-level

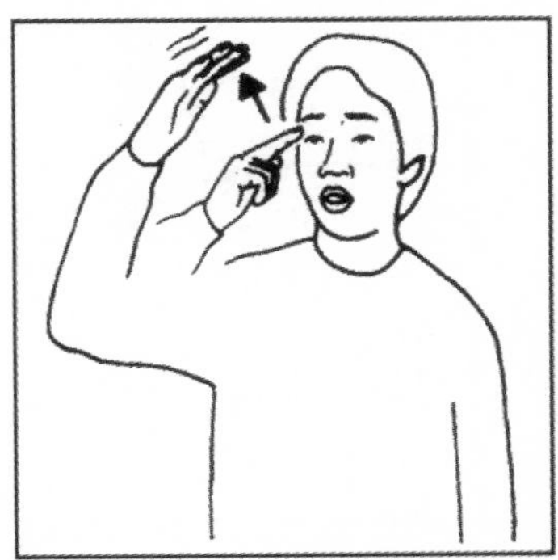

Nuisance

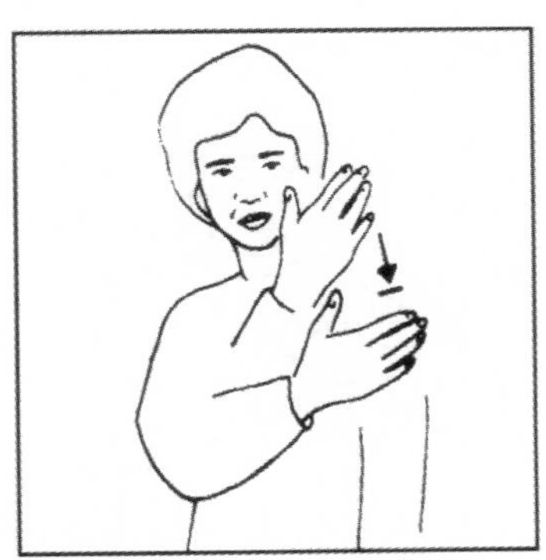

Don't Stir-up One's Heart

yàa kuaan jai (v.) อย่ากวนใจ

don't bother me (with idle talk), to cut off a person who is nuisance

Satisfaction

Satisfied Heart

krà yìm jai (v.) กระหยิ่มใจ
phOO jai (v., adj.) พอใจ

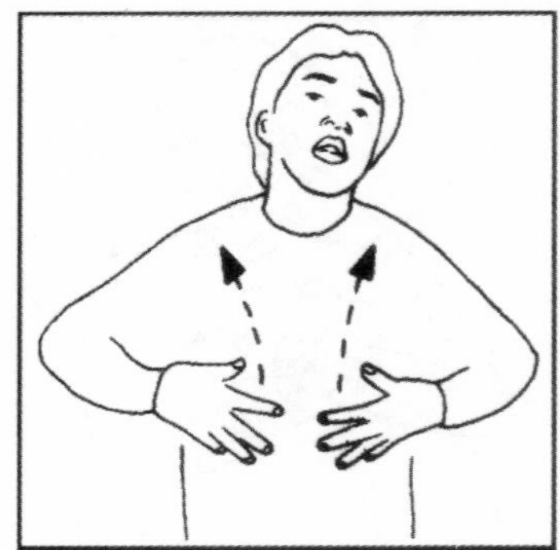

pleasant (generic), satisfied

The long, slow movement is for emphasis of feeling.

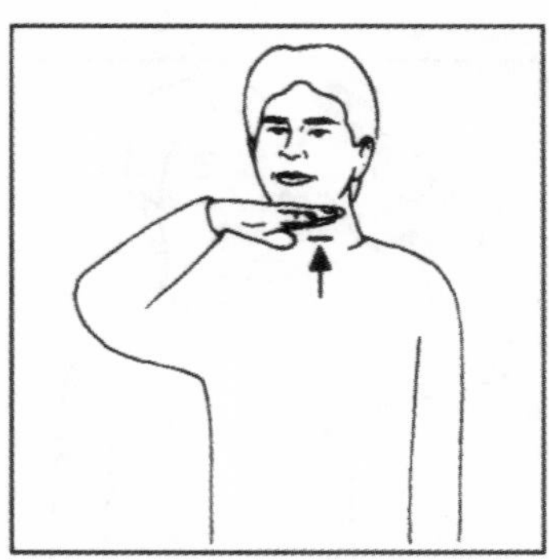

Satisfied Heart

phOO jai (v., adj.) พอใจ

satisfied, fulfilled

The movement in this sign ends in a stop.

Trust

Close to One's Heart

sà nìt jai (adj.) สนิทใจ (สนิทสนม)

to be close, to have a supportive relationship, intimate friendship

"Nit and Noi are very close friends."

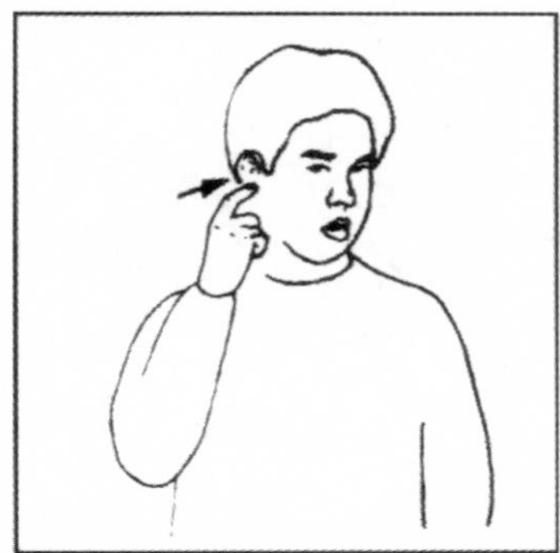

Trust with One's Heart
wái jai (v.) ไว้ใจ

to believe, to trust

Cannot Trust with One's Heart
wái jai mâi dâay (v.) ไว้ใจไม่ได้

(referring to) a person who is led astray from duty easily, uncertain, and unsure of duty or responsibility, or vacillates a lot

Understanding

Understand in the Heart
khâw jai (v.) เข้าใจ

to understand

Unfaithfulness

Cheating Heart
nÔOk jai (v.) นอกใจ
Heart with Many Rooms
jai mii lǎay hÔOng (v.) ใจมีหลายห้อง
Two Hearts
sǑOng jai (adj.) สองใจ

polygamy, polyandry, to have many wives/husbands

Unreliability

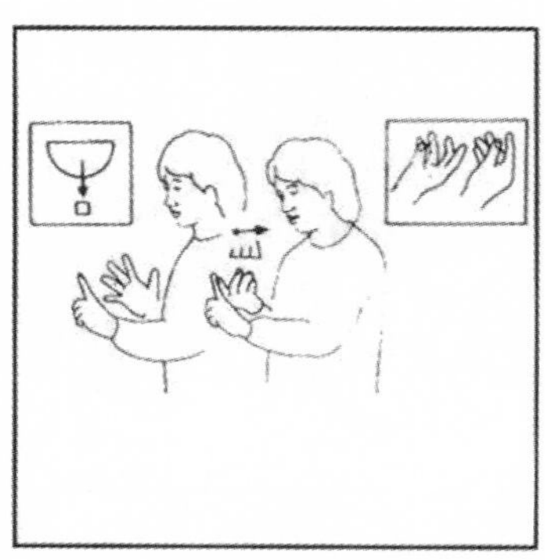

Fickle Heart
jai loo lee (v.) ใจโลเล

promiscuous

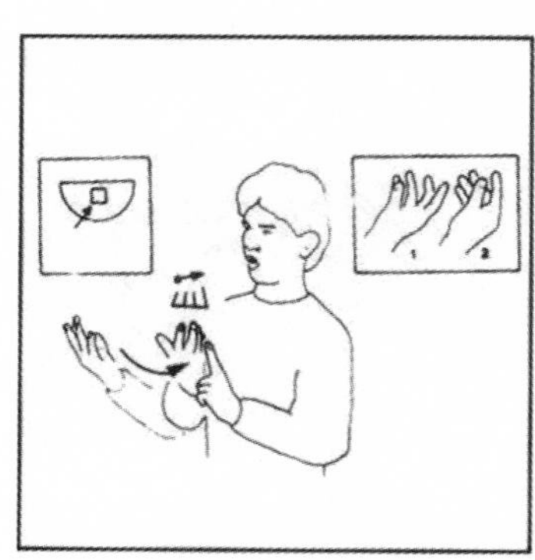

Fickle Heart
jai loo lee (v.) ใจโลเล

(I am) promiscuous

Vengefulness

Vengeful Heart

khÉEn jai (v.) แค้นใจ

rancor, hard feelings, umbrage, pique

GLOSSARY

A

à naa thOOn rÓOn jai อนาทรร้อนใจ	37
à nàat jai อนาถใจ	58
àan jai อ่านใจ	144
àan nai jai อ่านในใจ	250
aay jai อายใจ	60
aÈEp mii jai แอบมีใจ	164
am phooe jai อำเภอใจ	94
am phraang jai อำพรางใจ	163
ân jai อั้นใจ	217
àt ân jai อัดอั้นใจ	138
àt ân tan jai อัดอั้นตันใจ	49, 138
àt sà jan jai อัศจรรย์ใจ	242
aw jai เอาใจ	156
aw jai chûaay เอาใจช่วย	195
aw jai duu hŭu sài เอาใจดูหูใส่	207, 313
aw jai khăw maa sài jai raw เอาใจเขามาใส่ใจเรา	65, 315
aw jai ÒOk hàak เอาใจออกหาก	129
aw jai ÒOk hàang เอาใจออกห่าง	129
aw jai sài เอาใจใส่	207
aw jai yâak เอาใจยาก	136
aw òk aw jai เอาอกเอาใจ	156
aw tÈE jai เอาแต่ใจ	95
aw tÈE jai ton เอาแต่ใจตน	95
aw tÈE jai tuaa eeng เอาแต่ใจตัวเอง	95

B

baan jai บานใจ	19
bàat jai บาดใจ	130
bàat măang jai บาดหมางใจ	141
bàat taa bàat jai บาดตาบาดใจ	130
ban daan jai บันดาลใจ	27
bang kháp jai บังคับใจ	258
bàt dĭiaw jai บัดเดี๋ยวใจ	257
bàt jai บัดใจ	186
baw jai เบาใจ	209
baw òk baw jai เบาอกเบาใจ	209
bOO rí sùt jai บริสุทธิ์ใจ	69
bòoek baan jai เบิกบานใจ	19

C

chá lâa jai ชะล่าใจ	91
chà lĭiaw jai เฉลียวใจ	227
chá loom jai ชโลมใจ	66
chá ná jai ชนะใจ	28
cháang săan nguu hàw khâa kàw meaa rák mâi khuaan wái waang jai ช้างสารงูเห่าข้าเก่าเมียรักไม่ควรไว้วางใจ	176, 330
chák juung jai ชักจูงใจ	203
chàm jai ฉ่ำใจ	240
chám jai ช้ำใจ	150, 292
châng jai ชั่งใจ	269
chii wít jìt jai ชีวิตจิตใจ	157
chÔOk chám rá kam jai ชอกช้ำระกำใจ	151

chÔOp jai ชอบใจ 26
chÔOp tham taam am phooe jai ชอบทำตามอำเภอใจ 94
chûaa ùet jai ชั่วอึดใจ 257
chûeaa jai เชื่อใจ 172
chùk jai ฉุกใจ 226
chûm jai ชุ่มใจ 16
chûm òk chûm jai ชุ่มอกชุ่มใจ 16
chúp náam jai ชุบน้ำใจ 40
chuu jai ชูใจ 26
chúu thaang jai ชู้ทางใจ 307
chûuen jai ชื่นใจ 128, 298

D

daan jai ดาลใจ 27
dâay jai ได้ใจ 90
dàng jai ดั่งใจ 275
daw jai เดาใจ 175
dii jai ดีใจ 23
dii núeaa dii jai ดีเนื้อดีใจ 23
dii òk dii jai ดีอกดีใจ 23
don jai ดลใจ 27
doon jai โดนใจ 117
duaang jai ดวงใจ 169
duaang taa duaang jai ดวงตาดวงใจ 169
dûaay náam săi jai jing ด้วยน้ำใสใจจริง 167
dùeaat jai เดือดใจ 33
dùeaat núeaa rÓOn jai เดือดเนื้อร้อนใจ 36
dùeaat rÓOn jai เดือดร้อนใจ 36
duu jai ดูใจ 303

E

è jai เอะใจ 227

F

fài jai ใฝ่ใจ 282
făng jai ฝังใจ 234
făng yùu nai jai ฝังอยู่ในใจ 234
fŭuen jai ฝืนใจ 276

H

hâam jai ห้ามใจ 259
hăay jai หายใจ 215
hăay jai khâw หายใจเข้า 215
hăay jai khlÔOng หายใจคล่อง 216
hăay jai mâi ÒOk หายใจไม่ออก 216
hăay jai mâi sà dùaak หายใจไม่สะดวก 216
hăay jai mâi thûaa thÓOng หายใจไม่ทั่วท้อง 36, 217
hăay jai ÒOk หายใจออก 215
hăay jai thaang pàak หายใจทางปาก 216
hâi kam lang jai ให้กำลังใจ 194, 337
hàk hâam jai หักห้ามใจ 261
hàk jai หักใจ 261
hàk òk hàk jai หักอกหักใจ 261
hĕn jai เห็นใจ 66, 335
hĕn òk hĕn jai เห็นอกเห็นใจ 66
hŎOm chûuen jai หอมชื่นใจ 115, 218
hŭaa jai หัวใจ 214
hŭaa jai fÒO หัวใจฝ่อ 221
hŭaa jai jà waay หัวใจจะวาย 220
hŭaa jai kèp kòt หัวใจเก็บกด 164
hŭaa jai lîip หัวใจลีบ 58, 221
hŭaa jai phOOng too หัวใจพองโต 26
hŭaa jai rá thom หัวใจระทม 50

hŭaa jai ráaw raan
หัวใจร้าวราน 292
hŭaa jai sà lăay หัวใจสลาย 293
hŭaa jai tên rEEng
หัวใจเต้นแรง 223, 338
hŭaa jai thÊEp jà khàat
หัวใจแทบจะขาด 56
hŭaa jai waay หัวใจวาย 220, 337
hŭaa jai yùt tên หัวใจหยุดเต้น 219
hŭaa jìt hŭaa jai หัวจิตหัวใจ 131
hŭaa òk hŭaa jai หัวอกหัวใจ 131
hŭaa rÓ nai jai หัวเราะในใจ 200
húek hŏoem jai ฮึกเหิมใจ 90

I

ìik ùet jai อีกอึดใจ 257
ìm jai อิ่มใจ 16
ìm òoep jai อิ่มเอิบใจ 16
ìt năa rá aa jai อิดหนาระอาใจ 62

J

jà rooen jai เจริญใจ 25
jà rooen taa jà rooen jai
เจริญตาเจริญใจ 114
jai aa khâat ใจอาฆาต 97, 161
jai aa khâat mâat ráay
ใจอาฆาตมาดร้าย 97, 161
jai aa rii ใจอารี 80
jai am má hìt ใจอำมหิต 99, 120
jai baan ใจบาน 19
jai bàap ใจบาป 124
jai bàap yàap cháa
ใจบาปหยาบช้า 124
jai baw ใจเบา 110
jai bOO rí sùt ใจบริสุทธิ์ 83
jai bÒOp baang ใจบอบบาง 178
jai bun ใจบุญ 82
jai bun sŭn thaan
ใจบุญสุนทาน 82
jai chà kan ใจฉกรรจ์ 76
jai chûaa ใจชั่ว 122
jai chûaa ráay ใจชั่วร้าย 122
jai chùeaay ใจเฉื่อย 101
jai chúuen ใจชื้น 28
jai dam ใจดำ 106
jai dam am má hìt ใจดำอำมหิต 120
jai dèt ใจเด็ด 75
jai dii ใจดี 79, 184
jai dii kÊE dâay jai ráay kÊE măi ใจดีแก้ด้าย ใจร้ายแก้ไหม 188, 327
jai dii phĭi khâw ใจดีผีเข้า 79
jai dii sûu sŭeaa ใจดีสู้เสือ 70
jai diiaw ใจเดียว 174, 305
jai diiaw kan ใจเดียวกัน 145, 300
jai duaang níi ใจดวงนี้ 288
jai fàat jai khŏm ใจฝาดใจขม 141
jai fÒO ใจฝ่อ 43
jai hăay ใจหาย 47
jai hăay jai khwâm
ใจหายใจคว่ำ 47, 243
jai hêaam ใจเหี้ยม 120
jai hÊEng ใจแห้ง 40
jai hìiaw ใจเหี่ยว 40
jai hĭn ใจหิน 123
jai hòot hêaam ใจโหดเหี้ยม 99, 120
jai hòt hùu ใจหดหู่ 39
jai hùaang thŭeng ใจห่วงถึง 302
jai jing ใจจริง 179
jai jòt jai jÒO ใจจดใจจ่อ 228, 282
jai jùuet ใจจืด 107
jai jùuet jai dam ใจจืดใจดำ 107
jai kà rú naa ใจกรุณา 72

jai khăw jai raw ใจเขาใจเรา 158
jai khÊEp ใจแคบ 102
jai khem ใจเค็ม 103
jai khêm khĚng ใจเข้มแข็ง 85
jai khĚng ใจแข็ง 86
jai khlàat ใจขลาด 97
jai khOO ใจคอ 132
jai khOO dèt dìiaw
ใจคอเด็ดเดี่ยว 75
jai khOO kháp khÊEp
ใจคอคับแคบ 102
jai khOO kwâang khwăang
ใจคอกว้างขวาง 77
jai khOO nàk nÊEn
ใจคอหนักแน่น 73
jai khOO ruaan ree
ใจคอรวนเร 108
jai khót ใจคด 105, 133
jai khwaam ใจความ 248
jai klâa ใจกล้า 73
jai klaang ใจกลาง 208
jai klaang mueaang
ใจกลางเมือง 208
jai krà dâang ใจกระด้าง 108
jai kwâang ใจกว้าง 77
jai lá laay ใจละลาย 292
jai leew ใจเลว 121, 340
jai leew saam ใจเลวทราม 121
jai loo lee ใจโลเล 109, 344
jai lOOy ใจลอย 229
jai maa ใจมา 195
jai măa ใจหมา 122
jai maa pen kOOng
ใจมาเป็นกอง 196
jai maa pen krà bung
ใจมาเป็นกระบุง 196
jai maan ใจมาร 123
jai máay sâi rá kam
ใจไม้ไส้ระกำ 107
jai mâi dii ใจไม่ดี 38
jai mâi klâa ใจไม่กล้า 97
jai mâi yùu kàp núeaa kàp
tuaa ใจไม่อยู่กับเนื้อกับตัว 47, 230
jai mâi yùu kàp tuaa
ใจไม่อยู่กับตัว 230
jai mêet taa ใจเมตตา 72
jai mii lăay hÔOng
ใจมีหลายห้อง 308, 344
jai mòk mûn ใจหมกมุ่น 94
jai mueaang ใจเมือง 208
jai muue ใจมือ 213
jai nák leeng ใจนักเลง 76
jai nàk nÊEn ใจหนักแน่น 73
jai nÊEw ใจแน่ว 228
jai ngaam ใจงาม 78
jai ngâay ใจง่าย 109
jai nÓOy ใจน้อย 177
jai ÒOn ใจอ่อน 81, 298
jai òop ÔOm aa rii
ใจโอบอ้อมอารี 80
jai pâm ใจป้ำ 78
jai pÊEw ใจแป๋ว 43
jai pen mÊE náam ใจเป็นแม่น้ำ 77
jai pen tham ใจเป็นธรรม 196
jai phét ใจเพชร 85
jai phrá ใจพระ 82
jai plaa siw ใจปลาซิว 98
jai prà săan jai ใจประสานใจ 189
jai ráay ใจร้าย 99, 340
jai rák ใจรัก 281
jai rew ใจเร็ว 100, 272

jai rew dùaan dâay ใจเร็วด่วนได้ 100
jai rÓOn ใจร้อน 100
jai ruaan ree ใจรวนเร 108
jai sà lǎay ใจสลาย 51, 293
jai sà wàang klaang lôok mûuet ใจสว่างกลางโลกมืด 258
jai saam ใจทราม 123, 340
jai sàp sǒn ใจสับสน 133
jai sàt ใจสัตว์ 119
jai sěaa ใจเสีย 42
jai sǐng ใจสิงห์ 75
jai sÒ ใจเสาะ 98
jai sǑOng ใจสอง 308
jai sûu ใจสู้ 281
jai sǔung ใจสูง 83, 341
jai tàm ใจต่ำ 119
jai tàm cháa ใจต่ำช้า 120
jai tàm saam ใจต่ำทราม 120
jai tÈEk ใจแตก 319
jai tem rÓOy ใจเต็มร้อย 134
jai tên ใจเต้น 21, 223, 339
jai tên mâi pen jang wà ใจเต้นไม่เป็นจังหวะ 21
jai tên túm túm tÒOm tÒOm ใจเต้นตุ๊ม ๆ ต่อม ๆ 21
jai thá min ใจทมิฬ 124
jai thá min hǐn chaat ใจทมิฬหินชาติ 124
jai thǔeng ใจถึง 74
jai too ใจโต 104
jai tòoep ใจเติบ 104
jai trong kan ใจตรงกัน 145, 300
jai túm túm tÒOm tÒOm ใจตุ๊ม ๆ ต่อม ๆ 244
jai ûeaa fúeaa phùeaa phÈE ใจเอื้อเฟื้อเผื่อแผ่ 72
jai wǐw ใจหวิว 221
jai wÔk wÊk ใจวอกแวก 230
jai yài ใจใหญ่ 77
jai yài jai too ใจใหญ่ใจโต 104
jai yák ใจยักษ์ 123
jai yák jai maan ใจยักษ์ใจมาร 123
jai yen ใจเย็น 254
jam jai จำใจ 278
jam khûen jai จำขึ้นใจ 250
jàp jai จับใจ 114, 297
jeaam jai เจียมใจ 184
JÊEng jai แจ้งใจ 248
jèp chám náam jai เจ็บช้ำน้ำใจ 152
jèp jai เจ็บใจ 143, 153, 339, 340
jèp krà dOOng jai เจ็บกระดองใจ 143
jèp thÓOng khÔOng jai เจ็บท้องข้องใจ 203
jîi hǔaa jai จี้หัวใจ 146, 299
jing jai จริงใจ 84, 306
jing jai yàang nÊEw nÊE จริงใจอย่างแน่วแน่ 166
jìt jai จิตใจ 157
jìt jai chûaa ráay จิตใจชั่วร้าย 122
jìt jai hìiaw hÊEng จิตใจเหี่ยวแห้ง 40
jìt jai hÒO hìiaw จิตใจห่อเหี่ยว 40
jìt jai mâi yùu kàp núeaa kàp tuaa จิตใจไม่อยู่กับเนื้อกับตัว 244
jìt jai ngaam จิตใจงาม 78
jìt jai phÒOng phÊEw จิตใจผ่องแผ้ว 83

jìt jai phÒOng săi
จิตใจผ่องใส 83
jìt jai ruaan ree จิตใจรวนเร 108
jìt jai sà ngòp จิตใจสงบ 257
jìt jai sŭung จิตใจสูง 83
jìt jai sŭung sòng จิตใจสูงส่ง 83
jìt jai tàm จิตใจต่ำ 119
jÒ jai เจาะใจ 159
jon jai จนใจ 43
jong jai จงใจ 272
jù jai จุใจ 240
juung jai จูงใจ 203

K

kaan tòk long jai การตกลงใจ 271
kaaw jai กาวใจ 189
kam lang jai กำลังใจ 194
kang won jai กังวลใจ 39
kÊEw taa duaang jai
แก้วตาดวงใจ 169, 294
kèp jai เก็บใจ 303
khà yûm hŭaa jai ขยุ้มหัวใจ 290
khaa jai คาใจ 46
khàat jai ขาดใจ 219, 337
khàat náam jai ขาดน้ำใจ 103
khâi jai ไข้ใจ 300
khăm nai jai ขำในใจ 200
kháp jai คับใจ 49
kháp khÊEp ÈEp jai
คับแคบแอบใจ 49
kháp òk kháp jai คับอกคับใจ 49
kháp thîi yùu dâay kháp jai yùu yâak คับที่อยู่ได้ คับใจอยู่ยาก 317
khàt jai ขัดใจ 136
khâw jai เข้าใจ 247, 343
khâw jăi เข้าใจ๋ 247
khâw jai phìt เข้าใจผิด 249
khâw òk khâw jai เข้าอกเข้าใจ 147, 247
khÉEn jai แค้นใจ 97, 160, 345
khĕn jai เข็ญใจ 185
khĔng jai แข็งใจ 273
khîi jai nÓOy ขี้ใจน้อย 177
khîi ngùt ngìt jai ขี้หงุดหงิดใจ 101
khít nai jai คิดในใจ 245
khlEEng jai แคลงใจ 167
khlÔOng jai คล่องใจ 135
khlÓOy jai คล้อยใจ 191
khÓ kà laa hâi măa dii jai
เคาะกะลาให้หมาดีใจ 93, 316
khòm jai ข่มใจ 258
khòm khŭuen jai ข่มขืนใจ 276
khŏm khùuen jai ขมขื่นใจ 141
khÔO yài jai khwaam
ข้อใหญ่ใจความ 248
khÔOng jai ข้องใจ 46
khÒOp jai ขอบใจ 185, 334
khÒOp òk khÒOp jai
ขอบอกขอบใจ 185
khóp kan dûaay jai
คบกันด้วยใจ 197
khrOOng jai ครองใจ 291
khrûeaang lÔO jai
เครื่องล่อใจ 193
khrûeaang măay tòk jai
เครื่องหมายตกใจ 243
khrúem jai ครึ้มใจ 16
khrúem òk khrúem jai
ครึ้มอกครึ้มใจ 16
khŭaay jai ขวยใจ 64
khueaang jai เคืองใจ 34
khúek khá nOOng jai

คึกคะนองใจ 90
khûen jai ขึ้นใจ 238
khùn jai ขุ่นใจ 35
khùn khÔOng mŎOng jai
ขุ่นข้องหมองใจ 142
khûu jai คู่ใจ 299
khŭuen jai ขืนใจ 276
khwaam jing jai ความจริงใจ 246
khwaam nai jai ความในใจ 165
khwăn jai ขวัญใจ 296
kin jai กินใจ 115
klaang jai กลางใจ 168
klai taa klai jai ไกลตาไกลใจ 138
klân jai กลั้นใจ 217
klân jai taay กลั้นใจตาย 51
klàp jai กลับใจ 54
klÒOm jai กล่อมใจ 204
klÒOng duaang jai
กล่องดวงใจ 222
klOOy jai กลอยใจ 297
klûm jai กลุ้มใจ 38
krà dàak jai กระดากใจ 60
krà thueaan jai กระเทือนใจ 150
krà won krà waay jai
กระวนกระวายใจ 37
krà yìm jai กระหยิ่มใจ 17, 342
kreeng jai เกรงใจ 182, 334, 335
kreeng òk kreeng jai
เกรงอกเกรงใจ 182
krìng jai กริ่งใจ 167
kuaan jai กวนใจ 231

L

lá aay jai ละอายใจ 60
lá hèaa jai ละเหี่ยใจ 63, 139
lá laan jai ละลานใจ 268
lá laan taa lá laan jai
ละลานตา ละลานใจ 268
lá wái nai thăan thîi khâw jai
ละไว้ในฐานที่เข้าใจ 236
láang jai ล้างใจ 232
lăay jai หลายใจ 308
lam bàak jai ลำบากใจ 44
lam phOOng jai ลำพองใจ 90
lang lee jai ลังเลใจ 280
léaang náam jai เลี้ยงน้ำใจ 68
lêek khá nít khít nai jai
เลขคณิตคิดในใจ 246
lom hăay jai ลมหายใจ 214
lón jai ล้นใจ 300
long rueaa pÉ taam jai pÉ
ลงเรือแป๊ะตามใจแป๊ะ 324
long rueaa taam jai pÉ
ลงเรือตามใจแป๊ะ 324
lÔO jai ล่อใจ 193
lÔO taa lÔO jai ล่อตาล่อใจ 263
lOOng jai ลองใจ 176
lôong jai โล่งใจ 29
lôong òk lôong jai
โล่งอกโล่งใจ 29
lóp man pai jàak jai
ลบมันไปจากใจ 232
lŭeaa jai เหลือใจ 137
lúek lúek nai jai ลึก ๆ ในใจ 163

M

maan hŭaa jai มารหัวใจ 121
măang jai หมางใจ 142
măay jai หมายใจ 273
máay lam diiaw yang tàang
plÔOng phîi nÓOng yang

tàang jai ไม้ลำเดียวยังต่างปล้อง พี่น้องยังต่างใจ 314
mâi aw jai sâi ไม่เอาใจใส่ 96
mâi chà lǐiaw jai ไม่เฉลียวใจ 227
mâi chûeaa jai tuaa eeng ไม่เชื่อใจตัวเอง 336
mâi jèp jai ไม่เจ็บใจ 340
mâi khÉEn jai ไม่แค้นใจ 340
mâi mân jai ไม่มั่นใจ 336
mâi mii kà jìt kà jai ไม่มีกะจิตกะใจ 51
mâi núek è jai ไม่นึกเอะใจ 227
mâi sà baay jai ไม่สบายใจ 36
mân jai มั่นใจ 66, 173, 287
mâng mii nai jai lÊEn bai bon bòk มั่งมีในใจ แล่นใบบนบก 313
mát jai มัดใจ 290
mii jai hâi kan มีใจให้กัน 290
mii jai pen tham มีใจเป็นธรรม 196
mii kam lang jai มีกำลังใจ 194
mii kÈE jai มีแก่ใจ 199
mii lûuk kuaan tuaa mii phǔaa kuaan jai มีลูกกวนตัว มีผัวกวนใจ 45, 322
mii náam jai มีน้ำใจ 67
mii náam jai dèt dìiaw มีน้ำใจเด็ดเดี่ยว 75
mii phlĚE nai jai มีแผลในใจ 154
mít trà jìt mít trà jai มิตรจิตมิตรใจ 198
mŎOng jai หมองใจ 142
mòt kà jìt kà jai หมดกะจิตกะใจ 51
mòt kam lang jai หมดกำลังใจ 42
mǔeaan jai เหมือนใจ 296
muue wai jai rew มือไวใจเร็ว 93

N

nâa jàp jai น่าจับใจ 114
nâa kuaan jai น่ากวนใจ 35
nâa núeaa jai sǔeaa หน้าเนื้อใจเสือ 104, 329
nâa òk nâa jai หน้าอกหน้าใจ 214
nâa prà tháp jai น่าประทับใจ 116
nâa sûue jai khót หน้าซื่อใจคด 105
nâa yài jai too หน้าใหญ่ใจโต 104
náam jai น้ำใจ 67
náam jai an kwâang khwǎang น้ำใจอันกว้างขวาง 77
náam jai nák kii laa น้ำใจนักกีฬา 80
náam nùeng jai diiaw kan น้ำหนึ่งใจเดียวกัน 190
náam sǎi jai jing น้ำใสใจจริง 84
náam sǎi jai khOO น้ำใสใจคอ 132
nǎaw jai หนาวใจ 289
nai jai ในใจ 163
nák bun jai bàap นักบุญใจบาป 105
nàk jai หนักใจ 39, 208
nàk òk nàk jai หนักอกหนักใจ 39
nǎm jai หนำใจ 240
nâng nai hǔaa jai นั่งในหัวใจ 146, 316
nÊE jai แน่ใจ 174, 269, 305
nÊEn nâa òk nâa jai แน่นหน้าอกหน้าใจ 218
nĚEng jai แหนงใจ 143
ngan ngók tòk jai งันงกตกใจ 48
ngùt ngìt jai หงุดหงิดใจ 101

ní săi jai khOO นิสัยใจคอ 132
nîng nOOn jai นิ่งนอนใจ 92
nÔOk jai นอกใจ 307, 344
nÓOm jai น้อมใจ 192
nÓOy jai น้อยใจ 59
nÓOy núeaa tàm jai น้อยเนื้อต่ำใจ 59
nÓOy òk nÓOy jai น้อยอกน้อยใจ 59
nùeaay jai เหนื่อยใจ 61
nùeaay jai thÊEp khàat เหนื่อยใจแทบขาด 61
núek è jai นึกเอะใจ 227
núek yùu nai jai นึกอยู่ในใจ 245

O

ÒOn jai อ่อนใจ 62
ÒOn jìt ÒOn jai อ่อนจิตอ่อนใจ 62
ÒOn òk ÒOn jai อ่อนอกอ่อนใจ 62
òt jai อดใจ 261

P

pàak kàp jai mâi trong kan ปากกับใจไม่ตรงกัน 147
pàak praa săi (náam) jai chûeaat khOO ปากปราศรัย(น้ำ)ใจเชือดคอ 148, 326
pàak ráay jai dii ปากร้ายใจดี 137
pàak yàang jai yàang ปากอย่างใจอย่าง 147
pàk jai chûeaa ปักใจเชื่อ 270
pám hŭaa jai ปั๊มหัวใจ 220
pan jai ปันใจ 307
pen jai เป็นใจ 198
pen jâw hŭaa jai เป็นเจ้าหัวใจ 139, 277
pen khâi jai เป็นไข้ใจ 153, 292, 300
pen khon (thîi) chûeaa jai dâay เป็นคน(ที่)เชื่อใจได้ 117
pen khon (thîi) wái jai dâay เป็นคน(ที่)ไว้ใจได้ 117
pen thîi (nâa) phOO jai เป็นที่น่าพอใจ 117
phá lang jai พลังใจ 190
phâak phuum jai ภาคภูมิใจ 205
phâap khûen nai jìt jai ภาพขึ้นในจิตใจ 233
phák phÒOn yÒOn jai พักผ่อนหย่อนใจ 20
pheaang jai เพียงใจ 156
phÉE jai แพ้ใจ 96
phÉE jai tuaa eeng แพ้ใจตัวเอง 277
phim jai พิมพ์ใจ 116
phìt jai ผิดใจ 142
phìt jai kan ผิดใจกัน 142
phìt phÔOng mŎOng jai ผิดพ้องหมองใจ 142
phleaa jai เพลียใจ 63
phlĔE jai แผลใจ 154
phlŏoe jai เผลอใจ 279
phlooen jai เพลินใจ 19
phlôoet phlooen jai เพลิดเพลินใจ 25
phOO jai พอใจ 238, 342
phrân jai พรั่นใจ 140
phŭaa meaa lá hèaa jai ผัวเมียละเหี่ยใจ 63
phûeaan rûaam jai เพื่อนร่วมใจ 198

phûeng jà mùuk khon ùuen hǎay jai พึ่งจมูกคนอื่นหายใจ 326
phueng jai พึงใจ 238
phueng phOO jai พึงพอใจ 238, 263
phûu rûaam jai ผู้ร่วมใจ 191
phûu thîi wái jai ผู้ที่ไว้ใจ 170
phùuk jai ผูกใจ 290
phùuk jai jèp ผูกใจเจ็บ 97, 160
phuum jai ภูมิใจ 205
phûut aw jai พูดเอาใจ 118
phûut tEEng jai dam พูดแทงใจดำ 177
phûut thùuk jai dam พูดถูกใจดำ 177
plàap plûuem jai ปลาบปลื้มใจ 205
plèaan jai เปลี่ยนใจ 279
plÈEk jai แปลกใจ 241
plìiaw jai เปลี่ยวใจ 52
plong jai ปลงใจ 271
plong jai chûeaa ปลงใจเชื่อ 172
plong jai rák ปลงใจรัก 288
plÒOp jai ปลอบใจ 155, 335
plÒOy jai ปล่อยใจ 231
plueaang jai เปลืองใจ 43
plueaay jai เปลื้อยใจ 159
plùk jai ปลุกใจ 189
plùk jai sǔeaa pàa ปลุกใจเสือป่า 18
plûuem jai ปลื้มใจ 205
plùuk rueaan taam jai phûu yùu phùuk ùu taam jai phûu nOOn ปลูกเรือนตามใจผู้อยู่ ผูกอู่ตามใจผู้นอน 312
pòoet jai เปิดใจ 159, 298
prà làat jai ประหลาดใจ 241
prà loom jai ประโลมใจ 18
prà tháp jai ประทับใจ 116
pràp khwaam khâw jai ปรับความเข้าใจ 204
preem jai เปรมใจ 16
prìm jai ปริ่มใจ 205
pròong jai โปร่งใจ 29
pùaan jai ป่วนใจ 44
pùaat jai ปวดใจ 154, 292

R

rá aa jai ระอาใจ 62
rá khaang jai ระคางใจ 141
rá ngáp jai ระงับใจ 255
rá thom jai ระทมใจ 292
rá thom khǒm khùuen jai ระทมขมขื่นใจ 141
rá thúek jai ระทึกใจ 47
rá wEEng jai ระแวงใจ 167
râa rooeng jai ร่าเริงใจ 25
ráaw jai ร้าวใจ 56
ráaw raan jai ร้าวรานใจ 56, 152, 292
rák รัก 338
rák diiaw jai diiaw รักเดียวใจเดียว 303
rák jon lón jai รักจนล้นใจ 300
rák jon mòt jai รักจนหมดใจ 301
ram kaan jai รำคาญใจ 34
ráw jai เร้าใจ 21, 189
rEEng ban daan jai แรงบันดาลใจ 28
rEEng jai แรงใจ 195
rooeng jai เริงใจ 24
rôok hǔaa jai โรคหัวใจ 221
rÓOn jai ร้อนใจ 37, 334
rÓOn òk rÓOn jai

ร้อนอกร้อนใจ 37
rÓOn rûm klûm jai
ร้อนรุ่มกลุ้มใจ 37
rÓOy jai ร้อยใจ 190
rOOy phim jai รอยพิมพ์ใจ 235
rûaam jai ร่วมใจ 188
rúu hěn pen jai รู้เห็นเป็นใจ 198
rúu jai รู้ใจ 144
rúu kÈE jai รู้แก่ใจ 237
rúu sùek jèp jai รู้สึกเจ็บใจ 153
rúu sùek lá aay jai
รู้สึกละอายใจ 60
rúu sùek sěaa jai รู้สึกเสียใจ 53
rúu yùu kÈE jai รู้อยู่แก่ใจ 237
rúu yùu tem jai รู้อยู่เต็มใจ 237
rûuen rooeng ban thooeng jai
รื่นเริงบันเทิงใจ 19

S

sà baay jai สบายใจ 15
sà dEEng khwaam jing jai
แสดงความจริงใจ 166
sà dEEng kì rí yaa mâi phOO
jai แสดงกิริยาไม่พอใจ 162
sà dEEng náam jai
แสดงน้ำใจ 199
sà dùaak jai สะดวกใจ 134
sà dùt jai สะดุดใจ 226
sà jai สะใจ 202
sà jai kǒo สะใจโก๋ 202
sà khraan jai สะคราญใจ 289
sà kìt jai สะกิดใจ 226
sà kòt jai สะกดใจ 259
sà kòt òk sà kòt jai
สะกดอกสะกดใจ 259
sà lĚEng jai แสลงใจ 151
sà lòt jai สลดใจ 58
sà màk jai สมัครใจ 187
sà mǒoe jai เสมอใจ 188
sà nàt jai สนัดใจ 135
sà ngòp jai สงบใจ 254
sà ngòp òk sà ngòp jai
สงบอกสงบใจ 254
sà nìt jai สนิทใจ 173, 342
sà nùk sà nǎan bòoek baan
jai สนุกสนานเบิกบานใจ 19
sà phâap jìt jai สภาพจิตใจ 130
sà thÓOn jai สะท้อนใจ 218
sà thueaan jai สะเทือนใจ 57, 150
sà wǎn nai òk ná rók nai jai
สวรรค์ในอกนรกในใจ 291, 328
sà wǎn yùu nai òk
ná rók yùu nai jai
สวรรคอยู่ในอกนรกอยู่ในใจ 291
sà yǐw jai สยิวใจ 296
sǎa jai สาใจ 202, 239
sǎa kÈE jai สาแก่ใจ 202, 239
sâap súeng jai ซาบซึ้งใจ 128
sǎay jai สายใจ 168
sài jai ใส่ใจ 206
sák sÓOm khwaam khâw jai
ซักซ้อมความเข้าใจ 249
sǎm raan jai สำราญใจ 16
sǎm ruaam jai สำรวมใจ 255
sǎm ruaam kaay waa jaa jai
สำรวมกาย วาจา ใจ 256
sǎn yaa jai สัญญาใจ 287
sǎng hÓOn jai สังหรณ์ใจ 236
sâw jai เศร้าใจ 153
sěaa jai เสียใจ 53
sěaa jai phaay lǎng
เสียใจภายหลัง 55

sĕaa kam lang jai เสียกำลังใจ 42
sĕaa náam jai เสียน้ำใจ 55
sĕaa òk sĕaa jai เสียอกเสียใจ 54
sĭiaw jai เสียวใจ 48
sîn jai สิ้นใจ 219
sĭn náam jai สินน้ำใจ 81
sŏm dang jai สมดังใจ 22
sŏm jai สมใจ 22
sŏm jai núek สมใจนึก 22
sŏm jai rák สมใจรัก 22
sŏm khwaam tâng jai สมความตั้งใจ 22
sŏn jai สนใจ 209
sŏn jai yai dii สนใจใยดี 209
sòng jai ส่งใจ 194
sòng rEEng jai ส่งแรงใจ 195
sôo thOOng khlÓOng jai โซ่ทองคล้องใจ 169, 287
sŎOn jai สอนใจ 207
sŎOng jai สองใจ 308, 344
sŎOng jìt sŎOng jai สองจิตสองใจ 280
súeng jai ซึ้งใจ 128
sùk jai สุขใจ 24
sùt jà rìt jai สุจริตใจ 69
sùt jai สุดใจ 295
sùt khûaa hŭaa jai สุดขั้วหัวใจ 302
sùt sà wàat khàat jai สุดสวาทขาดใจ 295, 301
sûu jai khàat สู้ใจขาด 70
sûu jon khàat jai สู้จนขาดใจ 70
súue jai ซื้อใจ 185

T

tà koon nai jai ตะโกนในใจ 201
taa jai ตาใจ 235
taam jai ตามใจ 156, 275, 339
taam jai pàak lam bàak thÓOng ตามใจปากลำบากท้อง 264, 320
taam jai pàak mâak nîi ตามใจปากมากหนี้ 263, 321
tàang jìt tàang jai ต่างจิตต่างใจ 158
taay jai ตายใจ 174
tàm jai ต่ำใจ 59
tam taa tam jai ตำตาตำใจ 130
tâng jai ตั้งใจ 272, 282
tâng jai fang ตั้งใจฟัง 229
tâng òk tâng jai ตั้งอกตั้งใจ 282
tàt jai ตัดใจ 274
tàt kam lang jai ตัดกำลังใจ 41
tàt òk tàt jai ตัดอกตัดใจ 274
tàt sĭn jai ตัดสินใจ 270
tàt sĭn jai mâi dâay ตัดสินใจไม่ได้ 337
tem jai เต็มใจ 71
tem òk tem jai เต็มอกเต็มใจ 71
thà lăm jai ถลำใจ 149
thà lăm lông chák ngâay thà lăm jai chák yâak ถลำล่องชักง่าย ถลำใจชักยาก 149, 323
thà nàt jai ถนัดใจ 135
thà nŎOm jai ถนอมใจ 68
thà nŎOm náam jai ถนอมน้ำใจ 68
thá yaan jai ทะยานใจ 90
thaa run jìt jai ทารุณจิตใจ 92
thăam jai duu kÒOn ถามใจดูก่อน 268
tham hâi phOO jai ทำให้พอใจ 162

tham jai ทำใจ 274
tham jai khĔng ทำใจแข็ง 273
tham taam am phooe jai
ทำตามอำเภอใจ 201
tham taam jai chÔOp
ทำตามใจชอบ 201
than hĕn jai ทันเห็นใจ 221
than jai ทันใจ 186
tháng kaay lÉ jai
ทั้งกายและใจ 286
thee jai เทใจ 301
thEEng jai แทงใจ 146, 177
thîi phûeng thaang jai
ที่พึ่งทางใจ 200
thîm thEEng jai ทิ่มแทงใจ 130
thÓO jai ท้อใจ 41
thŎOn hăay jai ถอนหายใจ 30
thŎOn jai ถอนใจ 30
thŎOn jai yài ถอนใจใหญ่ 30
thÒOt jai ถอดใจ 96
thÔOt thŎOn jai ทอดถอนใจ 30
thŭeng jai ถึงใจ 239
thŭeng òk thŭeng jai
ถึงอกถึงใจ 239
thúk jai ทุกข์ใจ 57
thúk kaay sà baay jai
ทุกข์กายสบายใจ 57
thŭue jai ถือใจ 173
thŭue jai sûue ถือใจซื่อ 70
thùuk jai ถูกใจ 25, 117, 296
thùuk khà mooy jai pai
ถูกขโมยใจไป 289
thùuk òk thùuk jai ถูกอกถูกใจ 296
tìt jai ติดใจ 262, 295
tìt núeaa tÔOng jai
ติดเนื้อต้องใจ 295
tìt òk tìt jai ติดอกติดใจ 262, 295
tìt taa tìt jai ติดตาติดใจ 262
tìt taa trueng jai ติดตาตรึงใจ 116, 235
tìt trueng jai ติดตรึงใจ 235
tìt yùu nai hŭaa jai
ติดอยู่ในหัวใจ 341
tòk jai ตกใจ 243
tòk kà jai ตกกะใจ 243
tòk long jai ตกลงใจ 271, 336
tòk long plong jai
ตกลงปลงใจ 271
tòk núeaa tòk jai ตกเนื้อตกใจ 243
tòk òk tòk jai ตกอกตกใจ 243
tôn máay tàang plÔOng phîi nÓOng tàang jai
ต้นไม้ต่างปล้อง พี่น้องต่างใจ 314
tÔOng jai ต้องใจ 233
tÔOng taa tÔOng jai
ต้องตาต้องใจ 233
trà nòk tòk jai ตระหนกตกใจ 242
treaam jai เตรียมใจ 273
trong hŭaa jai ตรงหัวใจ 146, 304
trOOm jai ตรอมใจ 154
trueng jai ตรึงใจ 235
trueng taa trueng jai
ตรึงตาตรึงใจ 116, 235
tueaan jai เตือนใจ 145
tùuen jai ตื่นใจ 192
tùuen taa tùuen jai
ตื่นตาตื่นใจ 20, 192
tûuen tan jai ตื้นตันใจ 25

U

ùet àt jai อึดอัดใจ 50
ùet jai อึดใจ 256

ùn jai อุ่นใจ 30
ùn kaay sà baay jai
อุ่นกายสบายใจ 31
ùn òk ùn jai อุ่นอกอุ่นใจ 30

W

wáa wèe jai ว้าเหว่ใจ 52
wăan jai หวานใจ 295, 338
waang jai วางใจ 171
wâat phâap nai jai
วาดภาพในใจ 233
wái jai ไว้ใจ 71, 170, 306, 343
wái jai mâi dâay ไว้ใจไม่ได้ 343
wái núeaa chûeaa jai
ไว้เนื้อเชื่อใจ 172
wái waang jai ไว้วางใจ 71, 170
wăm jai หวำใจ 234
wàn jai หวั่นใจ 140
wang weeng jai วังเวงใจ 53
wát jai วัดใจ 175
wuaa săn lăng khàat hĕn kaa bin phàat kÔO tòk jai
วัวสันหลังขาด เห็นกาบินผาดก็ตกใจ 140, 318
wûn waay jai วุ่นวายใจ 44

Y

yaa jai ยาใจ 294
yàa kuaan jai อย่ากวนใจ 341
yàa nîng nOOn jai
อย่านิ่งนอนใจ 210
yàa wái jai taang yàa waang jai khon jà jon jai eeng
อย่าไว้ใจทางอย่าวางใจคนจะจนใจเอง 325
yâam jai ย่ามใจ 91
yàang jai อย่างใจ 156, 275
yàng jai หยั่งใจ 304
yáp yáng châng jai ยับยั้งชั่งใจ 260
yen jai เย็นใจ 15
yin jai ยินใจ 238
yin yOOm phrÓOm jai
ยินยอมพร้อมใจ 191
yÓOm jai ย้อมใจ 40
yÒOn jai หย่อนใจ 20
yÔOt duaang jai ยอดดวงใจ 169, 294
yûaa yuaan jai ยั่วยวนใจ 17
yuaan jai ยวนใจ 17
yûng yâak jai ยุ่งยากใจ 45, 280
yuuem jà mùuk khon ùuen hăay jai ยืมจมูกคนอื่นหายใจ 326

INDEX

A

abashed, 60
absent-minded, 229
accept, 36
accomplishment, 205
activism, 187
addicted, 295
addiction, 262
adultery, 307
adversity, 70, 273
advertisements, 203
aesthetics, 114
affection, 156, 289, 293, 338
afraid, 48, 140
agree, 36, 191, 271
aimless, 231
alarmed, 242
alert, 210
alliance, 198
alone, 52
alternatives, 280
altruistic, 167
amazed, 242
amorous, 164
amusement, 200
anger, 33-34, 142, 339
annoyance, 34-35, 101
anxiety, 36-39, 334
appetite, 320
appreciation, 128, 81, 113, 128, 186
appropriate, 188, 327
argument, 139, 142, 158
aroused, 234
arrogance, 90-91
ashamed, 60
aspire, 272
assignment, 188
assistance, 199
association, 197
assured, 174, 305
astonished, 241
attention, 207, 229, 313
attentive, 207
attracted, 262
attraction, 262, 289, 295
awareness, 210, 226-227, 256
awe, 182, 334

B

bad-hearted, 340
base, 119
battle of will, 276-278
beauty, 113, 114, 289
behavior, 65-72, 89-97
believe, 172, 343
belittled, 59
beloved, 168, 295, 301
benevolence, 312
betrayal, 129-130, 293
beware, 325
bickering, 63
bitterness, 141
blind, 258
blindly, 174
blunt, 177
body, 213

boldness, 74
bond, 191
bother, 341
bottled up, 49, 138
braggart, 104
bravery, 73
break up, 141, 153
breasts, 214
breathing, 214-218, 338
broad-minded, 77
broken heart, 50, 56, 58, 151, 292
bruised, 150
brutal, 99, 120, 123, 340
Buddhism, 82, 207, 255, 258, 328
burnt out, 63

C

calmness, 254-57, 260
capital, 208
captivated, 21, 114, 297
careless, 91
caring, 206
center, 168, 208, 214, 294
centered, 255
certainty, 269-270, 305
change, 279
changeable, 108
character flaws, 89
character traits, 72-86, 97-110, 132
cheating, 307, 344
cheer on, 195
cheer up, 40
cheerful, 19
childlike, 83
chill out, 20
choice, 268-269
clairvoyant, 235
clarity, 248
class, 181-187, 334
claustrophobic, 216
closeness, 173, 298, 342
comfort, 15, 30
comfortable, 15
comforting, 18, 66, 155, 204
commit, 271
commitment, 286-288
common good, 190
common purpose, 190
communion, 286
community, 187-191
compassion, 65-66, 72-73, 82, 315, 335
compatibility, 145, 296, 300
compel, 276
complacency, 91-92
complicit, 198
compliments, 65, 113-118
composure, 254-256
comprehension, 248
compromise, 192
con artist, 106
concealed, 163
concentrated, 228
concentration, 207, 227-229, 255, 313
concern, 335
condemnations, 89
condolence, 54
conduct, 65-72, 89-97
confederate, 191
confidant, 170, 198
confidence, 66-67, 73, 170, 336
confident, 173, 287
conflict, 139, 141-142
confront, 273
confused, 133
conscience, 237, 291, 328
consensus, 191-192
consent, 191, 271
considerate, 65, 199, 312, 315
consideration, 67-68, 183, 199, 324, 334
console, 155, 335
consumerism, 192-193, 263, 321
contentment, 15-17, 24, 57

contract, 287
contribute, 188
control 139, 277
control freak, 139, 277
conundrum, 44
convenient, 134
convenient, 134-136
conviction, 85, 170
convinced, 172, 270
cool-headed, 254
cooperative, 188
corruption, 81
couple, 299
courage, 73-76
courtesy, 68
courtship, 263, 303
cowardice, 97-99
credulous, 110
criminals, 120, 198
criticism, 89, 118
crook, 133
cross-examination, 159
crude, 137
cruelty, 92, 99, 120, 123
crush, 164

D

danger, 244
daredevil, 74
darkness, 258
darling, 297
daydreaming, 232, 313
dearest, 294
death, 51, 56, 219, 221, 293, 337
debt, 321
deceit, 104-106
deception, 93
decide, 270
decision making, 267-274, 336
decorum, 183
dedication, 282
defeat, 51, 70, 78, 277
defeated, 96
deference, 182
degenerate, 119
delighted, 205
demoralized, 40
dependence, 326
depraved, 119
depressed, 39, 60
depression, 39
desire, 17-18, 22, 234, 262, 279, 313
despair, 39, 154
despicable, 121, 340
despondent, 40
determined, 75, 281
devastated, 51
devil, 121, 123
devoted, 281
devotion, 286, 300-303
diabolical, 120
dictator, 139, 277
differences, 158, 314-315
difficult relationships, 136-139
difficulty, 33
diffident, 336
dignity, 317
disagreement, 158
disappointment, 292
disapproving, 162
disclose, 159
discomfort, 49, 318
discouragement, 41-44, 61
disempower, 41
disheartened, 42
dishonesty, 129, 133, 316
disobliging, 136
dispirited, 39, 43
displeased, 136, 162
disposition, 132
disregard, 95, 201
dissatisfied, 162

distant, 138
distinctive, 314
distraction, 229-30
distraught, 51
distress, 36, 204
distrust, 167
disturbance, 44-45, 322
disturbed, 44, 231
diversity, 158, 315
dizzy, 221
domestic pressure, 322
donation, 82
double-dealing, 129
doublespeak, 147
doubtfulness, 46, 167, 227
dying, 219-221, 337

E

earnest, 166
efficiency, 186
effort, 134
egocentric, 94
embarrassment, 60
emboldened, 90
emotional state, 6, 130-34
empathy, 65, 315-316
encouragement, 26, 194-196, 337
endearment, 293, 338
endure, 256
enjoyment, 19
entertainment, 19-20
erotic, 18
essence, 248
estranged, 141-142
ethical, 120
evil, 120, 122
evocative, 18
exasperated, 137
exasperating, 137
excitement, 20-21, 193, 217, 338
exclamation mark, 243
exclusive, 303
exhale, 215
exhausted, 43, 61, 139
exhilarated, 268
expectation, 22, 273
extract, 159

F

fainting, 221-222
fairness, 196-197
faith, 171
faithfulness, 301, 174, 305
false promise, 316-317
fatigue, 61
favors, 80
fear, 36, 47-49, 140, 182
fearful, 42, 47
fearless, 74
fickle, 109, 344
fighting, 281
firm, 73
flattering, 118
flattery, 114
follow, 191, 275, 339
fondness, 233, 290, 338
food, 264
forbid, 259
force, 276
forgetting, 232
forgiveness, 82
forgo, 261
forlorn, 52
fragrant, 115, 218
free will, 274-282, 339
Freedom, 139, 201, 317-318
Friendship, 197-201
Frightened, 47, 98, 140, 243
frustration, 49-51, 138
fulfillment, 22-23, 342
fun, 19
fussy, 136

G

gangster, 76
generosity, 72, 77-78, 80, 104
genitalia (male), 222
giddy, 221
gift, 81
gist, 248
giving, 298
gladness, 23
glee, 17
glutton, 264, 320
goodness, 78-80
grace, 80
grateful, 128
gratification, 239, 262
grief, , 50-51 56, 155
grudge, 97, 141-144, 339
guilt, 69, 318-319
gullible, 109

H

habit, 132
Hamlet, 108, 280
happiness, 15, 23-27
hard-hearted, 85, 108
harmony, 145, 190, 300
hasty, 272
healer, 294
heart attack, 218, 220, 337
heart connection, 144-147
heart disease, 221
heart, 1-3, 132, 214, 288
heartache, 151, 232, 292
heartbreak, 151
heartbreaking, 56
heartthrob, 296
heaven, 328
heavy, 208
hell, 328
helpful, 199
hesitation, 280
hidden, 163
hierarchy, 181-187
high-spirited, 90
homage, 182
honesty, 69-71
hope, 258
hopelessness, 49, 51-52
hubris, 90
human condition, 65, 89
humility, 184, 192
hunger, 264, 320
hurt feelings, 150-155
hurtful, 57
hurting, 57
hyperventilate, 217
hypocrisy, 147-148, 327

I

idle, 92
ignored, 59
imagination, 233
immaturity, 319
immediately, 186
immoral, 124
impatience, 100-101, 272
impetuous, 90, 272
implication, 236
important, 169, 294
impoverished, 185
impressed, 114, 116
impression, 116, 233, 235
impressive, 115
impulse, 259
in control, 73
inaction, 92
inattentive, 96
inconsistent, 108
inconvenienced, 44
indecision, 268, 308, 337
indecisive, 108, 280

indifference, 96, 107
indulgence, 156, 264, 320-321, 339
infatuation, 295-297
influence, 185
inhale, 215
injustice, 201-202
innocence, 69, 83
insecure, 336
insensitivity, 201
inspiration, 26-28
instant, 186
insults, 118-125, 340
integrity, 170
intellect, 4
intention, 272-273
interested, 209, 281
interruption, 35
intimacy, 115, 144, 297-299
intimate, 159, 173, 298, 342
intolerable, 49
intractable, 137
intrepid, 75
intuition, 235-237
irritation, 35, 101
isolation, 52

J

join, 189
joy, 23-27, 128, 298
judgments, 267
justice, 196, 202-203

K

keen, 281
kicking, 222-223
kindness, 79-81
kissing, 116
knowledge, 237-238

L

language, 2
laughter, 200
lazy, 101
lessons, 207
lie, 328
light-headed, 221
lion heart, 75
listen, 229
loathsome, 122
Loneliness, 52-53, 289
lonesome, 53, 289
loose, 109
loss, 261
love affair, 307
love interest, 300
love sickness, 153, 300
love, 299-302, 338
lover, 299
loyalty, 176, 185, 302, 331

M

malicious, 105
manipulated, 109
marriage, 322-323
materialism, 263
math, 246
mean, 99, 105, 122, 123
meditation, 255, 258
mellow, 15
memento, 145
memory, 234, 341
mental state, 131, 157
merciless, 120
merit making, 82
merry, 25
metaphor, 1
miffed, 55
mind, 2-3
miserable, 57
misfortune, 53, 58
miss, 302
misstep, 323

mistaken, 149
mistakes, 149-150, 323-324
mistreatment, 318
mistrust, 167
misunderstanding, 249
mobilize, 189
moderation, 321
monogamy, 174
monster, 123
moodiness, 101
moral lessons, 207, 311
motivation, 282
motive, 69
mutual attraction, 146, 290, 300

N

narrow-minded, 102
national identity, 2
nature, 132
naughty, 137
negotiation, 204
nervous, 217
nobility, 82-83, 341
nuisance, 341
nurturing, 68

O

obedience, 324
obligation, 184
obscene, 119
obsession, 94
openness, 159, 298
opportunistic, 119
out of control, 319
overawed, 336
overconfidence, 90
overwhelmed, 42, 336

P

pacify, 255
pain, 150-155
palpitation, 339
pandering, 18
panic, 244
panting, 218
passivity, 101-102
patience, 254, 256-257
patronage, 185
peace, 257-258
pep talk, 189
perception, 226
perseverance, 281
personality, 72, 132
persuasion, 203-205
perverted, 340
pestering, 35
physical attributes, 213-214
pickpocket, 93
pillow talk, 286
pique, 345
pitiless, 107
pity, 81, 335
pleasantness, 15, 342
pleasing others, 155-157
pleasing, 114, 233
pleasure, 16, 25, 238
polyandry, 344
polygamous, 308
polygamy, 344
popularity, 28
pornography, 120
possess, 291
power, 185, 190
powerless, 42
precious, 222
premonition, 236
preoccupied, 94
prepare, 273
pressure, 276, 278
pride, 205-206
pristine, 83
promiscuous, 109, 307-308, 344

promise, 93, 316
protected, 31
proverbs, 311
provocative, 18, 234
purity, 83-84

Q

quarrel, 141-143
quick, 93
quickly, 186

R

rancor, 339, 345
rancorous, 143
rape, 276
reach out, 192
read, 250
ready, 274
realization, 226-227
reassurance, 28, 257
rebellion, 319
recklessness, 74, 90
recollection, 238
reconciliation, 192, 204
recovered, 195
redemption, 54
reflection, 233
refuge, 200
regrets, 53-55
rejection, 43, 55-56
relationships, 127
relaxation, 19-20
relief, 28-30, 195, 209
remember, 145, 226, 250, 341
reminder, 145, 226
repentance, 54
reprehensible, 125
resentment, 141-144, 153, 339
resignation, 260
resolute, 75
resolve, 70-71, 273-274
respect, 157-158, 182, 192, 324
responsibility, 206-210, 313
restraint, 258-262, 324
resuscitate, 220
reticent, 334
retribution, 140, 160, 318
revelation, 159-160
revenge, 97, 160-161
reverence, 182
robust, 76
rogue, 76
romance, 286
rough, 137
rueful, 54

S

desirable, 296
sadness, 51, 56-58, 153
safe, 31
saintly, 82
satiated, 239
satisfaction, 17, 26, 117, 162, 202, 238-240, 342
satisfied, 238, 263, 342
savage, 124
scared, 48, 98
scatterbrained, 229
secrecy, 163-165
secrets, 159, 176
security, 30-31
seduction, 17, 193
selection, 268
self-absorption, 94
self-centeredness, 95-95
self-confidence, 90
self-control, 254, 320
selfishness, 102-103, 106-108, 201
self-pride, 90
self-reliance, 325
sensitivity, 59-60, 177, 316
sex appeal, 21

sexual desire, 18
sexy, 296,
shadenfreude, 202
shame, 60-61
shattered, 51
shock, 243
shout, 201
showing off, 104
sigh, 30
sign language, 333
silent, 250
sincerity, 84, 165-167, 197, 246, 306, 326-327
sinfulness, 125
single-minded, 228, 282
sinking feeling, 43
size up, 175
Skill, 188, 327-328
slighted, 59
sluggish, 101
sly, 177
smell, 115, 218
smooching, 116
society, 181
soft, 81, 298
solidarity, 187-191
soothing, 204
sorrow, 54
sorry, 53
soulmate, 198
spirit, 131, 134
spirituality, 125, 200, 328-329
spoiled, 95
spoiling, 156, 275
spontaneous, 186
sporting, 78
sportsmanship, 79
spouse, 299
startled, 243
stoic, 273
straight talk, 177
straight, 70, 304
strength, 85-86, 194
stress, 164
stricken, 49
strong, 85, 273
strong-minded, 85
struggle, 185
studying the heart, 303-304
stunned, 47, 243
submissive, 182
succumb, 277
suffering, 185, 328
support, 194, 337
sure, 174, 269, 305
surprised, 223, 241
surrender, 96
suspicion, 143, 167-168
sweetheart, 295, 339
sympathy, 58, 66, 147, 158, 247, 315, 335

T

temperament, 254, 260, 315
temptation, 17, 193, 234, 262-264
tenderness, 128, 147
test, 176, 304
Thai consonants, 11-12
Thai language, 4-13
Thai phonetic system, 8-13
Thai tones, 13
Thai vowels, 8-10
thank, 185, 334
thief, 93
thinking, 245-246
thoughtful, 65, 199, 315
thoughts, 165
thrilled, 223, 296
thug, 76
tickled, 299
timid, 98
tiredness, 61-63
titillated, 21

touched, 114, 146, 299
touchy, 59, 178
tranquility, 257
treachery, 104-106, 329-330
trembling, 48
trouble, 36, 49, 325
troubled, 45, 136, 280
true, 84
trust, 71, 170-176, 304-306, 325, 330-331, 342-43
trustworthy, 117
truth, 166, 177, 246, 304-306
truthfully, 70
turbulence, 44
turmoil, 33, 37

U

umbrage, 345
unappreciated, 55
unattainable, 313
unaware, 227
uncaring behavior, 96
uncertainty, 97, 108, 277-281
uncomfortable, 44, 50
unconditional, 286
unconfident, 336
understanding, 147, 158, 204, 247-250, 342
unfaithfulness, 306-309, 344
unfamiliar, 242
unfeeling, 108
unhappiness, 39, 57, 154
unity, 189-90
unkindness, 106-108
unmoved, 108
unreliability, 108-109, 344
unrequited, 289
unresolved, 46
untainted, 83
untrustworthy, 343
unusual, 242
unwilling, 278
unyielding, 70, 85
uplifting, 26

V

vengefulness, 97, 160, 345
vexed, 35
vicious, 92
vigilant, 210
villain, 122
vindictive, 160
violate, 276
violence, 92, 123
virtue, 83
vogue, 192
volunteer, 187
vulnerability, 177-178

W

waiting, 256
warmth, 30
wasted, 43
wavering, 280
weak-mindedness, 109-110
weariness, 43, 61-63, 139
well-being, 15, 57
well-mannered, 183
wicked, 122, 124, 340
will power, 281-282
willingness, 71-72, 135, 187
wish, 22, 156, 275
wit, 43
withdraw, 96
withdrawn, 60
women, 322
wonderment, 242
worn out, 62
worry, 36-39, 334
wound, 154
wretched, 56, 154